An Architectural History
London

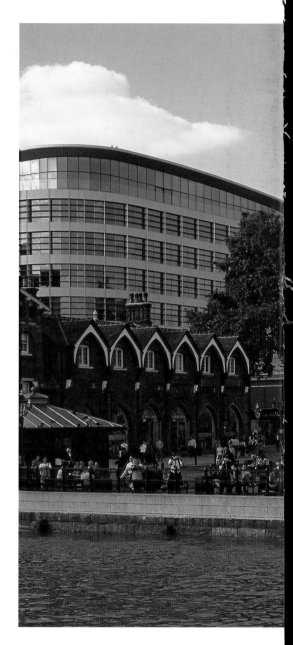

Yale University Press
New Haven and London

An Architectural History
London

Anthony Sutcliffe

Designed by Gillian Malpass

Printed in Singapore

Library of Congress Cataloging-in-Publication Data

Sutcliffe, Anthony, 1942–
    London : an architectural history / Anthony Sutcliffe. – 1st ed.
        p. cm.
    Includes bibliographical references and index.

    ISBN 0-300-11006-5 (alk. paper)

    1. Architecture–England–London. 2. London (England)–Buildings, structures, etc.
I. Title.

    NA970.S87 2006

    720.9421–dc22

                                                    2005028848

A catalogue record for this book is available from
The British Library

Page i   (*Top*) The Crystal Palace, Sydenham, c. 1890; (*bottom*) High Holborn
in the late nineteenth century, looking east with Staple Inn on the right.

Frontispiece   The eastern fringe of the City from the Tower of London.

In memory of Sir John Summerson

And for Telieah and Travan Dickson
without whom this book would not have been written
yet who may never see it

Contents

facing page   Merchants' houses in Cloth Fair, built in the late eighteenth century. They were stuccoed in about 1830. The contrast between City and West End residential building is striking here, with the new houses built into the existing street pattern.

Houses at 91–99, Upper Park Lane, dating from the 1820s. They followed the example of Brighton and other seaside towns where curved bays broadened the sea view. In this case, the view was over Hyde Park.

Preface

Iure sit gloriatus marmoream se relinquere, quam latericiam accepisset.

Lignea incepit latericia floruit.

In 1993 Yale University Press published my *Paris: An Architectural History*.[1] My editor, John Nicoll, encouraged me to write a parallel book on London but it was not until March 2002 that I started work. This book, however, really dates back to 1944, when a mother took a toddler on his first visit to Baker's Arms, Walthamstow, with its cavernous bus garage and raucous street market. As a schoolboy I often cycled into central London on Sunday mornings, reaching Westminster Abbey, Hampstead and Hyde Park, normally covering twenty-five miles of London streets before lunch. Much of what I saw then has helped shape this book.

Like my Paris book, *London: An Architectural History* seeks the distinctive character of a great city's architecture as it has evolved throughout its history. As I warned my *Paris* readers (p. ix), I do not offer 'the kind of specialised architectural history which seeks to describe and comment upon all the representative buildings of a locality or of a period in time, or to identify and *explain* the works of a single architect, or of a school of architects'. Instead, I want to introduce the reader to the whole of London's architectural evolution, looking more for causation, general features and lasting characteristics than for design highlights, great names, 'important' buildings and representative building types. I aim to explain London's architecture, allowing factors such as innovation, established practice, foreign influence, social and political contexts, controversy and changing opinions to contribute to the physical result. Certain lasting influences, such as the London climate, the Palladian tradition, the use of brick, the training of architects and foreign contributions, are emphasised. As in *Paris*, I seek an architectural identity through the ages. This book is written for the general reader, and the architectural specialist may well detect errors, omissions and questionable judgements. I have striven to control these, with the help of expert advisers, but this remains a historian's book, not an architect's book.

London's progress from outpost of the Roman Empire, with maybe forty thousand people at its peak early in the second century AD, to more than six million at the start of the twenty-first, means that a growing volume of new architecture confronts the historian, except for the years 400–900. How to put all this in one book has taxed me from start to finish. Like many historians of architecture I am not an architect and my approach is the 'aesthetic' one defined by David Watkin.[2] My main concern is to describe and account for visual and stylistic variations between buildings and townscapes over time. How they stand up is rarely my concern and interiors secure only incidental attention.

Most of the buildings and layouts in this book draw on earlier styles and I have thought carefully about what to call both the styles and the revivals. I make frequent use of the term 'Classical' to describe a whole range of designs inspired, even remotely, by the Ancient world and dating from the sixteenth century. Where appropriate, I identify categories within the Classical mode, such as 'Palladian' and 'Baroque', and I do the same with modern architecture, as in 'Modern Movement' and 'Brutalist'. Wherever possible I provide the name of the architect and the date of completion of a building. I sometimes provide the start date when the work takes two years or more from initial sketches to completion. First sketches, rather than footings, usually determine the start date. These dates will not necessarily agree with those given in other studies, as there is often some uncertainty, especially over start dates.

As in *Paris*, I have taken my own photographs wherever possible, to link the illustrations to the text. In many cases there has been a choice between an archive illustration and one of my own photographs. Where the quality has been equal and where the building has remained largely unaltered, I have normally preferred my own photograph, mainly in order to present London as a living city where there is much for the stroller to see. Interiors have been a big problem. It is now difficult to go inside most London buildings. Churches have been a problem for many years, but since 11 September 2001 security and general suspicion have made matters worse. My 'Stop and Search' by a City policeman near the Monument was entirely courteous and indeed informative but it took thirty minutes, by which time the light had gone. I often shied away from encounters with security staff and other employees. My tripod worried many, perhaps because they remembered *Day of the Jackal* (though the policeman did not and was more worried about my chunky 'Leningrad' light meter). In the end, I took many more hand-held shots than I had planned. Summerson, however, must have had bigger problems when photographing London buildings during the war.

This study concentrates on the architecture of London as an area of buildings which expands as time passes, reaching the inner edge of the post-war Green Belt in recent years. It excludes the broader London region extending up to forty miles from Charing Cross. Outlying villages and small towns are excluded until they are absorbed into the continuous built-up area, as Hampstead was in the nineteenth century. Buildings outside the built-up area figure only if they have a direct connection with London through ownership, use or patronage, such as great houses, airports and stadia.

At first, in Roman times, London was a small settlement which virtually disappeared from the fifth century until hesitant urban growth was resumed in the ninth and tenth centuries. From about 1000 building began to fill the gaps in the old Roman City and the outliers at Southwark and Westminster acquired a denser urban structure. Building along the Strand linked the City and Westminster, as did the houses on the rebuilt London Bridge which joined the City and Southwark from the twelfth century. From the thirteenth century London expanded on both banks of the Thames, centred on the City, Westminster and Southwark. Although not entirely concentric, London spread out in all directions, producing a classic 'ink blot' by as early as the sixteenth century. The Thames was the axis of London-related building from Teddington in the west to Tilbury in the east, projecting for miles outside the built-up area and often influencing building inland on both banks.

Every writer likes to think that his book is new but mine is merely one of a long line of writings on London architecture to which it owes most of its value. It has been inspired above all by Sir John Summerson, whose scholarship and acuity were combined with an appreciation of London as a human space. His often terse but always honest and informed judgements allow the best of London architecture to be distinguished from the ordinary. Frequent references to Summerson reflect my belief that his writings have never been surpassed and Summerson himself has not been replaced. However, special mention should be made of a number of books whose authors have laboured to produce – some over many, many years – comprehensive guides to London architecture. These authors are the foundation of the current volume: Nikolaus Pevsner and his associates and successors, Ann Saunders, and Edward Jones and Christopher Woodward. Alastair Service's *Architects of London*, though more selective in its method, covers the whole of the capital during most of its history, with a series of original interpretations. Renzo Salvadori's *Architect's Guide to London* is convincingly selective. Nicholas Bullock's *Building the Post-War World: Modern Architecture and Reconstruction in Britain* has been been my example for the twentieth century. I want to pay a special tribute to the doyen of British stamp design, David Gentleman, whose vibrant architectural drawings bring out the vigour of London building old and new.[3] Finally, I have drawn much inspiration from those who can laugh about architecture, including Osbert Lancaster, Louis Hellman and 'Piloti'. Would that there were more such people.

Architectural dictionaries deserve my special gratitude. Two stand out: John Harvey's *English Mediaeval Architects: A Biographical Dictionary down to 1550*, and Sir Howard Colvin's *A Biographical Dictionary of British Architects, 1660–1840*. Sir Howard's book is a gem of scholarship and has helped me more than any other source. Also very helpful has been the architectural content of Ben Weinreb and Christopher Hibbert, *The London Encyclopaedia*, one of the first great city encyclopaedias. Having drifted through many websites, all of them helpful, I want to give special thanks to Bob Speel's (www.speel.demon.co.uk), which is a mine of information and perception.

Ephemera, including television programmes, have made their contribution. I owe a particular debt to *Country Life*, mainstay of reading in the Nottingham University Staff Club, and the Saturday property section in the *Daily Telegraph* which have introduced me to many interesting buildings. The latter's interest in modern architecture has been especially welcome. BBC1's 'Wren: The Man Who Built Britain' was the outstanding architectural programme among the many broadcast while this book was in preparation.

I am grateful to the librarians of the Hallward Library, University of Nottingham and especially to Tony Dexter and Derrick Winfield for their encouragement and photographic advice. Julie Cochran and Anna Wright of the Museum of London were of great help in the illustration of the book, as were Lynne McNab, Hannah Wardle and the staff of the Guildhall Library, especially with their novel 'Collage' search engine. Theresa Calver of the Colchester Museum helped me with the Temple of the Deified Claudius. Gavin Jones, former Press Officer of the University of London, gave me generous help with Charles Holden's role in the planning and design of Senate House. Mr Joseph Scroxton of St Paul's Cathedral greatly expanded my knowledge and understanding of Wren's work when he gave me a personal Triforium Tour one rainy afternoon in 2004. Topsy Arlidge and Fierek Di Bello opened my eyes to Ernö Goldfinger during a tour of his Hampstead house (National Trust). The security director of the Hotel Russell taught me much about Fitzroy Doll. My great friend Professor Peter Fawcett's unrivalled knowledge of architecture has extended to reading my drafts and correcting many errors. Our arguments over pints of real ale have echoed through many a pub in the Nottingham area. My old friend from the Dyos era of urban history, Robert Thorne, has given me much encouragement. Ian Sutton has kept me on the right track in discussing building stone. Stefan Muthesius helped me identify the source of an important photograph of Carlton House Terrace.

My especial thanks go to John Nicoll, Gillian Malpass and Sarah Faulks of Yale University Press, who have encouraged me throughout. The book was greatly improved by two anonymous assessors. Finally, I want to thank my publishing partner of more than a quarter-century, Ann Rudkin (Alexandrine Press). Our combined telephone bills over the years must run into thousands of pounds but her advice, as always, has been crucial to the shaping of this book.

Nottingham, May 2005

1   View of the City from Bow church, c. 1895.

we often look for a distinctive or lasting character in a city's architecture. Sometimes we find it easily enough, as at Venice and medieval Bruges. In larger cities it is usually much harder to detect. Post-medieval Paris qualifies easily enough but London does not. London architecture has had only periods of coherence, as in its timber-rich Middle Ages, its extended Augustan Age in the seventeenth and eighteenth centuries and its Modern revolution since 1930. It has few impressive thoroughfares and many of its buildings are astoundingly ordinary, not to say ugly. The terraced suburbs of the nineteenth century have a common pattern but their architecture does not impress. Only the residential districts of the West End, the work of landowners, developers and architects of great vision, offer an aesthetic identity on Classical lines.

This book follows my *Paris: An Architectural History* of 1993. That book detected a coherent Parisian tradition from 1600 to 1950. It was based on Classical principles, quality construction, municipal supervision, a big state contribution, a trained corps of architects and popular pride in a traditional aesthetic. In London such generalisations are less applicable. London grew to be the biggest and richest city in the world by 1850 but much of its architecture struggled to reach the highest standards and no overall design aesthetic emerged, except in the form of a multi-faceted Classicism, which will often figure in this book.

In the absence of aesthetic continuity, this book emphasises a number of elements that have shaped London's architecture. These include building materials, squares, courtyards and enclosures, London architects, the climate, fire and flimsiness, and 'better inside than out'. Readers need to be aware of these now but I shall return to some of them in the last chapter.

★   ★   ★

STONE AND BRICK

Paris has access to a local building stone of great quality and character. It is a honey-coloured limestone (usually known simply as *calcaire*) which is easy to work and which resists the atmosphere well. For London, building stone was a problem. The only accessible stone was Kentish ragstone, chalk from the North Downs, Reigate stone and the chalky Beer stone from Devon.[1] Ragstone was normally used in the form of rubble or small, roughly shaped blocks. A wall built of Kentish ragstone would stand up well enough but it would look no more than rustic unless it were coated in plaster or mortar. It was used by the Romans and for some churches from the Middle Ages to the nineteenth century but it was useless for ashlar building (walls built of smooth, shaped blocks of stone). Chalk was scarcely used for building in London at any time, except for foundations and hardcore. The same was true of local mudstone.

London's good water access helped it to import stone, however. There were three main sources of stone with ashlar potential. One was the quarries near Caen, which supplied a very fine limestone to major London buildings in the Middle Ages and occasionally thereafter. Wren, who saw its results at old St Paul's, once described Caen stone as 'more beautiful than durable'.[2]

The second was the royal quarries in Dorset, which supplied an extremely hard limestone which came to be known as Portland stone. This stone was used in London from the sixteenth century. It resisted the London climate and pollution better than any other stone used in London except granite. Some levels of Portland stone could produce brilliant white blocks which were much valued in London. However, it was highly difficult to work. It could be shaped into ashlar blocks with some effort, but carving was rare.[3] It was generally used to create large, smooth, vertical surfaces

1

2 London brickwork at its zenith in Sloane Gardens, c. 1890. Many houses here in Brompton were influenced by Richard Norman Shaw whose love of fine red brick often encouraged craftsmanship in others. However, this multi-coloured sidewall is exceptional and the equivalent of the best Dutch work.

punctured by regular window openings. Granite was not normally used for ashlar at all but appeared from the nineteenth century in rough plinths, inserts, window surrounds or contrasting string courses. Strength and insensitivity are the hallmarks of both these stones.

The third source was the broad band of limestone and ironstone quarries from Dorset to the Humber. Their consistency and colour varied greatly. Most valued in London were the quarries of the Bath area which produced a beautiful honey-coloured stone which resembled Paris *calcaire*. Bath stone hardly appeared in London until the early eighteenth century but, appreciated by Adam and Nash, it was very popular between about 1780 and 1840. Unfortunately, with pollution much worse by 1850, Bath stone began to show its weaknesses and it went almost completely out

of use. The striking, brown ironstones of Northamptonshire and Oxfordshire were too vulnerable for use in London. As for the Midland limestones, they were used by the Romans but little thereafter. Transport was a problem until the railways came and by that time pollution was too big a threat.

After timber failed its ultimate test in the Great Fire in 1666, brick took over. Until the nineteenth century almost all of it was produced in London or nearby. Brick was a cheap and easy solution rather than an elegant one, but to import large quantities of good stone from long distances would have been too costly for all but prestigious buildings. The cities of the Low Countries faced a similar problem and answered it with brick and brick had been used on Hampton Court and other important buildings under the Tudors, so brick did not in itself condemn London to poor design. In fact, brick and its associated stucco helped give London a good measure of architectural coherence between about 1770 and 1870. However, the shortage of local stone, the London atmosphere, the threat of fire, rapid building serving accelerated urban growth and planned obsolescence, combined with the 'throw'em up' designing and building that brick allowed, all militated against the achievement of the highest architectural standards or even of any architectural standards.

Pollution became the enemy of London stone from the later Middle Ages. William Te Brake detects the import of coal into London, and the attendant pollution, from as early as the thirteenth century.[4] Air pollution seems to have been less of a problem between 1300 and 1550, perhaps because the population fell after the Black Death, but damage to stone must have continued.[5] Coal smoke did far more damage than wood smoke because of its sulphuric content and by the sixteenth century builders were choosing their stone carefully, with Portland stone already in use despite its high cost. Until the sixteenth century coal was used mainly by industry but domestic consumption grew rapidly thereafter.[6] Peter Brimblecombe, following J. U. Nef, estimates that the weight of coal imported into London increased twenty times between 1580 and 1680.[7]

Smoke damage began to cause concern in the seventeenth century. Dugdale quotes James I in 1620 as bemoaning the damage to St Paul's Cathedral, then said to be approaching ruin.[8] This was presumably the damage which Inigo Jones was asked to repair when he recased the whole of the exterior of the nave and transepts in Portland stone in 1633–42. In the eighteenth century a number of observers noted the deterioration of the stonework on major buildings, including the new St Paul's.[9] Inigo Jones encased the front and rear facades of his Banqueting House in Ketton Stone, a Midland limestone, with only the trimmings and the balustrade in Portland stone. In 1829 the whole was encased in Portland stone, suggesting that the limestone was being damaged.

The volume of smoke increased in step with London's population and industry until 1900. Smoke controls and prevention devices had almost no effect, though new heat and power sources reduced the generation of smoke from the end of the nineteenth century. The only defence was to use a resistant stone. By the mid-nineteenth century only Portland stone could do the job. This had major implications for London architecture.

STREETS AND SQUARES

Most urban buildings face streets and other public spaces, and London has been no exception. Grid plans dominated Roman London, the Classical West End and the Victorian suburbs. Elsewhere, and at other times,

looser patterns prevailed. None of this was unusual, at least in Europe, and street planning will not figure strongly in this book. In one respect, however, London was unique. This was in its squares and crescents. A product of the Italian Renaissance, the square spread over much of inner London from early in the seventeenth century, helping shape a Classical townscape which influenced even minor details of the architecture. By 1900 more than 150 squares swept on a broad south-west to north-east axis from Earl's Court to Kingsland Road.[10] No other city could offer such an array. The crescent, essayed by developers from the second half of the eighteenth century on the model of Bath, was scarcely seen outside Britain. Squares and crescents also encouraged landowners and developers to take care in planning linking and approach streets, encouraging harmonious design to spread across whole districts such as Bloomsbury and Belgravia. One might quibble about the quality of much of this mass architecture but the result in terms of urban design made London an example to the world in the eighteenth and early in the nineteenth centuries. The creators of even the cheapest squares, in the East End and south of the Thames, knew enough about their connection with the Renaissance to build in Classical styles, or at least to use Classical proportions, so they often produced a degree of Classical diffusion even in poor districts.

COURTYARDS AND OTHER ENCLOSED SPACES

Long before Inigo Jones brought the formal square to London in 1631, the city had a rich tradition of courtyards and other spaces defined by buildings. The Inns of Court, the legal institutions which grew up from the thirteenth century just to the west of the City of London, make up London's biggest system of courtyards. The Knights Templar, moving to their second site around 1160, created a large precinct to the west of the City. Four Inns of Court and ten Inns of Chancery, including Lincoln's Inn and Gray's Inn, were laid out to the north. Their foundation dates are unclear but the largest Inn of Chancery, Staple Inn, may have been in existence by 1283 and was definitely there in 1333.[11] By the fourteenth century they formed a cluster of buildings and spaces shaping the area to the immediate west of the City between the Strand and Holborn.[12]

In the City, the halls of the guilds and livery companies and the houses of rich citizens normally had courts. The great royal palaces were arranged around a number of courts and the houses of the nobility normally had a courtyard from the Middle Ages onwards. When the great London hospitals were founded or extended in the eighteenth century, their buildings were grouped round courtyards, following the medical practice of the time. The huge London prisons of the nineteenth century had a variety of enclosures, though few would have known about them. From the eighteenth century London was increasingly organised round streets but the enclosure heritage was strong enough to shape the environment of inner London until the present day.

LONDON ARCHITECTS

Until the twentieth century most architects did not go through a formal course of training. Instead, they qualified informally in the office of an established architect, to whom they were often articled and had to pay a fee. The better the mentor, the better the training and the higher the fee – and vice versa. Late in the eighteenth and in the nineteenth centuries more and more young architects attended lectures provided by institutions in central London. Only in the twentieth century did most architects acquire a formal qualification. Learning on the job is a British tradition and the lack of formal training was not necessarily a weakness for able young men. The weakness arose where mediocre young men were articled to mediocre masters and then went on to train new generations of mediocre young men. Mediocrity could be absorbed during the Classical era when rules and accepted practice kept most architects under control but in the Victorian 'battle of the styles' standards dropped among all but an elite of architects. The growth of formal training in the twentieth century produced a much more capable corps of architects which generated a new architecture, the Modern.

THE LONDON CLIMATE

London's air and light have shaped its architecture. Passengers flying from North America to London often note the huge banks of cloud moving eastwards towards Europe. Ireland gets the rain first but there is plenty left for England. Even London's dryer days are often afflicted by low cloud. Sunny days, though often grouped in a succession of up to three days in winter and up to ten days in summer, are few in number overall. This means that for nearly all the year London

3 *The Embankment*, 1874, by John O'Connor. This noted painter of stage scenery was a stickler for detail and the pollution visible here is probably realistic. On this sunny, summer mid-morning, the eastern part of the City is shrouded in smoke driven from Southwark by a southerly wind. There are some thin, white clouds but the hazy sky suggests a more general pollution which blurs the image of St Paul's. The Portland stone front of Somerset House, on the left, is weakened and yellowed even though it is in full sunlight. The yellow pollution near the ground recalls Mexico City and Los Angeles in our own day. Many of the London skies photographed in this book in 2004 and 2005 resemble O'Connor's.

4 *The Thames at Westminster*, 1871, by Claude Monet. This pollution is probably more an effect than an objective record, but Whistler, Daubigny and Atkinson Grimshaw soon joined Monet in painting foggy or nocturnal views of the Thames. French artistic interest in London's smoke, fog and gloom goes back at least as far as Bouton and Jaime in the 1830s, but it seems to have grown after 1860.

is a sombre city. Strong shadows are rare and the details of buildings tend to merge with their mass. Whereas in Italy the sun can produce large areas of bold shadow, contrasting with large, brightly lit surfaces, London is usually a sea of grey hues. In the winter, the mists and fogs which arise from the Thames Valley, sometimes strengthened by vapours rolling in from the estuary, darken the grey and hide the detail even more. On many winter days the observer in the street or at a window sees little more than a succession of dark silhouettes disappearing into a grey background.

London's natural vapours mixed increasingly with artificial gases. From the Middle Ages, wood and some coal smoke hung increasingly in the air above London. From the sixteenth century London began to build up a world reputation for its tainted atmosphere. Coal smoke, mixed with rain, created acidic fluids which damaged most types of stone. The smoke menace was brought under control from the 1950s but the new scourge of motor and heating fumes took its place from the 1970s. This air pollution further darkened the atmosphere over London and bit into the buildings, clouding windows, stripping paintwork and eroding stone and mortar. All this was a long way from Tuscany.

The architecture of the Italian Renaissance sprang from the bright sunlight, pure air and lush planting of Italy itself. Many British architects and clients soon found as much when, from early in the eighteenth century, they went to seek inspiration in Italy. The problems arose when they returned to London with their bulging folders and notebooks. In the country it was often possible through stonework and planting to simulate something of an Italian environment, at least in sunny weather, but London's atmospherics were a constant discouragement. Many architects, whether consciously or not, responded to these limitations, often putting little art into upper storeys and roofs because they were hard to see from below. Decorations, whether stone trimmings, carving or projections, were kept to a minimum. The Building Acts, meanwhile, discouraged ambitious decorations on safety grounds. These factors encouraged the use of the Palladian style and its variants. The Palladian could be expressed in simple forms without losing its Classical pedigree. It was especially useful for rows of identical houses. Other Classical varieties, of which the Baroque, the Neo-Classical and the Italianate will appear below in their London manifestations, could not rival the Palladian as an effective London style.

FIRE AND FLIMSINESS

London was prone to accidental fires, perhaps more than any city in Europe. The danger began in Roman times and lasted until about 1850. Candles and the open fires used for heating, cooking and industrial work were mainly to blame. Timber building in medieval London

5   Repainting at Nash's Carlton House Terrace, 1898. The columns, which are the last to be painted, carry up to five years of London grime.

increased the risk. The post-Fire building regulations reduced the number of fires but the open flames remained and the leasehold system encouraged flimsiness. Most of the great architecture of Italy was built to last but London's moderate equivalent was, except in the case of churches, built to fall down or burn down. Build cheaply and wait for the value of the land to rise was the common solution over much of London.

'BETTER INSIDE THAN OUT'

Fire and flimsiness had one positive result. This was that the interiors of most London buildings except government and commercial offices were usually of a high standard, higher at any rate than the exterior. Panelling and fittings could be moved on demolition to a new building so the 'hundred-year-rule' did not apply as rigidly as to the exteriors. Standards of comfort in London became the highest in Europe from the seventeenth century onwards. Even the open fires, defective in terms of warmth, ensured a fresh air supply. London interiors did not get caked in soot—it was the exteriors that suffered. Many distinguished foreign decorators were employed, while foreign architects were rare.

THE TWENTIETH CENTURY

Much of the above does not apply to the twentieth century. Coal smoke has declined and since the 1950s has been almost eradicated. The progress of leasehold reform has encouraged better building. Town planning has strengthened the confidence of builders and owners. Environment and conservation concepts have led to buildings surviving longer than they would have done before 1960. The growth of 'gentrification' has improved many older residential areas and the rise in house prices since the last war and the growth of owner-occupation has encouraged investment in existing buildings. Exterior appearance has become more important to owners and much residential building since the 1980s has been given an architectural sheen which can rival the latest office blocks in the City and Docklands. I shall look at these changes in the later chapters of this book.

If the reader will agree that a great architectural revolution occurred in London in the twentieth century, he will be able to discern four great stages in its history. They are Roman/medieval flimsy; London's Age of Augustus; Victorian pick-and-mix and, fourth, the twentieth-century Modern Renaissance. Rarely have two millennia been so simplified. But this is a simple book.

2 The Remote City, 43–1603

Most English people see the history of London as a glorious progression from Roman foundation to world city. In reality, London was a modest place until the seventeenth century and it was not until the second half of the eighteenth that its appearance began to reflect its imperial role. Nor was its development continuous. Roman London was in decline in the fourth century and almost deserted in the fifth. A revival of trade in the seventh century took place in a straggling merchant settlement, or *wic*, to the west and south-west of the Roman walls. By 900 repopulation was beginning in the old City, with most of the new buildings made of timber. By about 1300 the population had reached around 40,000 but the Black Death and other difficulties brought it down below that figure in the fifteenth century. The population increased to about 200,000 in the sixteenth century but London was becoming overcrowded, dangerous and ill-equipped. The great disasters of the seventeenth century–plague and fire–were already on the horizon. This was no entrée to a feast of architecture.

THE CITY ON THE EDGE OF THE WORLD

This chapter deals with the first 1500 years of London's architectural and building history during which the temporary, the accident-prone, the combustible and the undistinguished were common to London building. Wooden construction was often to blame. The timber of the London region, supplemented from the thirteenth century by growing Baltic imports, was the city's major building material. Much of it was used in a rough way at first.[1] However, the thirteenth century saw English carpentry advance to the point where timber could be used for tall houses and stout roofs. By the sixteenth century, London's carpenters had created a timber architecture without parallel in Europe. I shall return to this great timber tradition.

ROMAN LONDON

Roman London, founded from scratch in about AD 50, heralded much of what was to follow.[2] With Kentish rag and mudstone the only local stone, London saw a fair amount of rubble building, often with a plaster or concrete coating, but the limestone and marble needed for prestige structures had to be brought from further away. Dark, Purbeck marble came from quarries at Corfe, Dorset, and limestone could be obtained from Northamptonshire, with additional supplies imported from the Continent. In these cases, transport costs must have been a discouragement and London was probably not important enough to sustain much ashlar building or marble facing. However, limestone was a favoured material for altars and statues. Brick and tile were made locally, and later in Hertfordshire and north Kent, with tiles being used in walls as well as roofs. Bands of tiles were widely used in rubble walls to provide level seatings for the stones.

The most impressive structures were military and commercial. Most housing was flimsy with much use of timber and mud walls, though interior plaster treatment added a veneer in some cases and allowed painting. The extensive building of Celtic wooden huts, many of them circular in plan at least in the early decades,[3] suggests a non-Roman environment for much of London. Even the houses of the rich stressed weather protection with steep overhanging roofs, small courtyards and verandahs. Houses built round large courts as in Italy were rare and they seem to have been concentrated on Cornhill and westwards along today's Cheapside.[4] Temples and bath houses were small and infrequent, though some rich people had their own baths.[5] No theatres have been found.

There are signs that masonry was used more widely from the 120s, after fire had swept the city for the second time in sixty years, and it appears in larger houses from late in the second century.[6] Fragments of

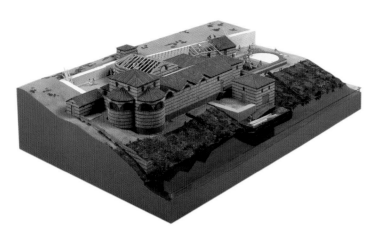

6 Huggin Hill baths. A large structure by London standards, it flourished in the late first and early second centuries but was disused by 200, perhaps following the desertion of some peripheral areas after the big fire in c. 120. It was surpassed in size and grandeur by the baths of Cluny in Paris, and those who knew the bigger baths of Rome itself would scarcely have recognised it.

one modest triumphal arch (some eight metres high) have been found. It may have been an entrance to a temple precinct, given that a carved limestone screen with pairs of gods in niches stood nearby. However, this screen was only 6.25 metres long and the 'temple' has never been detected.[7] The 'Baltic House' site, thoroughly excavated in 1995–6 after a terrorist explosion, turns out to have been used mainly for agriculture even though it lay within the walls and a mere 300 metres from the basilica.[8]

7 A reconstruction of the only triumphal arch to have been detected in London. Presumably built by the army, it was a greatly reduced version of the imperial arches of Rome. The projecting stonework is original but the smooth surfaces are conjectural.

This was no rival to Rome. A fairer comparison would be with Paris but Paris was larger, better built and above all more Romanised than London. Nor did it help that London's legal and administrative status within the northern Empire and even within Britain itself was never clearly defined. London took over many of the functions of the original capital, Colchester, but it does not appear to have become the official capital of the province or the permanent residence of the governor.[9]

The most impressive structures in Roman London were the riverside staithes, the forum and basilica, the Thames bridge, the fortress and the defensive wall. The amphitheatre or arena, which aroused much interest in the late 1990s when gladiators (including lady gladiators) were all the rage, was a modest affair. Sited near the fortress, it had earth banks held in by timber (later stone) revetments and seated no more than 8000 people.[10] It was probably used more for training and ceremonies by the army and by veterans and their families living near the fortress, than for public displays.

The forum and basilica were very big by the standards of the northern Empire, with extensive roofing, suggesting both a strong flow of trade and a goodly ration of rain, fog and snow.[11] The first forum was laid out in 70–80, enclosing 5459 square metres. It was a rectangular space, used as a market and for minor trading between merchants, surrounded to the east, south and west by a low arcade and bounded on the north side by a long basilica, an enclosed building containing a large space for assemblies, courtrooms and permanent offices. This forum was replaced by a much larger forum and basilica around 100. It was five times larger than the first forum, with a courtyard measuring 116 by 85 metres, suggesting a big growth in business.[12] The new basilica was huge – nearly 150 metres long and 52.5 metres wide externally – but it was very much a northern affair with a steeply pitched roof with clerestory windows, rising to 25 metres on Milne's calculations, and it bore little resemblance to the great basilicas of Rome itself (its closest parallel is the surprisingly large basilica at St Albans). It seems to have had no vaulted spaces and the visitor to the interior would have looked up to a steep timber roof. The windows would probably have been very small, with semi-circular arches and no glazing. Its walls were in brick.[13] The interior was divided into a nave and two

8 A reconstruction of the Temple of the Deified Claudius at Colchester (c. 50, and rebuilt after Boadicea's rebellion in 60). This was by far the biggest temple in Roman Britain, probably built with imperial funds. It would not have been out of place in Rome, with its external dimensions the same as the venerable Temple of Castor and Pollux on the Forum Romanum, which Claudius himself had restored after alterations by Caligula. Hopes of finding a similar structure in London faded long ago.

side aisles by two rows of brick piers and there was an apse at the east end. There were further ranges of rooms on the north side with spaces for tribunals here as well as in the basilica itself. The whole was impressive enough for the fringes of northern Europe but no Italian visitor would have troubled to write home about it, particularly in view of the probable absence of columns and capitals from the whole complex and the modest dimensions of the forum entrances.[14] However, it is probable that rows of statues in the basilica leavened the lump. A second, similar basilica was built on top of Tower Hill late in the fourth century but nothing is known of its use and suggestions that it was a Christian church remain purely speculative.

Temples were a disappointment. The only British example which could have stood comparison with the larger Italian temples was at Colchester, celebrating Claudius's victory there in 43. Its massive, vaulted plinth still supports the huge medieval keep, 46 by 33.5 metres. In London the only complete temple to have been excavated is the temple of Mithras, dating from about

240.[15] Although this was a large temple by the standards of the secretive Mithraic cult, its interior space measured only 16 by 6.5 metres, being divided into three compartments by two rows of seven columns. It was modestly built of rubble with a timber and tile roof, while the deliberately dark interior required few windows. It had an apse at its western end, like a basilica. It was, however, richly decorated and contained an array of statues.[16]

A small temple stood for a while outside the first forum but even this central site did not generate an impressive building. The temple was only 20.7 metres long and appears to have been of economical construction, probably without columns and capitals.[17] It did not survive the enlargement of the forum. It is always possible, of course, that one or more big temples lie undiscovered but it is more likely that London simply possessed few temples, perhaps because of the lack of rich Roman dynasties like those who founded many temples in Rome itself. Probably, London was never sufficiently Romanised to generate a temple culture, with public building undertaken mainly by the army and most worship taking place at home round the limestone altars which have been dug up in some numbers. There may, however, have been some small, Romano-Celtic temples built largely of timber.

Army building skills shone in two structures which conformed to the best imperial standards. One was the square (230 by 215 metres) legionary fortress to the north-west. Known today as the Cripplegate fortress, it was developed from the original legionary camp in about 100.[18] Its buildings were mainly low barracks but its walls, turrets and gateways had heavy, stone foundations and its double-arched gateways were constructed of large stone blocks including purple sandstone. The walls were up to about 1.3 metres thick and faced mainly with rubble over a core of lighter materials, with a shallow exterior ditch. The entrance roadways were of compressed gravel, perhaps owing to the shortage of paving stone in the London area.[19]

The other structure was the two-mile wall built round the city on the north bank of the Thames, early in the third century.[20] It enclosed about 133 hectares and rose to a maximum height of four metres. Like the fortress, which formed its north-west corner, the wall was faced mainly with stone, with six gates; a number of bastions were added in the fourth century. The wall stood on a plinth of purple sandstone blocks, resting in turn on a solid rubble foundation. It had a ditch, or ditches, outside it and a surfaced road inside. Like the fortress, the wall was built mainly of rubble but it included regular layers of tiles to provide a level seating

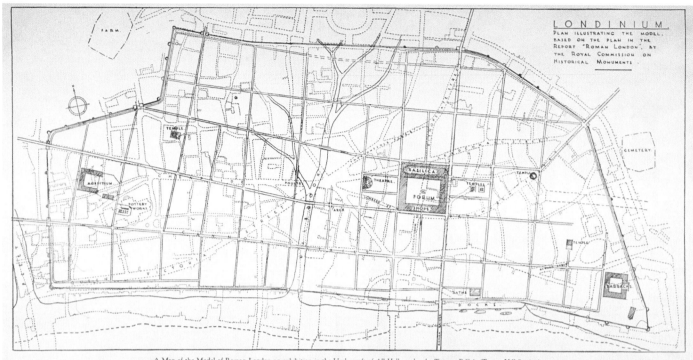

A Map of the Model of Roman London on exhibition in the Undercroft of All Hallows-by-the-Tower, E.C.3. (Tower Hill Station).

9 (*above*)   Map of Londinium at its fullest extent, c. 400, showing post-Roman streets and major buildings (dotted). The archaeological interpretation is out of date but the large street blocks suggest that much of the land lying off the streets was cultivated or fallow, except near the forum. British families and clans could have taken up residence without disturbing their lifestyle. Apart from the forum and basilica, and the mysterious fourth-century basilica near the Tower, large public buildings seem to have been rare, suggesting a low level of Romanisation. However, the streets, laid out and surfaced by the army provided a solid basis for movement.

for masonry laid above. There was an internal core variously composed of earth, smaller stones and clay, producing a total width of between two and three metres and a defensive potential much greater than that of the fortress walls.

London's Roman wall survived—except along its third-century extension on the Thames frontage—into the Middle Ages when it was raised and reinforced. For the rest, Roman London disappeared quite quickly. The Roman use of coatings for prestige buildings tended to accelerate decay when the coatings fell off. Looting of building materials doubtless played its part but one may wonder how much there was to loot and how much was needed.[21] The most plausible explanation for the physical decay of Roman London is that it had never been much Romanised, except by the army and military society.[22]

★   ★   ★

10   Remains of a bastion added to the wall in the late fourth century. These new bastions may respond to a greater threat of attack, but they may also be the product of developments in artillery and artillery tactics.

10

London's post-Roman emergence as a durable city seems to have begun in the 880s, when Alfred seized London from the Danes.[23] A revival of building within the Roman walls then took place. Given the prolonged desertion of the City, the survival of many streets of the Roman grid, albeit in distorted form in many cases, is striking. It may reflect their root-resistant surfaces, doubtless made of compressed gravel over hardcore, or the lack of disturbance by damage or redevelopment during the long desertion period. Whatever the cause, the survival of parts of the Roman street plan and the division of the Roman blocks by narrow lanes from the ninth century may have helped discourage the emergence of long burgage plots (crofts) in the City (though it is impossible to determine the shape and size of individual plots until the eleventh century).[24] Most redefined parcels, at least in the centre of the City, seem likely to have been roughly square or rectangular. This had implications for later London housing. Palliser and his co-authors believe that longer plots which may have been created just inside the walls from the eighth century were shortened in the twelfth and thirteenth centuries as the population increased.[25]

In southern Europe, Roman structures and ruins influenced barbarian building into the Dark Ages and beyond. By contrast, in Britain little but fortifications survived the sixth century while the Anglo-Saxon settlers built mainly in timber. In London, Roman brick and tile were re-used in walls and simple arches until the twelfth century, especially in churches such as All Hallows Barking, but Roman styles and methods were never revived except in defence works. Roman brick-making had been the work of the army and the skills were lost when the legions left in 410.[26] So the new, timber London drew almost nothing from its imperial past.

Single-storey houses must have been the norm at first, many with two rooms, one of them heatable with food stored in the other.[27] Some houses had cellars with timber supports. Living at ground level was cold and damp and occupants or owners gradually sought to create a first floor for eating and sleeping, leaving much of the ground floor for industrial or commercial use. At first, the extra floor was usually provided in the form of a 'solar', a shelf-like floor inserted at one end of a hall.[28] Its insertion in small houses probably began in the twelfth century. Soon the solar began to extend across the whole of the house and the walls were raised to allow the completion of a comfortable room on the first floor rather than a poky attic. These two-storey

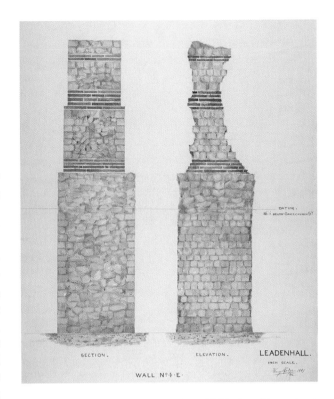

11 How the Roman wall was raised in the Middle Ages. Here at Leadenhall, a narrow piece of facing, and a cross-section, show the medieval builders using the Roman technique of layers of tiles separating rubble while the Romans, using shaped facing blocks, had not needed it.

houses multiplied from the twelfth century and they were still being built, off narrow lanes and courts and on tiny sites on major street frontages, in the sixteenth century. Most had small courts behind them. These houses generally had two rooms on each floor, though some of those squeezed in on street frontages or in the corners of courtyards had only one room on each floor.[29] They established a dwelling type that I have termed the 'London box house'.[30] These houses required a chimney, though sometimes it could be built of wood, and the kitchen was often a separate structure as late as the seventeenth century.[31] Many of the front rooms were used as shops or taverns and courtyards often contained a workshop, brewhouse, tannery or other workplace.[32]

With much land in the City occupied by the nobility and the Church, the height of houses tended to increase above two storeys. Many of the sites were probably shallow, with space only for a small house on the street frontage and a small yard behind or built back-to-back. Frequent references to party walls in building regulations and judgements from the thirteenth century suggest that all but large, courtyard houses were normally built directly next to an adjoining house or houses. This normally meant the erection of a single party wall, rather than two separate adjoining walls and this required a degree of regulation designed to secure strength and to apportion the cost. London party walls became increasingly strong and thick (and a declining proportion were built of timber) and it seems likely that many party walls were re-used after the demolition of timber-framed houses on either side.[33]

By the late Middle Ages there are signs that some builders were putting up two or more houses in rows within a single structure. In the fifteenth century there are some references to this practice, as at the four-storey Goldsmiths' Row off Cheapside, which may have been built in 1491.[34] Ralph Treswell's watercolour drawing of Paternoster Row in 1585 shows rows of houses with standard frontages and, as a surveyor, he may have provided an accurate picture.[35] What London declined to adopt was the North German and Scandinavian *wik*, which had come to mean a fire gap of up to a metre between two houses. London may have paid a price for this economy.

THE GROWING USE OF STONE

It took the Normans to bring stone building to London on a large scale. Edward the Confessor's reconstruction of Westminster Abbey (1050–65) and his early work on his new Palace of Westminster had been mainly of stone but they were the exception. The Normans were prepared to import limestone from across the Channel and they exploited English stone as the Saxons had rarely done. Their huge castles, abbeys and cathedrals launched an architectural revolution.

William of Normandy used architecture in a way, and on a scale, never seen before in London. One of his first acts was to build an earth and timber castle where the Roman wall met the Thames in the east. In about 1077 he decided to replace it with a great stone keep, completed in 1097 and soon to be known as the White Tower. It was probably modelled on the great tower of the Dukes of Normandy at Rouen and was intended to express Norman authority over the whole of England. Its curtain defences spread outwards between 1190 and 1285 and in the 1280s the mason, Robert of Beverley, completed the Byward and Middle Towers, thus completing England's earliest concentric castle, a type pioneered by Richard the Lionheart at the Château-Gaillard in 1196–8.[36] The whole fortress came to be known as the Tower of London.[37] A recent judge, James Campbell, concludes that as a palace-fortress with

several suites of rooms and an internal, two-storey chapel it had no equivalent north of the Alps.[38]

The White Tower was built of Kentish ragstone, Roman materials and local mudstone, with ashlar dressings in Caen and Quarr stone. Construction was supervised by Gundulf, Bishop of Rochester, who had come to England from the see of Caen in 1070.[39] It measured 32.5 × 36 metres and was 27.4 metres high. Its impressive residential accommodation may mean that William foresaw the danger of a rebellion which would have forced him to take refuge in what, by the standards of the day, was an impregnable fortress. Or he may have wanted to provide an impressive first port of call for visitors from the Continent.

William must have judged that Edward the Confessor's Westminster Abbey to the west was already impressive enough, especially as it symbolised his claim to be the direct successor of Edward the Confessor, and he had chosen to be crowned there in 1066. The abbey had emulated the latest Norman architecture, including the great abbey of Jumièges, though its master mason, Godwin Gretsyd, was an Englishman.[40] William must also have realised that the abbey and the nascent Palace of Westminster nearby, linked to the Tower by fast boats, would allow him to control the City while staying in personal contact with his nobles residing on the north bank of the Thames. This water axis, which had meant nothing to the Romans, then began to shape London. Many Norman lords and bishops built houses in London to be near the royal court. Probably the biggest was the Archbishop of Canterbury's Lambeth Palace. Built from the early thirteenth century opposite the Palace of Westminster, it could be quickly reached by boat. Senior churchmen's houses multiplied in the City and outside from the twelfth century and there were nearly fifty of them by the end of the Middle Ages.[41] According to Caroline Barron, most of the larger houses were built of stone on the courtyard plan and their design changed little during the Middle Ages.[42] Some of these houses had precinct walls and lookout towers, the towers often built of timber. Smaller noble houses were probably of the courtyard type from the twelfth century onwards, standing back from the street with a hall, including a buttery and solar, and a gatehouse.[43] Two Norman castles built in the City by powerful barons in support of the king—Baynard's Castle and Mountfichet Tower—were pulled down at the end of the thirteenth century during their owners' conflict with John (though the former was quickly rebuilt and again, by Henry VII, in 1496–1501). The river frontage of Henry's castle was impressive, with a number of projecting towers.

12 The White Tower, 1077–97. The four corner turrets were added in about 1400.

Henry VIII's confiscation of monastic property in 1536 and 1539 brought many of London's religious houses into the hands of the aristocracy and gentry. Most were built of stone and a number of these buildings were converted to residential use by their new owners, as at Charterhouse which was granted to Sir Edward North, a privy councillor, in 1545.[44] This work followed a period of artistic caution in which lords had done little to emulate the king's interest in French and Italian innovations. Their caution continued. Schofield detects new facing, glazing and interiors but apart from a number of new courtyards as at Charterhouse, he believes that the existing cramped layouts discouraged the creation of spacious palaces.[45] Moreover, many of the courts were disordered or ramshackle affairs which discouraged investment.

When London's modest cathedral church, St Paul's, had burned down in the big London fire of 1087, the Norman incumbent, Bishop Maurice, started work on a large structure resembling the biggest churches in Normandy. The twelve-bay Romanesque nave had an arcade, triforium, clerestory and (at first) a timber roof,

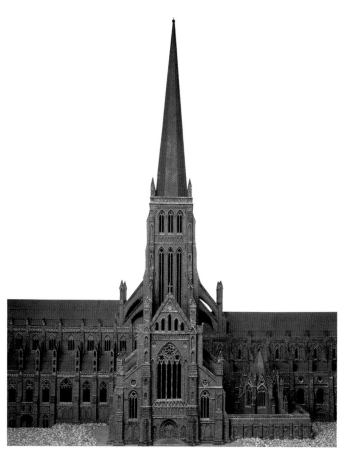

13 Model of the old cathedral of St Paul, showing its impressive dimensions. The refacing of the nave by Inigo Jones, including Palladian *oeils de boeuf*, is visible on the left.

14 The choir of the old cathedral, in a print by Wenceslaus Hollar, c. 1658. The artist's emphasis on symmetry and length may well give an over-schematic and elongated impression.

putting it on a par with the most important cathedrals of the realm.[46] Two towers stood at the west end, outside the lines of the aisles. There were three apses at the east end, one for the nave and one for each of the aisles. The nave and aisles together were about 30 metres wide and the impressive rib vault, added in the early thirteenth century, was about 27 metres high.[47] The choir and retrochoir, built between the 1250s and about 1315, were Gothic, producing a total length for the cathedral of 178 metres, just five metres shorter than St John the Divine, New York, the world's biggest Gothic cathedral.[48] The Perpendicular chapter house and cloister (1332–49) included all the main innovations of the day and influenced design elsewhere in England.[49] The spire, always vulnerable to lightning and rebuilt twice, was 149 metres high in its last version of 1444–62. This spire, destroyed in 1561 and not rebuilt, was only twelve metres lower than the world's tallest church spire at Ulm, which was not completed until late in the nineteenth century. This was a very

impressive building, perhaps a little cautious in its design, especially in its Romanesque nave, but one of the finest cathedrals in England none the less and well known throughout Europe.

At least one other new London church was of cathedral style and dimensions. This was the Augustinian priory of St Bartholomew the Great near the market of Smithfield, founded with an adjoining hospital in 1123 by Abbot Rahere, a companion of Henry I. Most of the three-storey choir, completed in 1145, still survives. Still little known despite starring as a location in the film *Four Weddings and a Funeral*, it is London's largest and finest Romanesque church. It also heralded the Gothic style in London with the pointed arches of its crossing, built between about 1145 and 1160. Comparable in scale was the church of the Augustinian priory of St Mary Overie (now Southwark cathedral), which was probably started early in the thirteenth century after an older building was burnt down in 1212. Although the dating of the thirteenth-

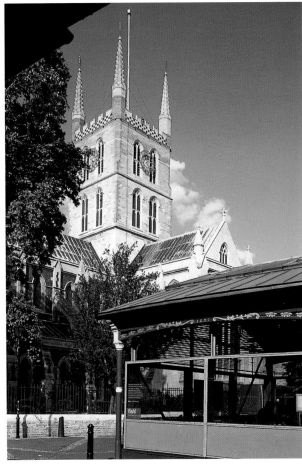

15 (*above left*) The choir of St Bartholomew the Great. This tripartite structure was common to most early Norman English cathedrals. Building probably lasted from 1123 to about 1160, producing the changes in treatment which are visible here.

16 (*above right*) The Augustinian priory of St Mary Overie was the largest church south of the Thames. It became Southwark cathedral in 1905. The tower dates from the fourteenth and fifteenth centuries and was restored in 1822.

century parts of the church is uncertain, this was a large church of very good, up-to-date Gothic design, mainly following northern France.[50]

Another fine church, though much smaller, was the circular Temple Church built by the Order of the Knights Templar in 1160–85. It was in a Romanesque–Gothic transitional style, the most innovative piece of churchbuilding in London at the time. Its rectangular

17 The Temple church. It was in the vanguard of the Gothic style in London, with pointed arches and arcading, foliage capitals, vaulting divided by slim shafts, and piers surrounded by shafts of dark Purbeck marble. The chancel of 1240 was in a more developed Gothic style with a vaulted nave and aisles, and large windows. This photograph dates from about 1940 when the threat of bombing led photographers to record what might be lost. Sir John Summerson was the most prolific of these.

chancel, added in 1220–40, was in exquisite Gothic, similar to the retrochoirs of Salisbury and other cathedrals of the time. The Templars' links across Europe and the Near East were probably the origin of this excellence.

In 1245 Henry III started to rebuild Edward the Confessor's Westminster Abbey. A great patron of the arts, he appears to have sought to emulate the huge French royal cathedral of Rheims, which had just been completed. Henry's church was much smaller but its Gothic design, the work of the master mason and keeper of the king's works, Henry of Reyns (or Reynes), who had probably worked in France as a young man, was fully comparable with the best French work and indeed bore a resemblance to the cathedral of Rheims while including some novel detail.[51] In particular, the east end was planned as a chevet of French inspiration (whereas the contemporary choir of St Paul's cathedral was given a flat east end in the English manner). English materials were used – Reigate stone for the body of the abbey and Purbeck marble for the interior dressings. Edward's building was gradually pulled down as the work proceeded. The huge chapter house, unrivalled in England, was built from 1245 to 1253, its vault supported by a central pier, with broad Gothic windows filled with tracery. With the king paying the entire cost of building, it is not surprising that baronial opposition, and his death in 1272, halted the work.

From 1269 the greater part of the nave was left unfinished, but under Richard II it was completed by the greatest master mason of the day, Henry Yevele.[52] After Richard II was deposed in 1399 work was interrupted again but the vaulting was completed in 1503–6. This was the tallest English vault, at 31.5 metres. It was lower than most of the French Gothic cathedrals but Yevele's self-effacing decision to persist with Henry of Reyns's design produced a unified structure with dramatic proportions.

Westminster Abbey was a major statement. It expressed London's status as capital of an important kingdom, not as rich and powerful as France by any means, but outstanding in comparison with the kingdoms and princedoms of the Low Countries, Germany and Scandinavia. Where the abbey differed from most French examples of its time was in its reduced width and narrowed bays, which produced an effect of great height. Safety may well have been the aim, with vault collapses common at this time all over Europe, especially on sedimentary subsoils like Westminster's.[53]

★　★　★

THE NEW CHURCHES

By the end of the twelfth century all the wooden churches and chapels had been rebuilt in Roman materials or stone. Their roofs were replaced in timber, though some of the big monastic churches may have had stone vaults, as at St Bartholomew the Great. The addition of aisles appears to have begun about 1230, as the population grew.[54] Many of the chapels of noble houses and of priories developed into parish churches, both before and after the Conquest. The total number of churches in the City reached 108 by 1300.[55]

The foundation of a number of friaries from late in the thirteenth century led to the building of a new type of church. Some, as befitted preaching orders, were large, with long, spartan naves. The Greyfriars' church, built in 1306 and probably the biggest, was 91 metres long.[56] Also on a large scale were many of the charitable religious foundations known as hospitals, founded from early in the twelfth century. The four major City hospitals, beginning with St Bartholomew's, had walled precincts.[57] Other religious houses and hospitals were founded outside the City and some had extensive buildings and precinct walls.[58] The benefactors of many religious houses created parish churches alongside them or vice versa, the two naves often being adjacent, as at St Helen Bishopsgate. Here, a Benedictine nunnery was founded in about 1200 next to an existing parish church. The combined naves had reached their mature form by about 1475.

18   St Helen, Bishopsgate. Two churches stand side by side here with a medieval parish church on the right and a nunnery church (c. 1200–15) on the left. The two naves could form a single space, as they do today.

19 St Ethelburga, Bishopsgate. This tiny church, much altered since the Fire and the victim of a terrorist bomb in 1993, is the only survivor of dozens of small pre-1666 churches.

Many churches added belfries from the thirteenth century. In the fourteenth century the larger churches acquired a square belfry tower at the west end. Most had a crenellated top and a corner turret at the top of the stair. The parish churches went through a period of radical repair, rebuilding or refurbishment in the fifteenth and early sixteenth centuries, when about fifty were transformed, mainly in the Perpendicular style.[59] St Stephen Walbrook, for instance, was partly rebuilt from 1429 by the most eminent mason of his day, Thomas Mapilton.[60] St Sepulchre, Holborn Viaduct, acquired a striking tower with four huge pinnacles in the mid-fifteenth century. The chancels became longer and wider in order to accommodate side chapels and funerary monuments. By the fifteenth century the common plan was a nave and one or two aisles ending with a chancel. In most cases, the nave piers supported a continuous clerestory and a shallow timber roof. Some of the larger ones, including St Andrew Undershaft, St Giles Cripplegate and St Sepulchre, were well-executed examples in their late medieval form.[61] Several of the fifteenth-century towers were very impressive.

To evaluate the architecture of chapels and churches in medieval London is very difficult since many were destroyed in 1666. St Bartholomew the Great and St Mary Overie were impressive churches of the second rank. In its parish churches, however, London was impoverished in comparison with many Continental cities. These buildings impress more in quantity than in quality. Conformity was a major feature and structure and decoration were ordinary. However, they reflected the wishes and life of the population of London, while the great urban churches of the Continent were much more the creation of the rich and powerful.

STONE AND TIMBER AFTER 1200

Stone seems to have come into wider use in the twelfth century but its application to housing was limited.[62] A passage in Stow's *Survey* suggests that rich London Jews were then building their houses of stone, as elsewhere in the kingdom.[63] John the Carpenter rented some stone houses from the Dean and Chapter of St Paul's between 1229 and 1241 but these lay just outside the churchyard and they may have been built for cathedral clergy.[64]

The repair of London Bridge made much use of stone. With the Thames much shallower than it is today, the construction of a bridge was not a frightening task and the Romans appear to have had a wooden bridge, built on piers rather than pontoons, by 100. The bridge decayed after the departure of the Romans but a crossing of sorts was re-established in about 1000. It was then rebuilt in stone on nineteen arches between 1176 and 1209. The work was organised by a priest, Peter of Colechurch. A chapel was built on one of the piers in the middle of the river and by 1201 houses were being built along the roadway (though they were all of timber). This London Bridge lasted, with many repairs and partial reconstructions, until the 1820s.[65]

The impressive repair and raising of the Roman wall also suggests that more stone was available. In 1215 the barons, in dispute with John, entered London through the ruinous Aldgate and, finding themselves in control of the city, repaired or rebuilt the walls and gates. A general increase in the height of the wall was achieved at this time. According to Stow, they used imported Caen limestone and small bricks from Flanders, known as Flanders tile, rather than local ragstone as might have been expected.[66]

Even as late as 1300, however, London was still a long way from the brick and stone city which it became after the Great Fire. However, the simple hutments of

20 The medieval Aldersgate on the London wall was rebuilt and embellished in 1617 and 1670 before its demolition in 1761. The resulting Mannerist effect was more impressive than scholarly. Most of the other London gates were raised and enhanced at much the same time in this Wicked Queen style. All but Temple Bar had been demolished by the end of the eighteenth century.

Saxon and early Norman times had now been surpassed by new methods. These were strong timber framing for walls and roof supports, and intricate carpentry for interior roofs. The first surviving English examples of timber framing date from the thirteenth century and it is likely that London saw them at that time.

Timber frames reached their apogee on the eve of the Fire, when they supported almost all the houses in London. Most seem to have been three storeys tall by this time. Jettying (overhangs) of the upper floors was normal. It is mentioned as early as 1246, though its widespread application probably had to wait until the fifteenth and sixteenth centuries.[67] Timber framing allowed walls, and combinations of wall and window, to be constructed as light panels which could easily be removed. It also permitted strip windows running right across the facade.

Three-storey houses were present in Cheapside, the main commercial street, in the late thirteenth century

and by the sixteenth century some houses there reached five storeys.[68] Extra rooms were provided in the roof, which normally presented a gable end to the street. Houses stretched further back into their sites than they had in the Middle Ages.[69] Staple Inn, in Holborn, is London's largest and finest example of timber framing. A row of houses built in two parts in 1586 and a little later produced a row of seven gables on the street. The facades have two levels of jetties. These buildings went through two major restorations in 1887 and 1936–8 but this impressive, close-studded frontage is probably an adequate representation of the original.[70] Many of the grander houses probably used this East Anglian method of close-studding, which may have spread to London in the fifteenth century. It meant that the timbers were set close together, and vertically. This was an expensive method, partly because additional, hidden timbers were needed to provide the necessary strength.[71] John Schofield suggests that a completely different method of framing based on small, decorated panels became fashionable in the second half of the sixteenth century but he may be confusing framing methods with applied plasterwork.[72]

From the fifteenth century, efforts began to create daylit accommodation in the roof. Schofield and Stell believe that dormer windows were being built by 1450, though the almost universal frontage gables would have been a discouragement.[73] By the sixteenth century some broader houses which would previously have had two or more gables were being equipped with a continuous attic frontage, often jettied and sometimes with a balcony. This hid the normal roof, or roofs, which stood behind, usually at right angles to the street. The house of the East India Company in Leadenhall Street, built in 1648, appears to have boasted an elaborate version of one of these attic screens.[74]

London's efficient timber framing may have postponed the use of brick. Brickmaking spread across much of western Europe from the twelfth century but brick and tile did not figure in London building until the fifteenth century when their manufacture revived in the London area.[75] From the sixteenth century brick was often used to fill the spaces between the timbers, in place of wattle and daub and other fillers such as plaster, and it was also used for chimneys. Richard Harris has suggested that brick was not evidently superior to wattle and daub; it tended to hold the damp and was a poor insulator, as well as being unnecessarily heavy for timber-framed buildings.[76] It was, however, fashionable and added lustre to a timber-framed house. Even by 1666 few London buildings were built completely of

21 Staple Inn's sunless north facade with its ever-present 'mystery van', seen from near 'The Cittie of York'. Some scholars question the authenticity of this restored frontage, but it is good enough for this author.

brick.[77] An exception was Clothworkers' Hall of 1549.[78] Summerson detects a growing use of brick in London buildings from the second half of the sixteenth century, in step with what he has defined as Artisan Mannerism.[79]

Timbers were probably left to weather to their natural colour, which would normally have been grey. If painted, they would probably have been ochre in colour. The panels would probably have weathered to light brown.[80] Blacking of the timbers became common in the sixteenth century, however. The use of glass became common, but not universal, and leaded lights could be bought by the rich.[81] The poor could use stretched linen, paper or shutters. In the richer houses, the upper panels of windows were often decorated with coloured glass bearing emblems. Bays and oriels projecting beyond even the jettied upper floors became

22 The jettied Inner Temple gateway and tavern (the Prince's Arms) at 17 Fleet Street, with double glazed bays. This building acquired its present appearance in 1611 when the gateway was inserted.

common, as at Inner Temple gateway, 17 Fleet Street. They let more light into rooms darkened by jettying and the increasing height of the houses. Two-storey timber bays like the ones surviving at 41–2 Cloth Fair seem to have been becoming more common in the decades before the Fire.

London's greatest achievement in timber was the broad roof or ceiling spanning a hall. English masons were slow to master the construction of stone vaults, so timber roofs were always a likely development. London had the biggest concentration of religious and secular halls in England. The hall was a large, heatable space used for meals, relaxation and meetings. Early halls were mostly small and crude and the construction of their roofs does not figure in the documentary evidence. The biggest London hall, Westminster Hall, dates from 1394–1401.[82] It was a radical reconstruction of a large hall built by William Rufus in 1097–9 which formed part of the Palace of Westminster. The master mason was Henry Yevele, who was just finishing the nave of Westminster Abbey, and the carpenter was Hugh Herland. Herland designed an unprecedented hammerbeam roof which permitted a span of 20.7 metres, which no stone vault could have achieved. Its key reinforcing element, the arch-rib, was rarely used elsewhere.[83] It weighed 660 tons and required heavy stone buttresses on the side away from the palace. It was prefabricated at the Frame, a 'framing ground' or

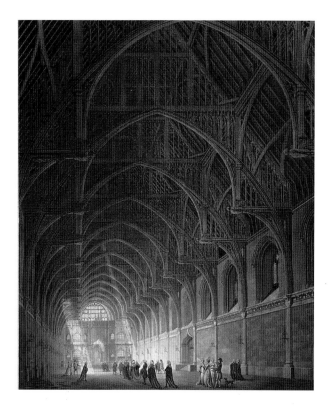

26 Westminster Hall in 1801. Its role in State ceremonies has made it so familiar that many no longer recognise it as one of the wonders of Europe.

carpenter Simon Birlyngham in about 1496, when he showed them several roofs so that they could express a preference for their new hall.[89]

Many halls were built in the fifteenth and early sixteenth centuries and their timber roof structures became more standardised. However, certain new features such as pendentives were developed, in line with the development of the Perpendicular style, and the roof sections became flatter. The hammerbeam roof and the double hammerbeam roof, which achieved greater height, proliferated. Carved decoration became more generous, and from the mid-sixteenth century it sometimes included Mannerist motifs. The halls of the Inns of Court and the Inns of Chancery had timber roofs. The hammerbeam roof of the great hall at Eltham Palace, Woolwich (1475–9), built for Edward IV from 1475 to 1479 by the senior carpenter Edmund Graveley, was an outstanding example of English carpentry.[90] Good examples of later hammerbeam roofs were Gray's Inn Hall (1556–60) and Middle Temple Hall's double hammerbeam roof, built between 1562

27 The Middle Temple hall, its double hammerbeam roof built in oak in 1573.

carpenter's yard at Farnham, Surrey, and taken to the site by road and river.[84] The Royal Commission on Historical Monuments deemed it 'probably the finest timber-roofed building in Europe' in the biggest understatement in this book.[85]

Westminster Hall was soon followed by the largest secular hall in the City. This was the Guildhall of about 1411–40, by the mason John Croxtone.[86] Replacing buildings dating from about 1125–50, and retaining an undercroft dating from about 1270, it was similar in style to Westminster Hall and for Pevsner it rivalled in scale the town halls of the big Italian and Flemish cities.[87] At 46 metres it was equal in length to the Salone dei Cinquecento in Florence. Its timber roof, perhaps the work of the carpenter Richard Bird, had a span of fifteen metres which was, after Westminster Hall, the largest in England.[88]

By the fifteenth century, timber roofs had acquired a standing in their own right, rather than being second best to stone vaults. This tradition of excellence meant that timber continued to be chosen for hall roofs even though the technique for building stone vaults was now more familiar. This was clear from the tour made by members of the Pewterers' Company with their

28 The Guildhall in 1921, after Victorian alterations and before war damage. It has the second widest single span timber roof in London.

and 1575 and judged by Saunders to be the finest in England.[91] Much of this new building sprang from the enhanced position of the Inns after the Reformation, and once their needs had been met, the building of halls declined in the later part of the sixteenth century.

The lawyers' halls were outnumbered by those of the City guilds, though some of these were much smaller. The guilds started to build or acquire halls in the twelfth century, and formal incorporation began in the thirteenth century. The first known hall was Goldsmiths', which dates from 1339.[92] Merchant Taylors' Hall followed in 1347. Some three to five companies are known to have possessed them by 1400. The numbers increased rapidly between 1400 and 1530, some of them having been acquired from noble families.[93] There were about twenty-seven halls by 1475, and forty-five by

1532–3, after which the numbers stabilised.[94] Many of the halls were developed from a courtyard house, bequeathed by a rich member.[95] Nearly all the livery company halls were set above ground level, so an external staircase was required to reach them. The only rich man's hall to have survived is Crosby Hall, built in Bishopsgate in 1466–75 by a cloth merchant and later owned by Sir Thomas More. The hall was moved to Cheyne Walk, Chelsea, in 1908–10. Its timbered vault is a fine example.[96] Most of these private halls seem to have been based on a gateway and courtyard, and they reinforced the enclosure as a widespread component of London's plan.

★　★　★

ROYAL, ARISTOCRATIC AND SHOW ARCHITECTURE, 1300–1603

We have seen that London was distinguished by three main design types—the timber-framed house, the low, aisled parish church with a bell tower and the stone hall with a pitched, timber roof. These were built in large numbers, without much variation, throughout the period and they were the main creators of the townscape. When we turn to buildings which were normally designed individually, and which were not reproduced on a number of sites in London, we find less coherence.

The biggest hotchpotch of all was the Palace of Westminster and its environs, including Whitehall Palace to the north, which Henry VIII acquired from Church ownership in 1529. As the seat of government and the court in London, it grew from its late Saxon origins into a mass of mainly modest, unrelated buildings, without even the coherent plan and design, say, of a large medieval monastery. The highlights, apart from Westminster Hall, were the Painted Chamber, a Norman structure equipped with a hanging ceiling and wall paintings under Henry III in the thirteenth century, and St Stephen's Chapel, Edward I's conventional attempt to outdo the Sainte-Chapelle, started in 1292.[97] As late as 1581, however, the building of a Banqueting House on Whitehall was executed in

30   The interior of Henry VII's chapel, 1505–12. The lush effect will enthral any visitor but there is no visual connection with the spartan purity of the abbey behind it.

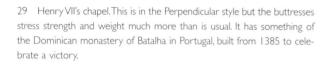

29   Henry VII's chapel. This is in the Perpendicular style but the buttresses stress strength and weight much more than is usual. It has something of the Dominican monastery of Batalha in Portugal, built from 1385 to celebrate a victory.

timber, with canvas walls painted to look like rusticated stone.[98] Only when the Stuarts came to the throne in 1603 did the Crown begin to encourage a new approach to the Palace on Classical lines, inspired by Inigo Jones.

Westminster Abbey, on the other hand, secured much attention. The pure, early Gothic abbey had been completed in the 1390s, but Henry VII had an interest in tall churches in the Perpendicular Gothic style. His master masons built fine examples at Windsor and Cambridge, and Henry went on to order a highly ornate chapel at Westminster. The design is probably by Robert Vertue, who showed a mastery of intricate decoration but who probably was not responsible for the decision to slap the chapel onto the east end of the abbey chevet. The interior of the chapel is almost invisible from the abbey, but from other points of view the new chapel is an insensitive intrusion. The heavy, over-built exterior of the chapel recalls some of the big Portuguese churches of the period. The ornate, fan-vaulted interior, however, is one of the gems of London.

31 Westminster Abbey nave, looking east. The black marble and reduced horizontal dimensions create a unique vertical effect.

32 St James's Palace gateway, 1532, a conventional Tudor design similar to that of Hampton Court and of some country houses of the aristocracy.

Large houses were not a feature of London in this period. The main exception was Somerset House, built in 1547–52 by the Duke of Somerset, briefly Protector of the young Edward VI. Somerset carved out a site of about two and a half hectares between the Thames and the Strand, a short distance downstream from the Palace of Westminster. His architect may have been the Italian John of Padua, though a more credible authorship is that of Sir John Thynne, Somerset's steward.[99] Summerson regards Somerset House as 'one of the most influential buildings of the English Renais-sance'.[100] This may apply to the enlarged house for which Inigo Jones would design the New Gallery, built in 1661–4, but the original structure was a quadrangle in the tried-and-tested Oxbridge college mode, very fashionable at the time for large houses.[101] It was surrounded by two-storey brick buildings with a balustrade and was entered from the Strand through a three-storey ashlar gateway with superimposed orders.[102] Two Mannerist pavilions stood on each side of the gateway. A continuous balustrade hid the low roof but the chimneys were prominent. The gateway is supposed to resemble that of the chateau of Ecouen but the design looks weak and uncoordinated, only remotely like its French contemporary. It was certainly a departure from the gateway of St James's, built for Henry VIII in 1532, with its tall flanking turrets in the classic, brick, Tudor country house style, but it did not offer a convincing alternative and appears to have had little influence on new houses, in London or outside.

Sir Thomas Gresham, the financier and diplomat, had a new house built in Bishopsgate shortly before 1566, which was formally arranged round a courtyard, as were Northumberland House (1605) in the Strand and the Derby house in Cannon Row, Westminster.[103] Northumberland House, built for the Earl of Northampton on the site of a former convent by Bernard Jansen and Gerard Christmas, was a spartan, symmetrical two-storey courtyard building with four corner turrets with pyramidal roofs, looking like the much earlier Syon House and recalling a fortress or prison. It had an awkward Mannerist gateway turret on the Strand frontage with a curved oriel. Sir Fulke Greville's house (Brooke House) in Holborn, supposedly designed by Inigo Jones in about 1617, was set on the street frontage. It was more Dutch than Classical and probably conformed to the wishes of the client.[104]

Public buildings responded to London's growth much better than the royal ones but their architecture was uncertain in style. The rebuilt Custom House of

33 Northumberland House in a print of 1753. The fashionable, curved oriel and the conventional lion with a rigid (iron) tail cannot rescue this banal frontage.

1559 was a rectangular, fortress-like building with no architectural distinction.[105] The Royal Exchange (1566–70), which revived the old Roman tradition of the forum, was built by Sir Thomas Gresham on lines similar to the slightly earlier Gresham College. Before this time, merchants had apparently done business while walking in Lombard Street and Gresham took his inspiration from the Low Countries, the main centre of foreign trade in northern Europe, with which he had close business and diplomatic contacts. Gresham brought over a distinguished architect, Hendryck van Paesschen, to build what Pevsner judges to be the City's 'first major Renaissance-style building', in stone.[106]

34 Model of Thomas Gresham's Royal Exchange, 1566–7. It resembled the Beurse at Antwerp.

His main model was the Beurse at Antwerp, built by Cornelis Floris in 1531. Some of the Exchange's stone was imported from Flanders.[107]

The Royal Exchange was based on a quadrangle of Doric columns topped by semi-circular arches leading to an arcade, with an Ionic pilastered storey above. It had a pitched roof with dormer windows and contained a hundred rental shops. Overall, the building was entirely Flemish in style. Schofield points out that courtyards surrounded by open arcades were becoming common in London.[108]

THEATRES

A completely new type of building matured in the sixteenth century. This was the theatre. London was the English centre of acting and the first permanent theatres were established there in the late sixteenth century. Plays had previously been performed in the courtyards of inns, some of which were later converted into theatres.[109] These origins produced the idea of the galleried theatre, galleries being normal in the courtyards of the larger inns. The first theatre was built at St Paul's in 1575. To avoid interference from City magistrates, theatres were set up in the suburbs, the first

35 The Old Tabard Inn, Southwark, in 1890. Some of the big City inns were taller, rising up to four galleried floors.

27

permanent example being the Red Lion in Stepney, built in 1567. By the end of the century, a cluster of theatres, open to the sky, had appeared in Southwark, including two very large ones, the Rose (1587) and the Globe (1599).[110] Further such theatres were built in the early seventeenth century.[111]

In terms of architecture these open theatres looked backwards rather than forwards. Some of them had an alternative use as bear-baiting pits. They had up to three levels of galleries. They were square, oval or round in plan, on a timber frame, sometimes with a thatched roof over the galleries. Enclosed theatres came on the scene in the late sixteenth century, with Inigo Jones and Wren designing several. The Globe burned down in 1613 but was rebuilt in a stronger and more elaborate form in the following year. The open theatre faded away in the seventeenth century while covered theatres became more common in the City as acting became more respectable.[112]

36 Model of the Rose Theatre, where Shakespeare performed. The foundations and lower walls have survived here, and a reconstruction was under consideration when this book went to press. Why London should want two rebuilt Tudor theatres is unclear, but Europe's richest city could probably afford them easily enough, together with the Olympic Games.

'THIS WOODEN O'

William Shakespeare wrote *All's Well That Ends Well* in 1602–3. His London was still a medieval city, its rapid growth merely adding to what had gone before. Soon most of London would be burned and rebuilt. There would be a fresh start after the Fire, on modern lines. We shall see what use London builders and architects made of this opportunity.

37 The Globe Theatre, the outstanding pastiche of the South Bank, opened in 1996, though not on the original site. To rebuild The Globe and perform Shakespeare's plays there was the ambition of the American filmmaker, Sam Wanamaker.

3 London's Augustan Age, 1603–1830

At the end of the Middle Ages Europe was swept by a great surge of interest in the world of Ancient Greece and Rome. It began in Italy and spread from the south of Europe to the north, reaching England by the mid-sixteenth century. Art, literature and culture were all affected. A new architecture emerged in the form of Classicism. This was the adoption of proportions, components, forms and details from the buildings of the Ancient world, together with their supporting philosophy—building 'in the ancient manner' as it was often termed. Ancient Rome was at first the main source. Strict laws of proportion were defined and features such as porticoes, columns, capitals, pediments, fluting, right angles, flights of steps, block cornices, statues, bas-reliefs, shallow or flat roofs, ashlar and rustication were brought into use. However, simple pastiches of Roman buildings were rarely attempted. Instead, Renaissance architects sought to create a modern, enlightened, Christian architecture using the best of the Ancient world. The result was usually highly convincing and the Classical quickly spread across Europe and into its overseas colonies.

THE BEGINNING OF CLASSICAL ARCHITECTURE

A number of Classical styles have emerged since the fifteenth century. In London, one has stood out. This is the Palladian style, an approach based on the work of the Italian architect and writer Andrea Palladio (1508–80). First introduced into London in the early 1600s by the royal architect Inigo Jones, Palladianism was revived in about 1720 by Whig aristocrats and their architects. The Baroque and other Classical variants figured in London in the seventeenth and eighteenth centuries but the Palladian was not replaced and it survived to sustain the Neo-Classical style of the late eighteenth and the nineteenth centuries.[1] The Gothic, dominant in London from 1200 to 1500 and occasionally in use thereafter, revived powerfully from the 1830s

38 'A Student conducted to Minerva, who points to Greece, and Italy, as the Countries from where he must derive the most perfect Knowledge and Taste in elegant Architecture.' This frontispiece to *The Works in Architecture of Robert and James Adam Esquires* (1775) is the very expression of Classical architecture. Admirers of Grand Central Terminal will know that a giant statue of Minerva figures on the pediment there, looking down Park Avenue. The ruins of a huge, domed temple of Minerva can be seen to the left of trains approaching the Termini station in Rome.

when it was the first radical challenge to Classical architecture but it went into sharp decline from 1870. A number of idiosyncratic styles, such as Queen Anne, Arts and Crafts and Free Style, made their claims from the 1870s but the Palladian carried on as one of a number of Classical styles. The Classical retained its important role until the 1950s, with the Palladian in particular contributing to Neo-Classical and even Modern architecture between the wars. In the 1980s the Palladian revived for a while under the influence of Prince Charles, albeit mainly as a pastiche form. By 2000 the magazine of the rich homeseeker, *Country Life*, was carrying advertisements for striking Palladian houses which, on examination, proved to be brand new.

In England, the Classical influenced four main building types from the mid-sixteenth century onwards. These were churches, the great houses of the Crown, aristocracy and gentry, the halls of livery companies and municipalities and the houses of ordinary people. The latter responded the most slowly. In London, however, an event unique in Europe—the Great Fire of 1666—provided an opportunity for the classicisation of the City of London. Although the result was incomplete, the reconstruction transformed the City, with the Gothic and the vernacular virtually eradicated.

INIGO JONES AND THE BIRTH OF CLASSICAL ARCHITECTURE IN LONDON

Classical design had not contributed much to London by 1600, except through the crude form of Mannerism, which meant little more than using disparate and dubious Ancient features, drawn from Italian, French and Dutch pattern books, to decorative effect. England was the only major European country to which an Italian architect had not been called to design a building.[2] In the new century there was some progress, beginning with the accession of James I in 1603 and continuing under his son, Charles I. Unlike Elizabeth, James was prepared to spend money on royal building and he was in closer touch with Italian and French fashion. In this new climate, one English architect, Inigo Jones, was able to bring Italian Classicism to England and make it respected there. Meanwhile, English traditions based on a refinement of Mannerism and the growing influence of Dutch Classicism after about 1625 continued to be influential at least until the end of the seventeenth century.[3] However, the work of Inigo Jones was a turning point in English architecture. It was also based in London, where Jones did most of his work. Jones certainly had the advantage of building for crown and court, where he had many influential admirers, but his main strength was his own genius.

Inigo Jones, the son of a clothworker, trained as a painter and went to Italy in 1601. He visited Denmark in 1604 and France in 1609. In 1613 he went to Italy again, returning through France in the following year, acquiring a growing interest in Classical architecture. No other English artist or designer had this rich experience and, with no major Italian architect working in England (in contrast to France), he was the main channel of Italian influence. In 1606 he started to work at Court, specialising in scenery and designs for masques and displays and supervising minor building tasks. In 1608 he

39   Inigo Jones's Banqueting House, planned as part of a larger Palace of Whitehall. It cannot be appreciated without viewing the double cube interior.

40   The interior of the Banqueting House, its double cube formula also used at the Great Hall of the Queen's House at Greenwich. The masques must have ceased early on, as the smoke would have damaged the ceiling.

41 The 'piazzas' (arcades) at Covent Garden in an engraving of 1777. Inigo Jones built awkwardly tall arcade arches which made the second and third floors look cramped. The absence of pilasters is surprising, but Jones may have sought a rustic or Etruscan effect on a site which lay near open land and markets. The origin of the tall arcades may be Palladio's farm buildings, where the arches and vaults had to accommodate loaded hay carts.

43 Inigo Jones built this gateway at Beaufort House, Chelsea, in 1621. It now stands in the gardens of Chiswick House. Jones was commissioned to build a number of gateways by owners who sought Classical distinction for their properties at low cost.

42 St Paul's, Covent Garden. The Doric columns and barn-like roof are probably a further expression of a rustic, Etruscan effect as defined by Serlio and Palladio. The church was originally in stucco.

made his first architectural designs in London under the patronage of Robert Cecil, the Lord Treasurer and Earl of Salisbury.[4] In 1615, just after his tour in Italy and France, he was made Surveyor of the King's Works, meaning that he became the royal architect. He was continuously engaged with official works from 1615 until 1652.[5]

Jones seems to have worked mainly on his own. He employed a variety of tradesmen but had no formal office with other architects assisting him. This meant that he apparently had no close followers or pupils, with the exception of his nephew by marriage, John Webb.[6] Jones's painstaking rendition of Italian Classical architecture thus remained focused on London. His influence was visible in other buildings but other architects and masons generally drew on the more muscular and vernacular-related versions of the Classical produced in Holland and in France.

Jones was a master of Classical detail and proportion.[7] His major works were the Banqueting House, Whitehall (1622), which Jones hoped would form part of a new Palace of Whitehall designed by himself, a new chapel for Henry VIII's St James' Palace (1623–7; now known as Marlborough Chapel); the Queen's House, an addition to Henry VII's Greenwich Palace; the recladding of the nave of St Paul's and a new west front with a Roman portico later much admired by Wren;[8] Covent Garden piazza and church; and a number of doorways and gateways, including the gateway from Beaufort House, Chelsea (1621), now at Chiswick House. From the 1630s Jones went on to prepare a number of designs for small houses and warehouses derived partly from Serlio's ideas, some of which were executed.[9] Their pitched roofs looked forward to Wren's designs for small buildings and would have been accepted by Serlio as necessary in northern climes.[10]

Most obscure of all is Jones's work in correcting or commenting on other men's designs. We know that he contributed to Nicholas Stone's rebuilt Goldsmiths' Hall in the 1630s, with Stone admitting that Jones 'did advise and direct before the perfectinge and finishinge of each

In an era of master masons and carpenters, Inigo Jones was London's only fully formed architect in the first half of the seventeenth century. Sir Christopher Wren, who became royal architect in 1669, enjoyed much the same status in the second half. His versatile architecture was Baroque (often referred to as English Baroque) rather than Jones's Palladian but both approaches were Classical and they did not conflict. Wren's Baroque was less geometrical and more decorative than the Palladian, using curves and depth and drawing on a variety of Classical components, often striving for effect rather than scholarship. His inspiration came from France and the Low Countries as well as from Italy. That London's Classical architecture should still be guided by one man in 1700, nearly three hundred years after Brunelleschi designed the cathedral dome at Florence, reflects London's delayed development, which sprang mainly from its northern location. Wren had more assistants and followers than Jones and his English Baroque was more widely adopted in London than Jones's Palladian had been but London's architecture, and the English architectural profession, were clearly retarded in comparison with France. Much therefore rested on the shoulders of Christopher Wren.

44 (*above*) The Queen's Chapel, Marlborough Gate (Marlborough Chapel) was built by Inigo Jones between 1623 and 1627 as a new chapel for St James's Palace. The first Classical church in England, its cramped interior and stuccoed exterior make it one of the least impressive of this architect's buildings. It is, however, utterly scholarly.

45 (*right*) Thanet House, Aldersgate. This was one of the houses that gave Aldersgate a reputation for aristocratic elegance in the seventeenth century. The pilasters give it a touch of Inigo Jones, who may have refronted it in about 1641. However, like Lindsey House (see below), this looks more like the work of a Mannerist artisan possibly following Jones's guidance.

piece'.[11] He also advised the parish of St Michael-le-Querne on the rebuilding of its church in 1638–40.[12] It is not known how widely he intervened in this way but his reputation, eminence and royal offices probably allowed him to exercise considerable influence, especially after 1618 when he served on the king's Commission on Buildings. Thanet House, Aldersgate Street (demolished), looks as though it benefited from Jones's advice without giving up all its Mannerist character, including strapwork. The pilasters, above all, suggested that Jones was pursuing his unifying aesthetic wherever he could.[13]

★   ★   ★

Wren had a scholarly background in mathematics and astronomy. In 1657 he became Gresham Professor of Astronomy in London. In 1661 he was elevated to the Savilian Chair of Astronomy at Oxford (where he gave his inaugural lecture in Latin).[14]. From about 1660 Wren started to show interest in architecture, mainly as an extension of mathematics.[15] In France meanwhile, the Académie Royale d'Architecture was founded in 1671 as part of the efforts of Louis XIV and Colbert to create a national culture. The new academy defined the functions and status of the architect, rewarded prowess and set up a programme of lectures on two days a week. The first director of the academy, the distinguished François Blondel, wrote that he wanted to create 'a sort of seminary of young architects'. As early as 1675, Blondel started to publish his lectures in a series of impressive volumes which became a practical as well as a theoretical guide for architects throughout France.[16] There were many master masons in France, as there were in England, but in France there was no longer any doubt that buildings were designed by architects, and by architects who were aware of a national architecture firmly based on agreed Classical principles and certain traditional features. Much more than mathematics was involved here.

Wren, England's greatest authority on the movements of the spheres, went to the Continent only once. This was in 1665–6 when he visited buildings and architects in Paris and its region. On the way, he may have travelled through Holland and Flanders. He had begun designing buildings, on mathematical lines, in Oxford and Cambridge in 1662 and from 1663 he had been a consultant to the new Royal Commission studying the repair of St Paul's. He may also have been working on a scheme for a new Palace of Whitehall. In France, however, he would have needed a guide or mentor (except when he could speak in Latin) and would have appeared to be a novice or dilettante. Bernini's refusal to let him have more than a glimpse of his big Louvre design suggests that obscure meetings with Mansart, Le Vau and other distinguished Paris architects – if they took place at all – were purely formal. However, the strong presence of Italian architects in Paris allowed him to claim that he had studied the best methods of Italian artists as well as of the French.[17]

LONDON'S BURNING

London had been burning down ever since the Romans founded it, though it did not usually all burn down at once. It was a chronic fire trap, with nearly all its houses built of wood and a combination of high densities and narrow streets which reached a dangerous peak in the early fourteenth century, before the Black Death and other disasters reduced the population, and an even higher peak by the middle of the seventeenth century. The only relief was that fires rarely spread beyond a few blocks and Londoners were used to being roused by shouts and screams as a fire took hold and turning over and going back to sleep unless the noise was very close.[18] Then came the Great Fire of London on 2–6 September 1666. This time most of the City and an area to the west burned down in a few days, producing 437 acres of devastation and the loss of 13,000 houses.

The Fire was the talk of Europe. The measures taken to prevent a recurrence were studied at the highest level in other cities, particularly in Paris where a similar risk was perceived. Europe rightly saw the Fire as a disaster, but London now had the chance to jump from its remote status to be the most advanced large city of its day. It was obvious that better water supplies, wider gaps between the buildings and fireproof building materials would be needed. That a new architecture might arise from the ashes was less obvious but it was clear that any innovations would be related to Classicism.[19]

THE FIRE AND WREN

The Great Fire of London destroyed five-sixths of the City within the walls and sixty-three further acres in the Fleet Street area. Most of London between the City and Westminster was untouched. The king set up a Royal Commission on the rebuilding of London, with Wren closely involved from the start. In 1667 the Fire Court was set up by Act of Parliament to decide boundary disputes. The Rebuilding Act, which fixed the lines on which London was to be rebuilt, was also passed in 1667 and owners started to rebuild in spring of that year, with serious reconstruction under way in 1668. A second Rebuilding Act in 1671 determined the fifty-one churches to be rebuilt.

Wren's contribution to the rebuilding was multiple. First, he was the main influence on the drafting of building regulations for the reconstruction of private houses, issued as soon as possible in 1667. Second, he took charge of the rebuilding of St Paul's. Third, he directed the reconstruction of the parish churches destroyed by the Fire. Fourth, he and Robert Hooke, one of three City Surveyors appointed after the Fire, built the Monument (1671–6), a powerful Roman column of which Blondel would have been proud. Fifth, he built the unassuming, brick Custom House (1669–71) with projecting wings,

The reconstruction of St Paul's was Wren's biggest and most frustrating project. It is also one of the most mysterious, for little of his correspondence and drawings have survived. Wren worked as sole architect from the start and Robert Hooke and his other architect friends have told us little. The initial cheap repair plan favoured by the cathedral authorities, based on the conversion of the surviving nave into a new cathedral and shopping arcade, opposed by Wren, did not survive a partial collapse in 1668. Wren now won his case for a completely new building.[21]

Wren was probably moved by two considerations. One was that large, prestigious buildings were becoming symbols of national pride. Louis XIV's France was the main seat of this sentiment. The other was that Wren wanted to build a tall dome at St Paul's. Charles II would have supported both these aspirations. The Dean and Chapter, representing the Archbishop of Canterbury, would also have wanted a cathedral to rival the greatest Roman Catholic churches on the Continent.[22] Outstanding was of course the basilica of St Peter's in Rome. St Peter's was about five times the area of Old St Paul's and all the parties must have agreed early on that it could not be emulated except in length, St Peter's being 211 metres long overall, not much more than Old St Paul's. That a dome at St Paul's could overtop the dome of St Peter's, as the old spire had done before 1561, may have been in Wren's mind. However, the cathedral would have to stand on a typical London subsoil of sand, clay and gravel, which raised serious problems of weight, especially for a tall dome.

There was no English design context for the new cathedral, owing to the lack of church building since Henry VIII's break with Rome in the 1530s and this gave considerable freedom to Wren. That the new cathedral should be in the Classical style seems, however, to have been quickly agreed by all the parties. Wren's first plan for the new church, the First Model, was presented in 1670. However, with the new City now rising around it, the design appeared too modest and Wren was allowed to review it. He then produced a variety of designs, most of them based on two contrasting concepts. One was a domed church on a traditional plan, roughly covering the site of the old cathedral. The other was a completely new approach, the Greek Cross design (1671–2). This was a church on the plan of a Greek cross, creating a huge central space, ideal for preaching, with a dome above. The concave quadrants between the arms of the cross were probably French in inspiration, derived from the work of Lepautre.[23] A version of the Greek Cross design

46   The Monument is one of the world's finest free-standing columns. However, the street vista from the Thames, planned by Wren, was never created and recent buildings have hidden or overshadowed it. The author's 'Stop and Search' complicated the taking of this photograph.

a central portico and triangular and curved pediments.[20] Unlike Inigo Jones, he did not try to do everything himself: he had an office and a house in the Palace of Westminster and he employed a staff there. However, he was a very hard worker and his hand can be seen in almost all the products of the Surveyorship of the King's Works. He designed more than seventy buildings in the London area. Most of his larger buildings were commissioned by the Crown or the Church.

47   St Paul's cathedral from the south. Wren's unique dome, achieving both height and bulk, makes a powerful statement here.

48 St Paul's cathedral interior looking towards the dome. The more conventional Baroque effect echoed a number of French, Italian and German churches around 1700.

heavy stone pinnacle, was as much a triumph of engineering as a work of art. However, Wren created a profile which would become the eternal symbol of London. In the end, Wren's dome, at 111 metres, did not quite beat St Peter's (138 metres). Moreover, the new cathedral was shorter, as the visitor to St Peter's learns from the marks on the floor.

Although Wren worked hard on the nave, chancel and transepts, they seem to have been of secondary importance to him. The Portland stone curtain wall of two storeys of constant height, a feature of the Warrant design, generated much repetition and the use of the upper storey to hide the vaults and supports of the nave and choir produced long runs of blank windows and niches. The great lengths of balustrade did not help, though Wren never wanted these and they were added by a new Surveyor in Wren's old age. The two western towers were, however, a great enhancement.[25] In old age, Wren often used to visit the cathedral, where he liked to sit quietly under his great dome.[26] We, in our turn, can dream of that Great Model, hidden above us in the triforium.

49 The dome of St Paul's in 1941. It was still under threat from the air and the fire watchers knew that just one incendiary could set the timber structure alight. Given that the dome must have been an aiming point, the bomb aimers were probably under orders to avoid it.

formed the basis for the Great Model (1673), which is still on display in the cathedral's triforium. Most commentators conclude that this is Wren's preferred design, clearly inspired by St Peter's. The Dean and Chapter, however, rejected it. They thought that it would be too small, too dark and lacking in processional space – a typical committee decision which in most respects was unjustified. Wren then submitted the cautious Warrant design (1675) on a plan similar to the old cathedral. Here, a thin and ungainly spire topped a low, saucer dome. The outer walls were divided into two tiers.[24]

Royal and ecclesiastical approval for the Warrant Design gave Wren a free hand in making adjustments but he never tried to return to the Greek Cross. He reinstated the dome but retained the nave and chancel plan of the Warrant design. The new St Paul's would not be completed until 1711 and the design was being altered until the last moment, notably with the addition of the two western towers (1705–8) in a Baroque style influenced by Bernini and Borromini. The dome, with its timber structure, false interior, and cone carrying the

The burned churches of the City presented a different problem. The Fire spared only twenty-two of 107 buildings. Many had been small and the diocese and the parishes agreed that nearly half should not be rebuilt. The rebuilding was entrusted to yet another Commission, which gave overall control to Wren. Wren's authority and ideas were not seriously challenged by other architects or the public. He ensured that the rebuilt churches were all broadly in the Classical style, though there were many variants.[27]

Funds came from a tax on coal imports first enacted in 1670 and renewed in 1686 and 1700. Wren was responsible for nearly all the fifty-one rebuilt churches, though in most cases he provided outline designs, or approved the designs of others, with the detailed work and the supervision of construction being done by his associates–of whom Hooke and later Gibbs and Hawksmoor were the most important–or by master masons. Hooke seems to have been sole architect for several churches. Several parishes rebuilt their churches themselves, using master masons of their own choice. The old foundations were often used and some of the plans did not diverge greatly from the old.

The Church of England required only one altar and no chapels, so most of the new churches had a simple, rectangular or square plan with a prominent altar at the east end and a simple interior suitable for preaching. Five were centrally planned, which meant that the altar was in the middle of the church or thereabouts.[28] Wren was usually behind these designs, which recalled his Greek Cross plan at St Paul's. The most impressive of these was the domed St Stephen Walbrook. Galleries, which had been introduced in some London churches from about 1620, were also related to the preaching requirement.

Flemish church architecture appears to have had some influence.[29] In the Netherlands the small area of many churches was compensated by tall spires. Once it became known that this formula was available in London, most parishes clamoured for their own towers or spires and in the end all the new churches were provided with them. Many parishes pressed for spires equal to their neighbours and were usually satisfied.[30] With the coal tax lasting until 1717, many spires were added to what had originally been mere towers. There was no equivalent in Europe for this mass of towers and spires, visibly relating to the dome of St Paul's. By 1701 there were many more tall towers and spires in the City than before the Fire, and Wren's dream of a vertical City had come to pass.[31]

50   St Bride's, Fleet Street. This is Wren's tallest City steeple. It resembles the tiered spire on his Warrant Design for St Paul's.

Apart from the towers and spires, the exteriors of many of the new churches offered little interest. Many faced narrow streets, lanes or paths. Few churchyards survived and they were usually too small to set the building off. Because they could not be viewed effectively, many elevations were of simple design. The interiors were carefully designed in almost all cases, though they could be repetitive and sometimes claustrophobic. Summerson detects in many of the City churches 'the rather gross aldermanish vernacular' which was also to be found in the rebuilt City halls: 'only occasionally does the lucid genius of Wren shine through with recognizable brilliance'.[32] Summerson, however, could pick out a 'gross alderman' at a hundred paces. Taken as a whole, Wren's cluster of new churches was unique in Europe and discussion here cannot do them justice. Perhaps the finest is St Stephen Walbrook (1672–80) with its domed interior. The tiered spire of St Bride's (69 metres) (1703) is one of the most striking in the City but St Mary-le-

Bow's great steeple (68 metres) (1678–80) is Wren's finest. St Andrew Holborn, rebuilt since the last war, has an intricate tower and a full interior array of barrel vault, arcades and galleries. The tower of St Vedast (1697) is an impressive exercise in angular Baroque. Among the work of other architects, Hawksmoor's tower at St Michael Cornhill in expressionist Gothick is outstanding.

Wren's achievement was nevertheless a compromise. It was his original intention to site all the churches at the end of vistas formed by new streets and houses and to distribute them evenly across the City.[33] In practice, no vistas or piazzas were created and with houses rising up to three or four storeys around a church, the spire or tower made the most visual impact. Overall, the spires and towers were much more varied and distinguished than the elevations of the churches, suggesting that Wren

52 (*below*) St Andrew-by-the-Wardrobe, rebuilt in brick by Wren in 1685–94, was close to a royal storehouse. Wren used this simple brick-and-stone style where workers might attend his churches.

and the other architects consciously catered for a still crowded city in which the observer's upward view could be most easily satisfied. This vertical aesthetic contrasted with the developing layouts of the West End where landowners concentrated on spacious new squares and approach streets, producing a horizontal aesthetic. In the City, verticality and spatial crowding have lived on to the present day, but the architectural example of the West End has spread to most of London in the form of the suburb.

INNOVATION AND CONTINUITY IN REBUILDING THE CITY

Immediately after the Fire, Wren drew up a plan for the reconstruction of the City. Other plans were prepared but Wren's was much the most thoughtful, detailed and carefully presented. However, it would have involved a massive re-allocation of land and no powers were available, or could reasonably be made available, to do the job. So the idea of radical replanning, which in Wren's case would have produced a Baroque layout on the latest Continental lines, was forgotten and the existing property and street lines were for the the most part retained, though with some new streets and many widenings. On 13 September 1667 a Royal Proclamation announced that the City would be rebuilt in brick and stone, with wider streets.

A committee of six, representing the king and the City, was immediately appointed. All six were architects or had a connection with architecture – Wren, Hugh May, Roger Pratt, Hooke, Edward Jerman and Peter Mills. They drafted the Act for Rebuilding the City of London and its liberties, passed in 1667. This building code, which was enforced by surveyors each responsible for a defined area, was the most ambitious in the world outside Italy.

London's houses had been influenced by building regulations since the twelfth century. When the population dropped between 1350 and 1500, the enforcement of regulations seems to have declined, but towards the end of Elizabeth's reign a burst of growth promoted a new wave of official concern. At first, Crown and Parliament sought to prevent the disorderly spread of London by a series of royal proclamations and an Act of Parliament of 1593. These enactments concentrated on forbidding the construction of houses on new foundations for up to three miles outside the City. However, the Stuarts went on to revive the medieval approach, requiring that new buildings were solidly built and as fireproof as possible. This aspiration was expressed in James I's Augustan proclamation of 1615 where he announced that he had found London of sticks but wanted it to be of brick.[34]

Building regulations tend to produce continuity of built forms. Later measures are generally accretions, with prior requirements often regarded as unalterable because building has already taken place with the approval of the law. In London, a continuous body of regulations dates from 1605, when brick or stone building was required, except on London Bridge. By 1630, each storey was required to be at least three metres high. The use of timber window surrounds was banned. To prevent strip windows, sections of wall between windows were to be not less than half the width of the windows. There were to be no jetties or oriels and walls were to rise vertically from their foundations. Open shop fronts were to be bounded by piers and shallow arches, to support the walls above and to ornament the streets. A standard specification and dimensions for bricks were laid down.[35]

A proclamation of Charles II in 1661 suggests that these regulations were not fully enforced during the Civil War and the Protectorate, with much timber building continuing. Moreover, the average height of London houses increased down to 1666. This allowed the builders some scope to enhance the design of their frontages and roofs. The parapet, hiding the roof, became more common. The gable survived, however, on most houses. A new feature was the gable with impure Classical features, which was imported from Germany and the Low Countries from the mid-sixteenth century.[36] These gables, which came to be known loosely as Dutch gables, were clearly fashionable in London after about 1610 and at that time were directly associated with Dutch practice, even though Dutch types were not directly copied.[37] Kew Palace (the 'Dutch House') (1631) was adorned by these gables and other Dutch features, all carried out in brick. The pergola (balconied window), deriving from examples in Italy and Paris, also became popular between about 1610 and 1666.[38]

Mannerist detailing started to appear on new houses from about 1550. By the seventeenth century, this crude phase was being succeeded by a more learned view of Classical architecture which sometimes allowed the creation of attractive designs even if the Classical rules were ignored or not understood.[39] In 1627–8, for instance, Sir Balthazar Gerbier built an extension of the Duke of Buckingham's York House, on the Strand, using Classical detailing of some quality, though not part of an overall design.[40]

Traditional approaches nevertheless survived until 1666. Palaces and houses just outside London were especially resistant to Classicism and even Mannerism.

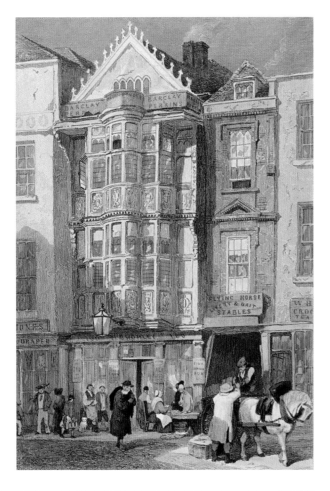

Holland House, Kensington, built in about 1607, was in the Tudor-Jacobean style with Dutch gables. At Charlton House (1607–12), an uninhibited Netherlandish columnar entrance with Mannerist detail did not detract from the overall Tudor-Jacobean effect, though the rigid plan and geometrical brick and stone elevations had no equivalent in the London area. Sir Paul Pindar's house in Bishopsgate, dating from about 1624, was a three-storey jettied house with a multiple curved oriel echoing the current fashion in country houses. Apart from a little strapwork, this house sprang from medieval and Tudor tradition.[41]

The Rebuilding Act of 1667 acknowledged many of the recent innovations in London building. It also took a big step forward by creating four building types. Three were determined by the class of street onto which they fronted: by-lanes ('the first sort'), streets and lanes of note ('the second sort') and high and principal streets ('the third sort'). The fourth building type, the mansion, did not front onto any street or lane. Each of the four building types had its own regulations.

Predictably, all houses had to be of brick or stone. The roofs of houses fronting lanes and streets had to be 'uniform', this being in effect a ban on gables, leading to their replacement by wooden eaves or cornices until these in turn were banned as a fire risk in 1707. For each of the first three building types, the number of storeys and the thicknesses of the outside and party walls were laid down. Houses of the first type were not to exceed two storeys. In the second type, three storeys were permitted and, in the third, four storeys. Mansions could rise up to four storeys at the discretion of the builder. The basic ceiling height was three metres except that in houses of the first type, and on the upper floors of houses of the second and third types, it was 2.75 or 2.6 metres respectively.[42]

One common feature did not spring directly from the Act of 1667, though it was probably encouraged by it. This was the wooden sash window, normally divided into small panes. With ceiling heights generally higher after the Fire than before, and strip windows banned, the larger houses began to admit light through taller openings of the type used by Inigo Jones, for instance at the Queen's House.[43] At first, the bottom part of these windows may have been filled with opening casements on hinges, with the upper part fixed. By the end of the century, however, the sash window was in widespread use on London frontages, even in smaller houses.

There were two main types of sash window. In one, the upper part of the frame was fixed, with the lower part rising behind it, and resting on wooden or metal supports. This system opened up to half the window. In

53 (*top*)   Sir Paul Pindar's House in Bishopsgate shown in an etching dating from 1851 (by now it had become the Paul Pindar Tavern),

54 (*above*)   A drawing of an upper room of the Paul Pindar Tavern in about 1890. The artist, Frank E. Cox, has portrayed the famous seventeenth-century ceiling but not the curved glazing of the oriel.

A NEW MAPP OF THE CITY OF LONDON &c. Anno 1716.

55 Map of London in 1716. The side streets, blocks and sites are crudely rendered. The main area of growth outside the City lies between the Fleet river in the east and the St James area in the west, on both sides of Piccadilly. Westminster remains a mere outlier.

the other, there were two mobile frames, each covering half the opening, and rising and falling on a system of pulleys, weights and ropes. The two-frame system may have originated in London but mobile frames were also in use in Holland and France in the second half of the century.[44] Before 1709 the glazing was normally flush with the outer wall of the house, as in medieval London, but the Building Act of that year required windows to be set back by ten centimetres in order to slow the spread of fire up the exterior of a building.[45]

★ ★ ★

THE NEW LONDON

These changes produced a degree of conformity in the rebuilt London which was without parallel in Europe. Nearly all the houses built in the fire zone between 1667 and 1700 have been demolished or degraded but a single design formula can still be seen in much of what remains. Three-storey lawyers' chambers built in Gray's Inn Square in 1678–88 are a good example. Nicholas Barbon, the prolific builder of small houses, erected a block of four-storey chambers at 2–3 Essex Court in the Temple in 1677. They were distinguished by stone trimmings and a Roman block cornice but looked much the same as at Gray's Inn. New Square, Lincoln's Inn (c. 1690) was another example. When Barbon built an entire, wide street at Bedford Row in 1680, he used simple, four-storey facades. Where houses were put up by individual

56   Great James Street, built in 1721 on the northern fringe of the West End just north of Holborn. Thoroughly utilitarian, these houses are standard products of the regulations of 1667.

57 (*below left*)   These lawyers' chambers in Gray's Inn date from about 1680 and conform to the post-Fire building regulations. Their pristine appearance reflects extensive repair after the war.

58 (*below right*)   Houses in Queen Anne's Gate, near Westminster Abbey (1704–8). The door canopies are 'carpenter's idiosyncratic' and there is no hint of the coming Palladian revival just a few years away.

builders, on narrow sites, complete conformity would be absent but an entire street would normally present the same general appearance.[46] Great James Street (1720–30) and John Street (1760) in Holborn show how the building of these simple four-storey frontages continued well into the eighteenth century. They were built for people of means, usually with mews behind, but not until the arrival of the Adams brothers in the 1760s and a new Building Act in 1774 did the facade treatments of larger houses move from post-Fire regimentation and

59 Smith Square, Westminster (1720s). Houses like these could be found in the outer London suburbs and in country towns. They did not necessarily require the services of an architect. A bricklayer or a carpenter could do the job.

60 Devonshire Square, built between 1678 and 1708 by Nicholas Barbon and others on the Duke of Devonshire's land. This engraving dates from about 1740 when the central area was still paved. The houses are equipped with areas, and tunnels lead through to the mews.

simplicity to the urban Palladian of Edinburgh and Bath. Inigo Jones's ideal elevation for an urban house, with giant order pilasters, disappeared after 1666. The tripartite horizontal division of the facade, promoted by Jones, figured in the Palladian revival of the 1720s but did not come into widespread use until the 1770s.

Most new houses were derived from the medieval box house, with front and back rooms, a staircase and an internal or external closet.[47] The number of storeys would depend on the building regulations, though in some cases houses were lower than the regulations would have allowed. Smaller houses often had a projection at the back containing the staircase and a closet. There was a cellar, lit by small windows at ground level.[48] Barbon put up many such box houses between 1670 and 1700. The frontages were usually three bays wide.[49] His biggest project was Red Lion Square, started in 1684, where all the houses seem to have been identical.

Although the Fire area seems to have been rebuilt mainly with small houses, they were larger than most of their predecessors. The Fire destroyed 13,200 houses but they were replaced by only 8000 houses, suggesting that

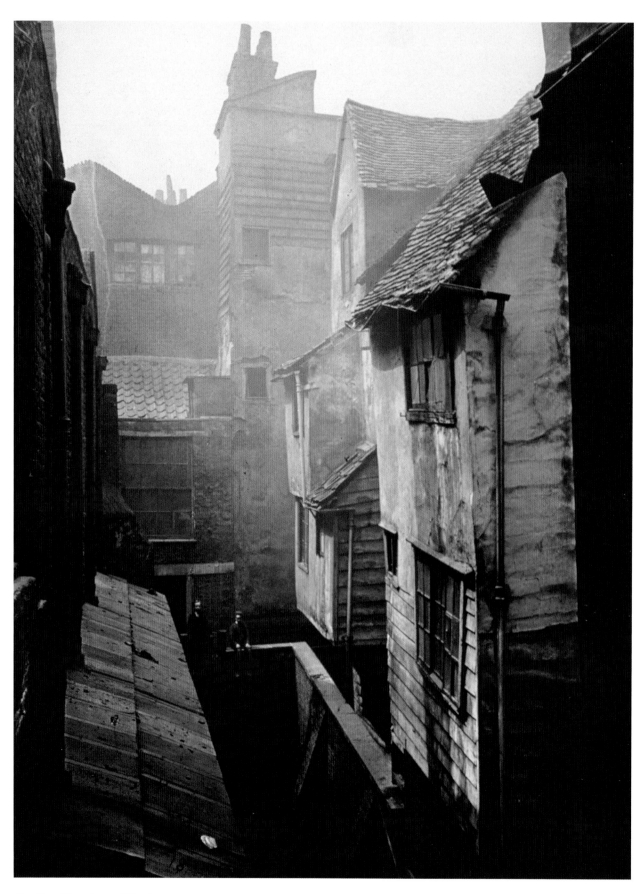

61   Cloth Fair backs in 1938. Staircase or closet projections like these were common in the Middle Ages and after the Fire.

many small sites were merged or deleted by street widening.[50] Few of the one-room-per-floor houses on street frontages that were common in medieval London appear to have been rebuilt. However, *A Large and Accurate Map of the City of London*, published by John Ogilby and William Morgan in 1676, shows many tiny square sites, some of them bearing houses apparently built back to back.[51] Peter Guillery's discovery of a surviving one-room back-to-back house in Smithfield is one of the revelations of his important survey.[52] Summerson stresses the poor quality of the small houses built after the Fire and suggests that this is why so many have disappeared.[53]

THE HOUSES OF THE RICH

The rebuilt houses of the City were mainly of two types. The larger ones normally stood back from the street, with a front courtyard, as before the Fire.[54] As such, they were not subject to most of the new regulations and many were very tall. Others were built on crowded street frontages such as Cheapside and Eastcheap, some of them reaching up to five storeys notwithstanding the regulations. New City houses were often more richly decorated than those of similar size in the West End, with Summerson lamenting their owners' pretensions and

62   Powis House, Drummond Street, built in 1685–6 by a military engineer and later used as the French embassy. This print may show a reconstruction after a fire. The repairs were financed by the French government without any obvious impact on the facade. A more flattering elevation appears in the first *Vitruvius Britannicus*.

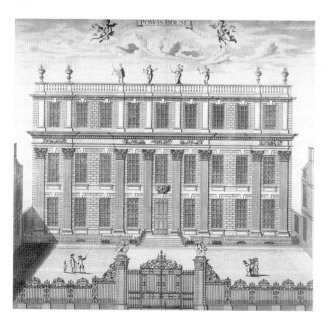

poor taste.[55] He concludes that most were designed by tradesmen, many of whom had moved into the City when conditions of citizenship were relaxed after the Fire in order to attract skilled workers.

Summerson finds much 'robust second-rate' in the City after 1666. Even the biggest new houses in the City, while grandiose and ornamental, were generally of poor taste. Number 73 Old Mansion House, with three bays, emphasised the central bay with carving and pediments, and thick horizontal bands divided the floors in a crude structure with some Mannerist detail. It was unusual in being stone-fronted. Larger town houses of five to seven bays often had a centre part standing forward and surmounted by a pediment, and sometimes with stone quoins. Summerson, with unusual generosity, sees these bigger houses as a mild reflection of the country house architecture of Pratt and May.[56] The College of Arms, built in two stages between 1671 and 1688 by Morris Emmett, later Master Bricklayer to the Office of Works, and other artisans, was a standard brick courtyard with

63   The College of Arms, with the dome of St Paul's in the background. The post-Fire norm of three storeys separated by projecting bands of brickwork is obvious here. Two projecting wings and a terrace, forming a fourth range in the foreground, were demolished when Queen Victoria Street was cut through in 1867–71.

the occasional Mannerist feature and central, pedimented bays standing slightly forward. An exception is St Paul's Deanery, Dean's Court, in which Wren may have had a hand. Built in 1672 or a little later, it is an impressive brick two-storey house with a decorated wooden cornice, dormers and a semi-basement. The tall windows, with their Dutch flavour, are its dominant feature.[57]

THE COMPANY HALLS

There were nearly one hundred halls in the City. In contrast to the churches, nearly all were rebuilt and without the guidance of a commission. Here, the master masons and the carpenters reigned supreme, though Wren's associate Edward Jerman, the City Surveyor and architect of the new Royal Exchange [1667–1671], designed some of them. Their work ranged from simple or very free Classical to Mannerist, with much use of

64 The Royal Exchange (by Edward Jerman, the City Surveyor, and Thomas Cartwright, the Master of the Masons' Company) in a drawing by Colin Campbell presented to the Lord Mayor of London. Pevsner rates it as 'the grandest monument of artisan classicism in the City'. Some Flemish influence survives from Gresham's Exchange a hundred years before.

heavy Classical detail, often on asymmetrical facades. The halls made little contribution to the development of London architecture but there were so many of them, and many were so large, that they did much to shape the new City.[58] Almost all were built on their pre-Fire sites and stood back from the street with subsidiary buildings forming a courtyard or they were approached through an alley. Most had a semi-basement, a ground-floor hall and an attic – as they had before the Fire. A few of the pre-Fire gardens, behind the halls, survived and were enhanced. The halls and their ancillary buildings, lying off the street, could rise up to four storeys under the

building regulations of 1667 and many had broad frontages of several bays.[59]

BUILDING IN THE WEST END

The West End boomed after the Fire. Since about 1600 many provincial aristocracy and gentry had spent part of the year in London and after the Fire some of the richer City residents joined them there. The growing gentility of the West End was reflected in its new houses.[60]

Three large houses were built in Piccadilly/Portugal Street in the 1660s – Berkeley House (1664) and Burlington House (1664–8) by Hugh May and Clarendon House (1664–7). The most impressive was Clarendon House, built for the Lord Chancellor on an eight-acre site by (Sir) Roger Pratt, a gentleman architect who had travelled widely on the Continent in 1643–9.[61] Its symmetrical elevations and plan were of a type known to architects as 'double-pile', and it looked like a large country house, of which Pratt built five between the Restoration and 1667. Its overall effect, with two projecting wings beside an open courtyard, and a central triangular pediment, was French but the detailing drew on the work of Inigo Jones. It was probably the finest house built anywhere in England in the mid-1660s, and cost £50,000, far more than the largest country houses of the day.[62] It was demolished in 1683, after Clarendon's fall, and replaced by more profitable streets and sites. Berkeley House was a similar concept, built of brick with stone trimmings and a hipped roof. It had a forecourt with quadrant colonnades linking to outbuildings.[63] Burlington House lay back from the street on a big site and had a forecourt in the French style.

Montagu House in Great Russell Street, Bloomsbury (1674–9), was designed 'after the French pavilion way', as John Evelyn put it, at the request of the Duke of Montagu who served as ambassador at the court of Louis XIV and was a great admirer of French art. The architect was Wren's friend and fellow scientist, Robert Hooke. It had mansard roofs and pavilions at each end, and was planned round an open forecourt. It had a coach entrance in the middle of the street wall and the main range had a square-domed centre, the whole recalling Choisy-le-Roi.[64] An (obscure) French architect, Bouget, and French decorators carried out a reconstruction in 1686–7 after a fire. Hooke's admiration for French design, and for pavilions in particular, was also reflected in his Royal College of Physicians (1672–8) in Warwick Lane and the impressive frontage of his Bethlehem Hospital (Bedlam) (1675–6) which stood on the site of the present Finsbury Circus, just outside London Wall.

NEW BEDLAM IN MORE FIELDS

HOSPITIUM MENTE CAPTORUM LONDINENSE.

65 (*above*) Bethlehem Hospital in an engraving of about 1714. The foreign influence, if any, looks French but any connection with the Tuileries is very tenuous. The long range was partly the product of ventilation concepts of the day.

Bedlam's long range (153 metres) was probably intended to minimise encroachment on the Moorfields park to the north and to encourage ventilation. It was articulated by pavilions in the middle and at each end.[65] It has been suggested that Hooke was inspired by the Tuileries but some have seen Dutch influence here.

Summerson's judgement on the surge of building in the west and north-west is that it was uncertain in style and retained 'a vernacular roughness'.[66] This was not true of the great houses just discussed but Schomberg House, Pall Mall (c. 1698), built for a German duke, bears him out. It resembled some of the the four-storey houses built for merchants in the City, particularly Fitch's House at the southern end of the Fleet.[67] Some guidance was eventually given for smaller houses by the City building regulations, which were extended to the City of West-

66 (*right*) Schomberg House, Pall Mall, built for a German aristocrat in 1698. Some of the big merchants' houses built in the City after the Fire, and especially Fitch's House at the southern end of the Fleet, had similar frontages.

minster in 1727, together with the parishes of St Maryle-bone, Paddington, Chelsea and St Pancras. This left the East End and Southwark without up-to-date regulations but from then on most of London tended to generate similar street and building forms.[68] With London and Paris now the largest cities in Europe, it was London that created the more harmonious townscape.

WREN AS ROYAL ARCHITECT

Three of Wren's greatest works lay outside London, on the silver ribbon of the Thames. Here he came into his own as Surveyor of the King's Works, working for one powerful client. Charles II was a great admirer of Louis XIV but as the king of a smaller country, constrained by Parliament, he could not afford to build on the same scale as the French king. However, he was prepared to contemplate building smaller equivalents of some of the great French royal works, as were his successors, James II and William and Mary. The result was a smaller Invalides (Chelsea Hospital), a reduced version of Versailles (Hampton Court) (commissioned by William and Mary) and the finest architectural landscape of its day, or any other day (the Royal Hospital for Seamen and the Queen's House, Greenwich), a long-term project with contributions authorised by several monarchs.

Greenwich

Though Greenwich was the work of at least five great architects, it joins St Paul's as one of Wren's greatest masterpieces. He made an embryonic palace into a mighty symbol of English seapower in the early years of its full flowering. The great expanse of the Thames before it, criss-crossed with shipping and with naval dockyards and armouries nearby in Deptford and Woolwich, and the great ascent of Observatory Park from the Queen's House to Wren's Royal Observatory (1675–6) at the summit were as important as the Classical buildings and spaces of Wren and others. Thanks to Wren's authority as an astronomer, time starts here. And it is a British time – *le monde entier à l'heure anglaise*, as the French might put it. Seen from across London's mighty river, already half ocean, it rivalled anything that Venice had to show.

The embryo of Wren's Greenwich was a late medieval house next to the little town of Greenwich near the water's edge, which came into royal hands in 1423. Henry VII liked it and Henry VIII added to it, producing a standard rambling brick Tudor palace with a tennis court, no doubt reflecting the king's early vigour. The name favoured by Margaret of Anjou, Henry VI's queen,

was Placentia or Plaisance. This suggested calm and Italian luxury and suited the connection of the palace with a series of queens. Elizabeth often stayed at Placentia but, predictably, spent very little money on it. In 1613 James I gave the palace and manor to his dissatisfied queen, Anne of Denmark, as a peacemaking gesture. She appears to have wanted a more convenient and modern home than Placentia and in 1616 Inigo Jones was asked to design a house for her, uphill from the old palace.

The Queen's House (1616–35) must have been the product of lengthy discussions with Anne, who had brought the masque to the English court and who had worked closely with Jones on set designs and costumes for the masques performed at the Palace of Westminster. It was built astride the Dover Road on the boundary between the palace grounds and the royal park which stretched up the hill behind it. There is some talk about this being the spot where Sir Walter Raleigh laid his cloak over a puddle to stop Gloriana getting her feet wet. Whether or not this is true, the choice of location is curious, unless it was intended to secure privacy from travellers on the road.

Jones built a modest villa, a model of Palladian principle though externally restrained and even spartan in comparison with Palladio's villas and palaces in Italy. It has something of the Palazzo Chiericati in Vicenza. It seems to express independence or even deliberate solitude and may reflect the queen's idea of a feminine or tasteful building. The identical 'windows in line', a novel and correct Palladian feature, will live on throughout this book. The big cube hall with a gallery recalls the Banqueting House and suggests that Anne and her friends performed masques here. The first-floor loggia on the south front, added between 1632 and 1635 when Henrietta Maria owned the house, was an advanced feature for England. The spiral staircase ('Tulip staircase') with its metal balustrade was utterly timeless and, in this author's opinion, the best thing that Jones ever did.

The next stage in this history came after the Restoration. Charles II was yet another monarch who valued the palace but this was more for its location than its fabric. The king soon decided to demolish Placentia and build a new palace in an up-to-date style. John Webb made several versions of the plan, with an open layout based on two long, parallel ranges at right angles to the Thames. In 1662–9 he built the King Charles Block, which he clearly intended as part of the western range. Hailed by Downes as England's first Baroque building, mainly because of its search for effect and the decorative use of Classical features, its low profile and stolid massing are disturbing.[69] Its dumpy silhouette may have

67 Webb's and Wren's Greenwich vista (1992). The Royal Observatory lies out of shot, to the top right.

deferred to the Queen's House but Webb's planning was never going to solve the problem of the southward vista from the Thames. Nor was Inigo Jones's assistant an obvious master of the Baroque.

Wren was the dominant figure when work resumed on what was now the Royal Hospital for Seamen (founded 1692) in 1696 but Hawksmoor and Vanbrugh made important contributions in their distinctive Baroque styles between 1699 and 1721. The main problem faced by Wren was the termination of the vista formed by Webb's parallel ranges, which took the form of four blocks.[70] Wren sketched a plan for a large, central

71 and 72 (*above*)   The King William Block (Webb) and the almost identical Queen Anne Block (Wren and his associates), face each other at the northern end of the vista.

73 (*facing page top*)   The complete Greenwich vista, with the Royal Observatory just visible by the right-hand dome.

74 (*facing page bottom*)   The Greenwich vista at sunset, enhanced by a telephoto lens which reinforces the Queen's House as the focal point. Wren would have liked this view.

68, 69 and 70 (*left, top, centre and bottom*)   The Queen's House, from the south, from the north, and in low light. The loggia traps the weedy southern sun but Inigo Jones built a formal entrance on the darker, northern side. The result was a bland northern frontage which weakened the perspective from the Thames which Webb and Wren worked hard to create. The loggia needs frequent maintenance, mainly because of damp.

75 (*left*) Wren's eastern colonnade and dome.

76 (*below left*) Vanbrugh's closing block to Wren's west court. This and Hawksmoor's equivalent block on the other side of the vista are freely designed in Baroque styles.

inal stocky block by Webb had to set the standard here. Wren tackled this problem to the south where the distance between the blocks is smaller and the colonnades create an impression of grandeur and horizontal movement.

The Greenwich story does not end with Wren and his fellow architects, for further building and alterations were carried out in the nineteenth century.[71] The care which was taken to make these conform to the original scheme is visible throughout. The Royal Naval Hospital and Queen's House are a triumph for London architecture. Louis XIV could boast of nothing so fair.

Chelsea Hospital

Work on the Royal Hospital at Chelsea started in 1681 and the chapel was consecrated in 1691. It was inspired by Louis XIV's Hôtel des Invalides, founded in 1670. Work lasted from 1682 to 1683. There are many echoes of Greenwich, including the Wren–Hawksmoor collaboration. The main frontage faced the Thames, with two long wings running towards the river. Brick was used throughout except for porticoes, quoins and another of Wren's height-seeking domes, which were of Portland stone. The heavy, closed courtyards of the Invalides were not emulated and both the open plan and the colonnades echoed Greenwich.

Hampton Court

Cardinal Wolsey acquired the site of Hampton Court in 1514. He built a brick Tudor palace to a high standard and the new owner, Henry VIII, started to enlarge it in 1530, building another of his tennis courts. Always an elegant and well-built palace, Hampton Court remained a welcome retreat from London for monarch and court until William and Mary decided in 1689 to make it their permanent home. Wren rebuilt and extended the palace between 1689 and 1694. His plans for a new palace on Versailles lines could not be financed so he retained most of the Tudor structure but rebuilt the third courtyard in brick with Portland stone dressings. There was indeed a touch of Versailles in the long, geometrical frontages and the related park perspectives but the new building was on a much smaller scale and was domestic in its effect.

block and dome, flanked by smaller domes on each of the two parallel ranges, but there was great reluctance at Court to hide the Queen's House. The Queen's House could of course be used to terminate the vista but it was too low and horizontal to do the job in Baroque style. Wren secured some peripheral verticality with two tall, thin domes (1704 and 1735) which stood on the corners of his great hall and chapel roughly halfway along the vista, at the point where it narrowed. This allowed the Queen's House to do what it could visually even though it was some distance beyond the end of the Wren buildings. The striking hill behind the Queen's House, topped by Wren's Royal Observatory of 1675–6, might be seen as part of the vista but the whole arrangement is unusual, even in the Baroque mode which Wren had come to favour. Summerson is a bit dismissive of Wren's domes, which he sees as crowded in a small area while straining for height. The four block buildings seem a little low in relation to the great spaces around them but the orig-

77　Chelsea Hospital, seen from inside the main court. This economical brick building is strengthened by the domed vestibule seen here but the grandeur of the Invalides is lacking.

Under Henry VIII in particular, courtiers (and boatmen) must have been aware of Hampton Court and Placentia as a balancing pair of palaces upstream and downstream from Westminster. More courtiers lived upstream than downstream but Henry was often at Greenwich supervising the development of his navy. In other reigns the oscillation was perhaps less clear but Greenwich was ideal for receiving foreign visitors and launching expeditions. Hampton Court was always more of a retreat for court and guests.

WREN'S ACHIEVEMENT

For sixty years Wren was the leader of English architecture, more than Jones ever achieved. Yet the quality of Jones's work has never been seriously questioned, where-

as Wren's has been attacked from time to time since the beginning of the Palladian revival around 1720. His defenders—and they are many—have sometimes tried to portray him as the founder of a national architecture, but their efforts have not always helped him. The criticisms are so varied that they cannot be fully reviewed here. The general drift, however, is that Wren was a mathematician rather than an artist and that his architecture was a collection of elements and motifs, held together by formulae. The result was 'inconsistency' and 'uncertainty of control' generated by English empiricism, as Summerson has put it.[72] However, Wren's architecture evolved during his long career and it offered a rich variety of responses to multiple design problems. There are both French and especially Netherlandish influences (Wren was not impressed by the often exuberant Italian architecture of his day), and the distinctive character of English Baroque became clearer in his work as he became older.[73] By 1700 Christopher Wren had created an architecture which, while firmly Classical, was flexible and decorative. It also represented a powerful, Protestant country and Europe's largest city. There was a touch of the Dutch about it at times which gave it a cosy, domestic feel but it was a national style which was generally valued by the educated classes and which had a reputation abroad. Although normally regarded now as a version of the Baroque, the term was rarely used of Wren's architecture in his own lifetime.

Wren's 'inconsistency' fades when set against his great, driving vision. He had a strong sense of the order of the universe within which he served an enlightened monarchy. His vision of London as a dome surrounded by spires, with ordered streets and houses, had a heavenly tinge. Outside the City, the gleaming ribbon of the Thames led to the king's great palaces and hospitals. He was an outstanding planner when he had the chance, as at Greenwich and Chelsea. Louis XIV had no better servant.

BAROQUE VERSUS PALLADIAN IN THE AFTERMATH OF WREN

No sooner had Wren's national style reached full maturity than it was challenged by two purist movements drawing directly on Italy. There was an episode in full-blooded Baroque which made Wren look tame and a Palladian (or Neo-Palladian) surge which swept all alternatives out of the way.

★　　★　　★

From the beginning of the eighteenth century a number
of architects moved from Wren's restrained English
Baroque to an expressive style which drew more directly
on the Continent. Kerry Downes calls this new architecture 'late English Baroque', acknowledging the continuing influence of Wren, but some of it was
revolutionary in English terms, meriting the title of
Baroque.[74] The leaders of the Baroque were John Vanbrugh and Nicholas Hawksmoor, who were joint architects of Castle Howard, near York (1699–1713). Vanbrugh
was a society figure, successful playwright and set
designer, while Hawksmoor was Wren's senior assistant
at the Office of Works. Downes sees Hawksmoor as the
best-trained architect of his day and Summerson rates
him as a better architect than Wren.[75]

In London the Baroque was used mainly for churches.
In 1711, Parliament passed an Act for Building Fifty New
Churches across London, to equip new or expanding
districts with churches comparable to the new City
churches. It was a Tory measure and much of the resulting architecture had political implications. As usual in
post-Fire times, a commission was set up and Hawksmoor was appointed as one of the two surveyors. Only
twelve churches were built but most were large by
London standards. Hawksmoor built six of the churches
under the Act between 1712 and 1733 and shared in
others. His dramatic Baroque churches marched east
across Stepney, and he built one of two similar churches
across the river at Greenwich. He also built the west
towers and gable of Westminster Abbey in a convincing
Baroque-Gothic style, probably inspired by Wren's Tom
Tower at Oxford, in 1734–5. Hawksmoor could master
a wide range of styles but his forte was the creation of
impressive masses related to Roman precedents.[76] He
never left Britain, which may explain why his version of
the Baroque moved towards the development of pure
form. It appears that he usually had plenty of money to
build with.

Hawksmoor's London churches were all in his
muscular, inventive Baroque. As Colvin has put it, no
one in England understood better 'the dynamic deploy-
ment of architectural form or the dramatic possibilities
of light and shade', while his London churches were
as 'eloquent as anything by Borromini'.[77] His three
East End churches (St Anne, Limehouse (1714–30),
St George-in-the-East (1714–29) and Christ Church,
Spitalfields (1714–29)), built to serve new districts in

78, 79, 80, 81, 82 and 83 (*this and facing page*)   Hawksmoor's trio of East End churches. A new approach to worship, and a new city, are implied here: Christ Church, Spitalfields (*facing page*); St George in the East (*top left and right*); St Anne Limehouse (*left and above*).

84 and 85   St Alfege, Greenwich, by Hawksmoor. The church was rebuilt after a storm and was financed under the Fifty New Churches Act. The Commissioners rejected Hawksmoor's plans for a tower and steeple but he adapted them for St George in the East. The steeple was eventually built by John James in 1730 in a polite but weedy, sort-of-Wren style. On this constricted site, Hawksmoor's elemental style is an expression of first and last things. Local children must be frightened of it at night.

Stepney, were massive structures with London's highest parish spires. Built of the best Portland stone, they offered one massive side to the southern sun and on sunny days they gleamed as did no other buildings in London. Hawksmoor favoured large, box-shaped preaching areas with galleries, yawning entrances and tall, fantastic towers and steeples. His interiors were dominated by lengthy galleries which reinforced the rectangular plan but the coffered ceilings recalled the interiors of Blenheim and Castle Howard. He liked to create simple geometrical forms such as squares and circles, while his elevations recalled Alberti's Tempio Malatestiano at Rimini.

The smaller St Alfege, Greenwich (1712–14), lacks the steeple that Hawksmoor designed for it and is less well known. St Luke, Old Street (1727–33), by Hawksmoor and John James, looks like a reduced, restrained Hawksmoor design, as does the demolished St John, Horsely-down. St Mary Woolnoth (1716–24), in the City, and St George, Bloomsbury (1716–31), were also smaller than his East End churches but they showed similar invention. Wren's influence was clearly present in Hawksmoor's churches but London had seen nothing like them, nor would it again.[78] Hawksmoor had no pupils and by the time he died in 1736 his work had moved

back towards the Palladian. London church design now returned to a more restrained Wren style, for instance at Henry Flitcroft's St Giles-in-the-Fields of 1731–3 and at John James's cautious tower on Hawksmoor's St Alfege, Greenwich.

The more ornate Italian or German Baroque was almost completely absent from London except in the work of Thomas Archer, a gentleman architect with a sporadic output. He was one of the commissioners for building Fifty New Churches. Archer had travelled and studied extensively in Italy and possibly in Germany and Austria and was influenced above all by Bernini and Borromini.[79] His St Paul's, Deptford (1712–30), with its Wren-like tower, had much in common with Hawksmoor's church of St Alfege but drew partly on Continental Baroque. Archer built another commissioners' church, St John's, Smith Square, between 1713 and 1728. This had more Continental Baroque in it than any church in England, with towers based on Borromini's Sant'Agnese in Agone in Rome. With his garden pavilions at Chatsworth and other decorative works charming the aristocracy, he looked to have a great future in country house design. Burlington's Palladian revival put a stop to that after 1715 and Archer took up the life of a country gentleman.

87 (*above*) St John's, Smith Square. built in a Continental Baroque style by Thomas Archer between 1713 and 1728. It had little influence in London.

86 (*left*) St Mary Woolnoth, rebuilt by Hawksmoor in 1716–27. This church had been partially rebuilt after the Fire and Hawksmoor's frontage on this small site combines the modest qualities of Wren's City churches with a vertical emphasis using Classical features and box-like forms. Like Hawksmoor's other churches, it was expensive to build and had little influence.

Vanbrugh built little in London but his house with prominent round-arched fenestration in Whitehall (Goose-pie House) (c. 1700) and his turreted Vanbrugh Castle in Maze Hill, Greenwich (1717–26) sought effect above all. He made a bold, martial contribution to the Greenwich Hospital in brick and stone. His Model Room at the Royal Arsenal, Woolwich, built in 1719, allowed him to develop his powerful brick arches in an industrial context.

THE PALLADIAN REVIVAL

The progress of the Baroque was soon stopped in its tracks by an unexpected development. This was the successful promotion in Britain of Palladian design, 170 years after Andrea Palladio had first applied it in Vicenza and its region and had gone on to publish one of the most influential architectural statements of all time, *I quattro libri dell'architettura* (1570). This Palladian revival was linked to the tastes of the Whig aristocracy which displaced the Tories as the main political force in the early eighteenth century.

In 1715–20 Giacomo Leoni, an architect of Venetian origins who had recently come to London and was working under the patronage of the Duke of Kent, pub-

lished the first English translation of Palladio's *Four Books of Architecture*. At much the same time, an able architect and publicist from Scotland, Colin Campbell, published a portfolio of drawings called *Vitruvius Britannicus* (1715–25). The drawings were mainly facades, including many of his own designs, but Campbell's main aim was to revive interest in the architecture of Ancient Rome and that of Palladio and his followers, as well as to secure country house commissions for himself and his friends. He included Italian examples and much English work, not all of it obviously Palladian, but this may have been due to the hurry in which the portfolio was prepared. Inigo Jones, the first English Palladian, was prominent but Vanbrugh also figured. Utterly rejected was recent Italian work, with Bernini stigmatised as 'affected and licentious' and Borromini held to be 'wildly extravagant'.[80] Hence the return to Roman purity.

Vitruvius Britannicus was not entirely unheralded. Since the turn of the century certain English architects, patrons and thinkers, such as the Earl of Shaftesbury, had been extolling Roman virtues and the aristocratic practice of the Grand Tour had begun.[81] Shaftesbury believed in 'taste' and in 1712, while in Italy, he wrote to Lord Somers attacking the Baroque and the influence of Wren. These enthusiasts were in many cases associated

88 and 89 St Botolph, Bishopsgate (*above left*), rebuilt in 1725–8 by a consortium of masons including George Dance the Elder, and St Botolph Aldgate (*above right*), built by George Dance the Elder in 1741–4. These churches show how little the Baroque influenced London churches after the Palladian revival began in the 1720s.

with the Whig or country party. Country houses were the first Palladian buildings to be undertaken after 1715, with Campbell building a number himself.

By 1730 Palladians controlled the Office of Works, thanks mainly to Burlington's patronage, and the Palladian style achieved general supremacy among the aristocracy and those who served them.[82] For the first time, English architects and their aristocratic patrons were visiting Italy in large numbers. The Palladian style was disseminated by the publication of books of architectural drawings, including supplementary volumes of *Vitruvius Britannicus* in 1717 and 1725. Between 1725 and 1759 roughly one architectural book was produced every year.[83] According to Elizabeth McKellar, published drawings were not used to design houses until about 1725 but thereafter the use of 'pattern books' was common, resulting in repetition.[84] Summerson believes that books were the main factor in establishing Palladian taste and in allowing masons and carpenters to develop into complete architects, though many of the books are rudimentary and incomplete, sometimes leaning on French designs presumably lifted from the great French publications.[85] After 1760 the books grew fewer as the number of competent architects increased.[86]

London Houses and the Palladian Style

Classical styles come and go but the Palladian had something special about it. It dominated London in the eighteenth century and beyond, especially in domestic architecture for which, for technical reasons, it was well suited.

The Palladian style quickly proved successful in big country houses, which were built in large numbers between 1710 and 1750 for an increasingly rich aristocracy. Burlington's concentric, domed Chiswick House (1720–26), inspired by Palladio's La Rotonda just outside

90 Chiswick House (1730). This was inspired by Palladio's Villa Rotonda (1565–9), a short walk from Vicenza. The lapse of 165 years between Burlington's Italian model and his recreation of it at Chiswick was unparalleled in British architecture until the Gothic revival.

91 A side wall of Chiswick House.

92 Chiswick House. This scene could be in Italy or on Olympus though the white Portland stone and the veiled sun produce a grey effect.

Vicenza, brought the best of the Italian Renaissance to the edge of London. Intended for entertainment and display, it was not planned as a residence but it attracted more visitors than any other house in the London area.[87] Colin Campbell built several country houses between 1715 and 1724, confirming that an acceptable Palladian treatment could be applied in the English context. In almost every case, these designs centred on a portico with a triangular pediment and four columns, with steps rising up to it. The facade stretched out for an equal distance on each side of the portico, with equal fenestra-

tion using tall, rectangular windows. The shallow roof was hidden by a balustrade. Pavilions were sometimes added at each end of the range, and turrets or cupolas could sometimes be included, as at William Kent's Holkham Hall, though these were not at first sight Palladian features. Stone was normally used throughout but the sides and rear of the house were often given a simpler and even cursory treatment. The exterior walls could be built cheaply, apart from the portico, given that the essence of the Palladian was classical simplicity. Here lay its potential for urban housing.

The most important Palladian statement in London at the time the first volumes of *Vitruvius Britannicus* were published was the rebuilding in about 1717–20 of the front of Burlington House, Piccadilly. Richard Boyle, third Earl of Burlington, had inherited the house in 1704. Burlington was an enthusiast for Italian culture and wanted to transform English culture by importing the Italian in its pure form. Burlington made his Grand Tour in 1714–15. Excited by the revival of interest in Palladio generated by Campbell and Leoni, he decided to rebuild his London house. In 1716 he engaged James Gibbs, whose five years in Rome under Carlo Fontana, a pupil of Bernini, gave him a qualification unique in England. Gibbs started work on buildings in the front courtyard but Burlington soon dropped him in favour of Colin Campbell.

Campbell may have persuaded Burlington that Gibbs's Baroque experience in Rome would prevent his designing a truly Palladian building, though the affair remains mysterious. Campbell enhanced Gibbs's front courtyard with curved colonnades on the Parisian model, but the new facade of the house was pure, scholarly, Palladian, based on the Palazzo Porto-Colleoni at Thiene near Vicenza.[88] It was two storeys high with a balustrade topped by classical statues, in Portland stone. There was a giant order of attached columns rising from the rusticated ground floor, with pavilions at each end, each with a striking Serlian window on the first floor. The effect was subdued and scholarly, rather than striking, and the central door was surprisingly small.

The aristocracy were impressed by Burlington House and some Whig aristocrats followed it into the Palladian manner if they had suitable sites in London. However, most of them concentrated on their country houses and no other equivalents to the big Strand palaces of pre-Fire London were undertaken.[89] Where their houses could not be built in or near Piccadilly, the Strand or Whitehall, even the richest lords settled for a site on a new development such as a West End square (see later under 'Palladio Victor'). If they could secure a broad frontage, their fashionable Palladian architect might provide an impressive result. One such was Harcourt House, Cavendish Square (demolished), built in about 1720 by Thomas Archer. It had a screen wall and a courtyard, with an elegant Palladian facade behind it. Most Palladian town houses, however, struggled with the problem of narrow sites. Where the house was freestanding, a shorter range was used than was usual in the countryside and the portico was often emphasised to compensate for it. An early example was Pembroke House, the villa built by Campbell for Lord Herbert in Whitehall in 1717–24 (demolished). Its strongest feature was a central portico with accommodation stretching back into the depths of the site.[90] When William Kent built 44 Berkeley Square in 1742–4 for Lord Burlington's cousin, Lady Isabella Finch, he had room for only

three bays on the street frontage and eschewed the solution of a four-column portico embracing the whole of the facade, perhaps because it would have looked pretentious or out of proportion with the rest of the square. His simple, three-storey facade was mainly of brick but his stone dressings, pediments and cornice gave it distinction. It had a fine interior with an ornate, top-lit staircase with Ionic columns and strong structural features. The interior had some raised ceilings on Louis Quatorze lines and the result has been called the finest terraced house in London.[91]

Where the house formed a continuous frontage with other houses, an impressive palazzo effect could be created with repeated pilasters, pediments or other decoration but continuously designed Palladian frontages were rare before 1750. Burlington gave a lead when he laid out streets and sites on his lands (Ten Acre Close) to the north of Burlington House between 1718 and 1739. Burlington designed adjoining (though contrasting) houses for Lord Mountrath (about 1721) and General Wade (1723) (both demolished), while Camp-

93 The garden front of General Wade's House (1723), built by Burlington for the greatest soldier of the day. It was based directly on a Palladio drawing in Burlington's collection. The site lay on Burlington land north of Piccadilly, at 29, Great (now Old) Burlington Street. The top floor must have been added later, perhaps when the house became part of the Burlington Hotel. This photograph was taken in 1935, just before demolition. Wade also owned the first Palladian house in Bath, a step from the abbey (where the author and his family once stayed, courtesy of the Landmark Trust).

94 Harley Street, looking north. Long lines of First Rates.

95 First Rates on New Cavendish Street, built by John Johnson in c. 1775–7. The balconies and canopies were probably a response to the direct southern aspect of these houses. Alfred Waterhouse, the innovating Victorian architect, lived here, at no. 61.

bell built a regular facade of four houses alongside them at 31–4 Old Burlington Street (nos 30 and 31 survive) in 1718–20. This block had three storeys with a dormer roof above a cornice and was thirteen bays long. A broad band separated the ground floor from the upper floors. These facades moved beyond the simple grids of the post-Fire years and re-introduced the Palladian tripartite division, once favoured by Inigo Jones, into street housing. The height of the windows, reducing at each storey, helped combine height and elegance and encouraged palazzo designs in long rows. Inigo Jones's pilasters returned to occasional favour and Leoni built a house with a giant order of pilasters for Lord Queensberry at 7 Burlington Gardens in 1721–3.[92] Most of these houses fronted long sites which ended at another street, so that their garden facades were visible to strollers. They were fully fashioned by the architect in consequence. Yet the streets were of modest width and, given that some of these houses were occupied by aristocracy, Burlington's planned environment was surprisingly modest. In Vicenza, however, the streets were of similar width.

Palladian architecture also contributed to the design of more modest houses. Nearly all were built in terraces

or rows on the street frontage, with short, narrow sites laid out by developers. Most had three or four main floors and were built of brick. There was an emphasis on the first floor, where the windows were often higher. The builder set many of these houses behind a series of standard facade designs stretching across a number of houses. Deliberate palazzo effects were rare but informal perspectives were common. Palladian features included the horizontal division of the facade into three parts, rectangular windows in portrait format, standard window dimensions on each floor, continuous parapets and (sometimes) attached pillars and capitals or pilasters with bas-relief capitals. Cruickshank and Wyld see much Baroque in these houses but Palladian was always the cheaper way to build. The main Baroque features were the doorcases which added character to simple facades.[93] An order was not obligatory but, where there was one, it rose through two floors to a cornice. It was seen at its best on four-storey houses (First Rates), which were the top class of house on street frontages recognised by the Building Act of 1774. Where there was no order, a projecting band marked the first-floor level. Shallow, segmental arches topped many windows after 1700. Parapets

96 4 St James Square (1726–8), by Edward Shepherd. Not a success visually, but the client's ceiling-height requirements may be to blame.

97 Nos 9, 10 and 11 St James Square. These houses were designed by Henry Flitcroft, Lord Burlington's assistant, in 1734. The big, square attic floors, with roofs concealed by parapets, lacked the charm of the gambrel roofs with dormers which multiplied in Paris from the early eighteenth century. The balcony and the lowered first-floor windows of the middle house date from the nineteenth century.

replaced eaves and cornices, increasingly harried by the Building Acts, with roofs and dormers set back behind them.

Builders appear to have adopted this new formula for terraced houses from the beginning of the Palladian period, succeeding the simple post-Fire boxes and rows. Most were, however, a long way from the mature Adam style of the 1760s. For instance, when Edward Shepherd built 4 St James's Square in 1726–8, his grotesquely tall attic floor upset the whole of the frontage. The general use of brick encouraged conformity. As we have seen, the Crown was prepared to sell its Portland stone but it was expensive and difficult to work. Many owners consequently opted for brick, even in large houses. The results were often ordinary, as the following examples will suggest, and there is a possibility that the use of brick was associated with other design economies.

The five-bay Chesterfield House (demolished), built in 1749–52 by Isaac Ware, was of brick with stone dressings, with two small buildings on each side and joined to it by colonnades parallel to the front of the house. This forecourt plan was a cheap variant of Parisian practice. The brick was a definite weakness, especially when combined with a cramped elevation which could have been found on a country rectory. The main house and two forecourt outbuildings were awkwardly narrow and overstressed the vertical. The stone pediments over the windows on the first floor suggested an attempt to secure Palladian distinction when so little was to be found elsewhere. The miniature gateway and wall on the street frontage would have suited a modern golf club but would have been a joke in Paris. Ugly ancillary buildings and chimneys to the rear, as so often the result of short London sites, did not help (though some of these may have been added later). This was an awkward and cheap composition. The grand staircase and upper landing, however, came from the Duke of Chandos's country house which had been demolished in 1744 to pay family debts. Ware designed the ante-room which became the best known of the French-style interiors carried out in England in the 1740s.[94] There were some good ceilings in a style transitional between Louis-Quatorze and Louis-Quinze. This was one of the first of London's 'better inside than out' houses.

Devonshire House, Piccadilly (1733–5) (demolished), had much in common with Chesterfield House. Built for the third Duke by William Kent, an experienced, Rome-trained painter starting out in Palladian architecture under Burlington's patronage, it was a long brick box with a central entrance, modest terminal pavilions and a large forecourt. Economy ruled on the exterior, where decoration was cut to an absolute minimum

and there was a high ratio of wall to window. Kent's bold painting enlivened the simple interior but this was Palladianism on the cheap.[95]

Leicester House by Sutton Nicholls (1727) (demolished) had a broad but undistinguished frontage with a front courtyard bounded by a variety of side buildings. Norfolk House (demolished), St James' Square, built by Matthew Brettingham in 1748–52, was another modest exterior but its interior was innovative, with a circuit of rooms round a central staircase and landing. According to Worsley, this arrangement was a turning point for London. York House (demolished), also built by Matthew Brettingham in 1760–63, had the same plan.[96] Londonderry House (1760–65) (demolished) off Park Lane, by James Stuart, was an oblong, three-storey brick box, sparse both inside and out. Stuart then took a commission from the rich Mrs Montagu to build a house just off Portman Square for her lavish entertainments. Work started in 1769 but Stuart soon sank into his notorious indolence (drink?) and the client's first party was not held until 1782. The house was another brick box and though it was noted for its interior fittings, most were portable apart from Stuart's attractive Adamesque ceilings.[97]

Other Palladian Buildings

The Palladian revolution also affected public buildings, especially after Burlington helped the Palladians to take over the Office of Works. This was not an important period for government building but the prolific William Kent's Treasury in Whitehall (1733–6) had an impressive though mannered Palladian facade. However, Kent's flanking wings were not built and the main interior rooms were sparsely fitted out and decorated, notwithstanding Kent's skills as a painter.[98] Kent went on to design the Horse Guards for the Board of Works in about 1745–8, drawing on the broad frontage of his Holkham Hall with its terminal pavilions and big central feature (1734).

The Horse Guards was built with many changes by John Vardy in 1750–58.[99] It was an extensively rusticated building in Portland stone symbolising martial vigour, with a dominating central block and a tall, heavy, stone lantern. At each end of the frontage stood two bold, three-bay pavilions with steep triangular pediments. The fenestration, including large Serlian windows set within the rustication, was highly varied. Given that it was intended as part of a ceremonial route to Westminster, the central arch was ludicrously small and William Chambers's Rococo state coach could not pass through it.[100] This design has generated mixed comments over the years but Kent's adoption of the 'country house range' with central and terminal features is permissible

99 (*right*) The Horseguards. One of London's clearest examples of a 'camel'.

in a building of such unusual function and the picturesque, slightly rustic, effect is not necessarily unwelcome even in a military building. However, at the Office of Works it was a common practice for all the staff to contribute to major design projects and the result looks more a classic 'camel' (a horse invented by a committee) than an integrated work of art. Wren would have done it much better.

London churches offered good opportunities to the Palladian architect. Funds were normally available for a portico and interior columns and a rectangular or square plan had been normal since Wren's time. Free decoration in the style of Wren, in the absence of full archaeological knowledge about Roman interiors, was acceptable. A steeple was always required but if all these features were provided, parishioners were not likely to complain about the result.

James Gibbs recovered from his disappointment at Burlington House by turning to church design, building four London churches. In 1713 he had become, with Hawksmoor, one of the two surveyors to the Fifty New Churches commission and had designed St Mary-le-Strand to great public acclaim before he was dismissed on political grounds (as a Tory and Scot, he thought) in 1715. Later he kept his already quite restrained Baroque inclinations in check. In 1720–26 he rebuilt the sixteenth-century St Martin-in-the-Fields with Wren-like walls and interior but a novel combination of Classical portico and Wren-like steeple above. The immediate success of this formula launched more than a century of porticoed churches with frontal spires or towers and rectangular preaching spaces behind. An early example was St George, Hanover Square (1721–4) by John James, while Hawksmoor's St George, Bloomsbury (1716–31), also used the formula. Its striking success in America shows that it had a broad appeal but its popularity in London sprang from its ability to meet the standard Palladian requirements of the day.

★   ★   ★

100 (*facing page bottom left*)   St Martin-in-the-Fields. Seen here under the best of conditions, it is a convincing candidate for selection as one of London's finest monuments, with Portland stone responding well to the low, western sun. No wonder the portico-and-spire formula was such a success in America.

101 (*facing page bottom right*)   St George, Hanover Square, by John James. Its portico was built shortly before that of St Martin-in-the-Fields. This was a Commissioners' church and, as usual, money does not appear to have been lacking.

NON-RESIDENTIAL PALLADIAN

The simplicity of the revived Palladian style after 1715 was both a strength and a weakness. It was soon modified, not so much in housing as in public buildings, where complex uses and site problems were bound to lead to modifications. Disagreements arose among architects, scholars and aesthetes. The Mansion House, built between 1739 and 1753 by George Dance the Elder, Surveyor to the City of London, was the work of a mason turned architect and was damned for its heavy and cramped facade (though no one could have followed the rules more closely than Dance). The Bank of England (1732–4) (demolished) by George Sampson, Surveyor to the Bank of England, was a simple Palladian design but was generally respected.[101] Theatres, which were constantly under construction, many of them after fires, were classic candidates for Palladian facades with porticoes or pilasters. The Theatre Royal, Haymarket,

102   The Mansion House, in subdued mien, on the left, with Foster's No.1 Poultry in the centre.

103   Side wall of the Mansion House.

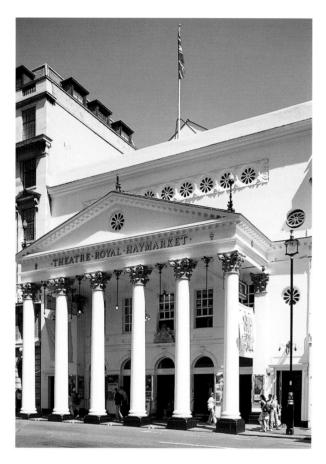

104 The Theatre Royal, Haymarket. Very few of the bigger London theatres lacked a classical portico in the late eighteenth and nineteenth centuries.

remodelled by John Nash in 1816–18, had a huge Corinthian portico with six columns but like most London theatres it had a narrow site, hemmed in by neighbouring buildings. In many other cases the Palladian was corrupted, becoming a caricature which lasted until the end of the nineteenth century in London theatre building.

PALLADIO VICTOR

By 1750 Palladian architecture was sweeping across London, mainly in the form of houses. Where the site and the setting allowed it, impressive results were achieved. Spencer House, built by John Vardy between 1752 and 1760, faced St James's Place but Vardy was allowed to build a rear elevation worthy of the view from Green Park. No expense was spared on this column-bedecked Portland stone facade in the Palladian style and it appeared in a volume of *Vitruvius Britannicus* in 1767.

The main rooms, overlooking the park, were decorated by James Stuart in the newly fashionable Roman manner, drawing on recent archaeological evidence. The 'Painted Room' with its coffered ceiling vault and the 'Alcove Room' with its Roman-inspired palm-tree columns and fronds were outstanding.[102] The broad east frontage, with Serlian windows and engaged porticoes, though incomplete, shows Vardy working well in an urban Palladian mode. London had little as fair as this and Spencer House is generally recognised as London's finest surviving eighteenth-century house, the equal of any Paris mansion of the day.

Even minor architects could do well in the Palladian manner. Richard Edwin, who exhibited at the Royal Academy in the 1770s, secured only one major commission.[103] This was Stratford Place, off Oxford Street, where he built a five-bay Palladian frontage in stone in 1773–5, at the top of a short approach lined by Palladian buildings. The powerful, attached portico and the fenestration have been compared to Adam but really this was a standard Palladian design for a town house with country characteristics, apart from the ambitious decoration of the cornice and pediment.

Sir William Chambers's Melbourne House, built in 1771–4, was a more limited achievement. It faced the standard Piccadilly site problem, exacerbated by client cost-cutting. The house stood back from the street at the bottom of a courtyard narrower than the frontage of the house. Chambers's drawings looked noble enough albeit in the reduced urban Palladian style with pitched roof and seven narrow bays which became acceptable in mid-century, with a rusticated ground floor and half basement, modest front entrance, a pediment and, apparently, stone construction.[104] It looked as though it would be a distinct improvement on Chesterfield House though designed to the same formula. Chambers took much trouble over his design for the gateway onto Piccadilly, which drew on Jonesian precedents.[105] Predictably, however, the house was finally built entirely of brick apart from the entrance and window dressings, with even the rustication sacrificed. The width of the bays was further reduced, producing a cramped verticality which the tall sash windows did nothing to allay, though the height of the frontage was in itself impressive.

This was an extremely cheap job. Lord Melbourne claimed that he had spent nearly £100,000 on the house and contents but this is hard to believe.[106] The best feature of the interior was a central, top-lit staircase atrium. Only the statues in the niches looked expensive but it is possible that they were made of plaster or came from some demolished house (or both).[107] The bas-reliefs and other commissioned decorations were costly but

105   Spencer House. This is the park frontage.

most could easily have been moved out, as could the statues and even the staircase. From 1791 the house was known as Albany House after Melbourne exchanged it with the Duke of York and Albany. In 1802 the duke sold the house to a young builder who converted it into apartments as the Albany. At least it was spared demolition for its materials, though they would probably not have raised much money.

The many aristocratic houses which formed part of a row were less demanding for their architects because only the frontage was normally visible. Anson (later Lichfield) House, at 15 St James's Square, built by James 'Athenian' Stuart in 1763–5 after his visit to Greece, was a weighty design in Portland stone with an attached four-column Ionic portico and triangular pediment. This expensive solution, which observed Palladian proportions, contrasted with Stuart's spartan Londonderry House. Robert Adam's 20 St James's Square (1772), was

a frontage of similar dimensions but with four Corinthian pilasters, a cornice and a balustrade. Sir Robert Taylor's Ely House in Dover Street (also 1772) drew its distinction mainly from three first-floor windows with

106   The Greek frontage of Lichfield House (1764–6), 15 St James's Square, by James 'Athenian' Stuart.

67

107 The interior of the Rotunda at Ranelagh Gardens, as portrayed by Canaletto in 1754. The artist has greatly exaggerated the proportions.

balustrades and triangular pediments over pilasters, with cartouches above. The ground floors of all three houses were heavily rusticated with round-topped window arches. All three solutions were influential in the Adam manner.[108]

A tour of large Palladian houses in London suggests that, whatever the quality of the exterior, their interiors were usually of a high standard. A monumental staircase hall and staircase were often included. Top-lighting of staircases, and later of certain rooms, began in about 1760. The main rooms were often decorated by Italian or French artists, whose numbers in London contrasted with the paucity of foreign architects. One of the most impressive interiors was at William Jones's Rotunda (1742) at the Ranelagh pleasure gardens, Chelsea (though this was an assembly room, not a house).

From about 1760 many clients began to see brick as an ignoble material and wanted it covered in stucco, given the continuing high cost of stone. The term 'stucco' was applied to versatile coatings made from a variety of materials including gypsum, sand, clay, chalk, cement, oil or lime. It had been brought to England by Italian craftsmen in the late 1500s and English plasterers continued to use it thereafter. Inigo Jones rendered several of his buildings in lime mortar but the practice was not generally adopted. A suitable stucco for London buildings had, however, become available, after many experiments, by 1775.[109]

The first big user of stucco was Robert Adam, who patented his own recipes, and it came into widespread use around 1800. Stucco was used by John Nash on most of the buildings in his Regent's Park and Regent Street development, after he gave up the idea of using Bath stone. He scored the stucco to simulate stone blocks and 'frescoed' each block to suggest the weathering of Bath stone. Nash was able to mould fine Classical details in stucco and paint stucco surfaces in light oil paint. Summerson detects a 'stucco age' inaugurated by Nash in 1812 when he used 'Parker's Roman Cement' at Park Crescent.[110]

As development with squares and adjoining streets spread across London, the planning of interiors became more difficult. At Covent Garden the buildings had been divided into large apartments on French lines but this solution did not prove popular. With many terraced houses rising to three or four floors, tenants and servants had much climbing to do. One answer was to create more space on the lower floors by pushing the rear walls towards the back of the site, producing deep, dark interiors. The resulting stepped effect at the back meant that the artistic design of rear walls became pointless. Cheaper materials were used there and random extensions, outbuildings and balconies proliferated. As the backs could not normally be seen from the street, owners and tenants were usually indifferent to the result. 'Queen Anne front, Mary-Ann back', as they used to say.

THE NEO-CLASSICAL

Around 1750 an important development occurred within Palladianism. A new burst of excavations in Italy revealed other periods and styles of Roman architecture, including interior design. The latter, as uncovered at Pompeii and elsewhere, was a revelation, especially in its use of intricate motifs and bright colours. Many more architects began to visit Italy. Palladio's engravings of Classical frontages could now be supplemented by an awareness of Roman life and of interiors which were much more varied than the exteriors. At the same time, a mature architectural profession emerged, with most of the masons, carpenters and artists dropping out of view. This allowed the architect to be in complete control of the design, inside and out.[111] Some architects, such as James Paine and Sir Robert Taylor, began to take articled pupils into their offices.[112] Sir William Chambers, architect of Somerset House, strove for years to organise the profession. The Royal Academy of Arts, founded in 1768, was partly inspired by French practice. Located in a new Adam building at the Adelphi, it included four architect Academicians. Other architects exhibited there, while Chambers was a leading member from the start.

This more professional approach to architecture is often linked to Neo-Classicism, a term coined at the end of the nineteenth century. Neo-Classicism is associated with the Enlightenment and developments in art, science, archaeology and philosophy. The whole of Europe warmed to it but it took different forms in each country. In Germany much Greek inspiration was visible. Complete near-facsimiles of Greek temples and gateways were erected there, some extremely large. France was also influenced by Greece but there a particular interest was shown in pure, geometrical forms. Its English exponents tried to express Reason, which normally was achieved through authentic Classical forms, colours, elegance and lightness of touch. Exteriors were simple, with limited decoration, but many interiors were meticulous creations and, in the hands of Robert Adam and his admirers, even an enhancement of the finest that the later Roman empire could offer. This meant much use of bright, rich colours and intricate patterns in a way which had not previously been associated with Classical architecture.[113]

In London the main exponent in the early years was Robert Adam, a Scot who began his Grand Tour in 1754.[114] After a fruitful period in Rome, 'the most glorious place in the Universal world', he sailed to Dalmatia to record the ruins of Diocletian's palace at Spalato, the highlight of later Roman architecture. In 1758 he set up a practice in London with his brothers James and William, because London offered him more scope for Classical architecture than did Scotland.[115] In 1761 patronage secured Adam one of the two new posts of Architect of the King's Works. Although the rivalry of Chambers, the Palladian Neo-Classical who obtained the other Architect's position, prevented Adam's obtaining big public commissions, his reputation among the aristocracy was unrivalled.

Adam sought to achieve a simple but grand Roman architecture, moderated by 'taste'. Although the main principles of his facades followed the Palladian, he sought to create movement and variety, something which formal Palladianism could not offer.[116] In practice this meant variety of detail using sometimes eclectic motifs, variations of silhouette and advancing and recessing of the plan across the frontage of a building. He made much of the portico and the pilaster. His main contribution, however, was interior planning and decoration, which confirmed the preference of the London client for an interior which outshone the exterior. In designing street facades, Adam favoured long blocks which could be split into five sections, with emphasis on the central and terminal sections, but with a plainer treatment of the bays in between. This distribution repeated that of his country houses. However, he could also build rows of conforming First Rate houses, as defined by the Building Act of

1774, which are sometimes hard to distinguish as his work.

Adam remodelled three country houses just outside London – Kenwood, Osterley (possibly with Chambers) and Syon. These were close to Chiswick House and strengthened his reputation in the capital. Adam's first London triumph was a commission from the Earl of Bute, twice prime minister in the early 1760s, for Lansdowne (formerly Shelburne) House, Berkeley Square (1762–8) (mostly demolished). The exterior was well up to Adam's standard, an attractive Palladian three-storey villa of thirteen bays in Portland stone with a tall attached portico, a rusticated ground floor, a richly decorated cornice and two symmetrical wings of two storeys, facing a forecourt. It was partly isolated and Saunders describes it as 'a country mansion strayed into a London square'.[117] The interior was a fine example of his Roman style, with more niches and inset arches than usual, holding a wealth of classical statuary. The highlight was the gallery, which included a coffered vault and two rotundas with coffered domes, smaller versions of his dome at Kedleston Hall. The wealth and variety of decoration could have filled a large country house, and must have publicised Adam's work in London.

However, most of Adam's London houses were terraced. Among the best was the three-storey 20 Portman Square (Home House) (1775–7). It had a broad frontage of five bays and the interior treatment was equal to many a country house. A soaring staircase, lit from a dome, was a high point. Most Adam houses were much narrower than this. So much accommodation had to be provided at the back of the site that the depth of many of his plans was five or six times greater than the width. This meant that an open, central, top-lit staircase was often essential.

The Adam brothers' Adelphi (1768–72) (almost completely demolished) was their biggest development of tall, deep, terraced houses. It stood partly on arches between the Strand and the Thames foreshore and measured 122 by 110 metres. It was on the site of Durham House, leased from the Duke of St Albans. Adam and his brothers built this partly to show how they would respond to the challenge of a big public commission. The brothers hoped to lease the space under the arches to the Ordnance Department but no agreement was reached and it had to be let out more cheaply. Instead, the brothers launched a lottery which proved enough to finance the scheme. The houses had a common height of four storeys, most of them with two further floors below street level.

For the frontages the brothers used a simple but effective design formula. Groups of four pilasters in the portico manner were separated by plain but elegant

108   No. 7 Adam Street, one of the surviving fragments of the Adelphi. This intricate, pedimented front is used to divide a long row of houses in the manner of a pavilion. This method would often be used by Cubitt and other builders of rows in the nineteenth century.

brick frontages. The pilasters were decorated with terracotta panels dressed with ornate, Ancient motifs, similar to Robert Adam's new interior style.[118] These motifs were repeated inside. Most of the interiors were a simplified version of the Adam style used in luxurious mansions. The premises of the Royal Society of Arts

(1772–4), built within the scheme, had an attractive Serlian window and a portico of attached columns within the frontage.

In 1773 the Adam brothers began work on a speculation at Portland Place, though they were not the developers. The original plan was for detached houses but poor business conditions during the American War of Independence led to a switch to brick terraces in 1776–80. The frontages were modestly built but they had all the marks of Adam work and included Corinthian pilasters. Robert Adam went on to build the east and

109 (*above left*)   Mansfield Street (nos 1–10), planned and built by Adam in the early 1770s as part of the Portland Place scheme. Some of the more distant houses are the work of other builders. These houses are fine examples of First Rates, with the 1774 regulations tending to encourage the Palladian style and a greater conformity. No. 16, built by Adam, was for sale in 2003 for £10.5 million after a film producer had redesigned the interior for use as a film set (*Telegraph Property,* 11 October 2003). Adam usually built well.

110 (*above right*)   Mansfield Street: the arched doorways mark the houses built by Adam.

south sides of Fitzroy Square in stone in 1790. This was a development of the Adelphi formula, with monumental pavilions and striking Diocletian windows, but Adam was never able to build the other two sides of the square, which were completed in stucco in 1827–35.

Adam made the most of one unusual opportunity, the rebuilding of the Drury Lane Theatre in 1775. The interior had a flat, hanging ceiling with Roman decoration and a wide auditorium with a circle and gallery and further seating and boxes on either side. The frontage was so predictable that it hardly needs describing–five deeply rusticated round–topped arches (though of two different dimensions), two further storeys with rectangular windows and six Ionic pilasters, four of them paired, and a triangular pediment. A commodious bal–

111   Mansfield Street: conventional areas and bridges on the Adam houses.

cony topped the ground floor. At least the paired pilasters were a bit of a surprise.

Few London architects of distinction have limited themselves to houses to the extent that Adam did. Yet in Summerson's judgement, no house was built in the West End that did not bear some mark of Robert Adam.[119] By the time of Robert Adam's death in 1792, however, taste was moving away from his 'gingerbread', as Horace Walpole described it, to the more 'chaste' Neo-Classical of Henry Holland's Brooks's Club and Dover House.[120]

Sir William Chambers, Robert Adam's rival, took a more purist approach to Neo-Classicism. He had studied in Paris and Rome from 1750 to 1755, including a period at J.-F. Blondel's academy, and was a highly trained architect with strong roots in France.[121] He was a convinced Palladian with a rooted respect for Inigo Jones but constant admiration for his distinguished Parisian contemporaries. His finest work was a villa, Manresa House, in Richmond Park. Built in 1760–68, it was a Palladian gem, similar to Palladio's Villa Foscari. He served in the Office of Works from 1761 to 1796 and was Surveyor General and Comptroller from 1782 to 1796.[122] He worked mainly on houses but his biggest project was Somerset House (1776–96), a huge block of government offices built on an arched, rusticated podium above the north bank of the Thames a little downstream from the Adelphi. There are indications that Chambers wanted to outshine Adam with an equally large, but more disciplined, structure.

As the leading official architect of his day, Chambers saw Somerset House as the highlight of his career and he concentrated on it over twenty years.[123] It was bigger than the latest public offices in Paris, which Chambers inspected in 1774 and possibly again after 1784.[124] It was arranged round a large courtyard with distinguished Classical facades. The inner and outer facades of the Strand block were modelled on the Queen's Gallery of 1662 which was demolished to make way for the new Somerset House. Although built by John Webb, the design of the Queen's Gallery was essentially the work of Inigo Jones and dated back to the 1630s. Extended sympathetically to the east and to the west in 1830–35

and 1856, Somerset House was especially impressive when viewed from the Thames, though its vertical features above the cornice were too weak for its length, probably owing to government economies.

Most critics opine that Somerset House failed to outshine Paris. Summerson saw Chambers as a domestic specialist who could not master monumental architecture.[125] However, buildings of this scale are rare and the extended Somerset House can be ranked with the Louvre, the Palace of Westminster, Grand Central Terminal, Federal Triangle, Lutyens's Viceroy's House and the Rockefeller Center. The completed river frontage of 244 metres posed similar problems to those faced by Barry at the new Palace of Westminster. Barry was allowed to build two towers and one spire to enliven the frontage. Chambers was expected to build London's first multi-purpose government offices in an era when there was no practical use for towers or for a large dome. Two monumental staircases – Chambers's speciality as at Melbourne House – were highlights of the building. French innovations are much more important than many critics allow. The generous courtyard recalls the Louvre and the Palais-Royal and is a striking answer to the cramped and

112 (*above*)   The north front of the courtyard of Somerset House, with the Inigo Jones formula spreading to the wings.

113   The Strand front of Somerset House, in a print of 1798. Apart from the top-lighting structure above the cornice, and the windows filling the arches on the ground floor, the elevation is modelled on the Queen's Gallery of the old Somerset House. The original Palladian design was first drafted by Inigo Jones in the 1630s.

stuffy Adelphi plan. Its pavilions and porticoes owe much to Gabriel's long frontages at the Place de la Concorde and to Antoine's Mint. However, Chambers's decision to use Inigo Jones elevations, albeit reinforced, on the Strand side may well have restrained the whole design. Chambers was, however, neither the first nor the last

114 Somerset House and the Adelphi from the Thames in 1790. This was one of Europe's finest river views and artists often emphasised its sublime character.

116 (*right*) The east front of the courtyard of Somerset House, with the portico showing French Neo-Classical influence in its paired columns and flat pediment.

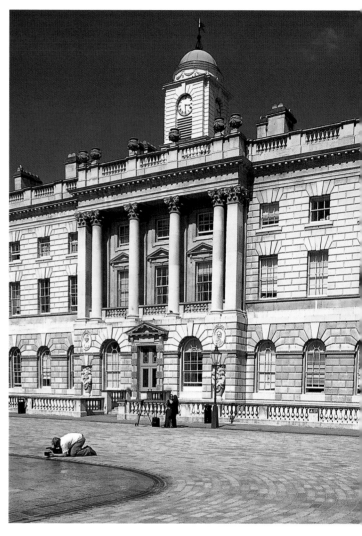

115 The south front of Somerset House, seen from the Embankment, completed in 1872. No longer rising directly from the Thames, Somerset House has lost some of its impact.

architect to find that working for the State was often a frustration and a restriction. He clearly wanted to build a big dome over the central portico of the river frontage but the extended range could well have incorporated three such features. The great, rusticated, riverfront arches added height at first when seen from the Thames but the Victorian Thames Embankment truncated them and made the building rise from a utilitarian roadway.

Summerson's explanation of English Neo-Classicism deserves consideration. He detects a generation of Neo-Classical architects growing up around 1750 who sought to consolidate rather than to innovate. They included Sir Robert Taylor and James Paine, who practised mainly in London. Chambers was a leading member of this group and the restrained elevations of Somerset House may reflect these conservative, Neo-Palladian tendencies, though some of his unexecuted palace designs had much of the French Neo-Classical about them.[126] Taylor's wings for the Bank of England

118   The west front of Stone Buildings.

117 *(left)*   Stone Buildings by Sir Robert Taylor, 1774–80, completed by a southward extension in the same style by Philip Hardwick in 1842. This restrained building by one of London's main Neo-Classical architects is Palladian in character.

(1766–83) and Stone Buildings (1774–80) at Lincoln's Inn were further examples of this careful conservatism.[127] Certainly, the powerful Neo-Classicism of the buildings painted and sketched by Chambers in Paris was not obviously reflected in Somerset House, though some features were created on a more modest scale.[128]

Summerson goes on to detect a new generation of architects practising in London from around 1775. By then, the big wave of Adam influence was over and Chambers was preoccupied by Somerset House.[129] Many of these younger architects were determined Neo-Classicists, much inspired by French interest in logic and form. Among the most active was George Dance the Younger. He studied in Rome with great success from 1759 to 1764 and was always a more sensitive architect than his father. Dance was noted for his aisle-less, barrel-vaulted All Hallows, London Wall (1765–7), and his powerful, rusticated Newgate Prison (1770–78) (demolished), which was one of the few English buildings to be included by Jean-Nicolas-Louis Durand in his *Recueil et parallèle des édifices* (1799).[130] Much of the detail was drawn from sixteenth-century Italy, especially from Giulio Romano, from whom Dance derived the niche in a blocked window, much applied at Newgate as part of the building's studied symbolism.[131] The Gothick facade which he added to the Guildhall in 1788–9 was one of the most original achievements in London at that time. He also engaged in housing development, begin-

ning at Vine Street (1765–70) and working on a number of sites until about 1790.

Among other examples of this new Neo-Classicism were the Hall of the Freemasons' Tavern, built in 1775–6 by Thomas Sandby, the first Professor of Architecture at the Royal Academy.[132] In 1776 Henry Holland built the brick Brooks's Club, St James's Street, whose Palladian

119   The new entrance to the Guildhall by George Dance the Younger. This exotic Gothick composition typifies Dance's confidence and versatility and his ability to convince his client. Like Chambers, Dance was admired in France.

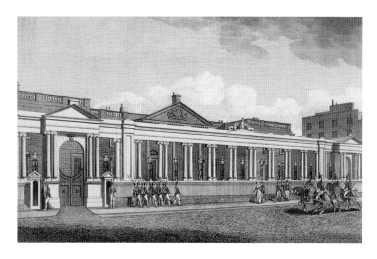

120 Carlton House in an engraving of 1813.

121 The salon and drawing room at Carlton House. Most of the contents and fixtures could be removed in the event of sale or demolition.

reflecting the artistic and social tastes of the prince in their public form. The interior expressed the prince's sybaritic private life and taste for art collection, a riot of caprice with no obvious style, but shaped mainly by French artists and craftsmen. However, Holland's leading assistant, J. P. T. Trécourt, was French, and he used a French foreman, French furniture makers and French decorators.[134]

122 Prince George (the larger figure) rides past Carlton House in a cartoon of 1804.

In 1770 James Wyatt won the competition for the Pantheon, a big place of assembly in Oxford Street. It had a coffered dome on Pantheon lines and internal colonnades. Samuel Wyatt built it in 1770–72 and it was hailed by Horace Walpole as 'a winter Ranelagh'. It burned down in 1792, which is not surprising given the quan-

123 The Theatre Royal, Drury Lane, 1810–12. Benjamin Wyatt strove to provide generous, elegant internal spaces and the exterior was a simple box with Classical trimmings. Even the ugly low porch and colonnade were a later addition by another architect.

facade leaned towards Neo-Classicism. Here he came into contact with leading Whigs, some of whom became his clients and patrons.[133] The Gallic sympathies of this group soon led Holland to study French architecture through publications and contacts with French professionals working in London, following the example of Sir William Chambers.

In 1783–95 Holland rebuilt Carlton House as a London residence for the Prince of Wales, who had admired his work at Brooks's Club. Holland's two-storey, rusticated, balustraded exterior was French Neo-Classicism in all its simplicity and purity, with a huge Corinthian portico and an Ionic screen of paired columns,

124　Trinity House by Samuel Wyatt, 1792–4. This Ionic frontage is one of London's most original Neo-Classical designs.

tities of wood and plaster it contained.[135] In 1811–12 Benjamin Dean Wyatt rebuilt the Drury Lane Theatre, now the Theatre Royal, Drury Lane, with an interior coffered dome in the Pantheon style with Cor-inthian columns supporting ceilings over the public areas.[136] This was the most advanced theatre in London, with elaborate arrangements to separate the social classes and a water-sprinkling system.[137] Its spacious public areas contrasted with those of most London theatres of the time or indeed since. Equally unusual was its lack of a portico.

In 1796, as Surveyor to Trinity House and builder of lighthouses, Samuel Wyatt designed the new Trinity House on Tower Hill. The main front was a charming, simple Neo-Classical design in Portland stone with engaged Ionic columns and decorative panels in Coade Stone. The segmental windows in the rusticated podium were the only curved lines in the structure.[138] Despite its unassuming dimensions, this was one of the best Neo-Classical buildings ever erected in London.

London's most original Neo-Classical architect was the imaginative Sir John Soane. The son of a Reading bricklayer, Soane joined the office of George Dance the Younger in 1768 and became his main pupil. He studied at the Royal Academy School of Architecture under William Chambers from 1771 and won its Gold Medal in 1776 and the King's Travelling Scholarship in 1778. Like some other winners, he chose to spend three years in Italy, from 1778 to 1780. He enjoyed a number of official positions from 1790, obtained mainly by patronage. His position as Surveyor to the Bank of England (1788–1833), which he owed to William Pitt, gave him a firm foundation for his career.[139] A series of government appointments led to his becoming one of three Attached Architects to the Office of Works. For many years Soane sought a modern style rooted in Classical simplicity, drawing on French and German Neo-Classicism and Greek precedents. Its main expression was at the Bank of England where Soane's great interior halls were unprecedented in England. Soane's work was unique, a landmark in the history of world architecture, but it was little emulated.

More conventional Neo-Classical architects con-

125 The Bank of England from the Mansion House, c. 1895.

127 (right) The Old Dividend Office at the Bank of England.

tinued to work into the nineteenth century. The Royal Mint (1807–9), completed to the designs of James Johnson by Sir Robert Smirke, did not put a step wrong. David Laing, a pupil of Soane, built the new Custom House in 1813–17 but it was much improved by Smirke who reconstructed the river frontage after a major col-

126 The new Custom House, built in 1813–17 by David Laing, surveyor to the Board of Customs. Laing was blamed when the central Long Room collapsed in 1825. Robert Smirke rebuilt much of the building in 1825–8. This southern, Neo-Classical facade is nearly 150 metres long.

lapse in 1825–7, putting in a third portico. The result showed much French influence.

THE GREEK REVIVAL

Yet another variant of Classical architecture reached a peak in the early 1800s. This has come to be known as 'Greek Revival' architecture, a curious title given that all the other Classical styles were also revivals.[140] It was associated with the Neo-Classical movement and sustained by studies in Greece. The London branch of the Greek Revival was led by Sir Robert Smirke and William Wilkins. Smirke, son of the distinguished artist Robert Smirke and a pupil of George Dance the Younger, travelled on the Continent from 1800 to 1805, including a productive period drawing ruins in Greece. In 1808 he rebuilt the Covent Garden Theatre after a fire, creating London's first building in the pure Doric style.[141] In 1813, thanks to Tory patronage at the highest level, he was appointed architect to the Office of Works and this brought him some big commissions, including the United Service Club (1816–17), the Union Club (1822–7) and the Royal College of Physicians (1824–7) on Nash's nascent Trafalgar Square, the British Museum (1823–47), the General Post Office (1824–9), the Custom

House reconstruction (1825–7), St George's Hospital at Hyde Park Corner (1827–9) and King's College, the Strand (1830–35) (the eastern extension of Chambers's Somerset House). His practice became one of the biggest in London. Although his stylistic preference was for the Greek Revival, he was always prepared to work more widely within the Classical mode.

Wilkins built less but had two huge commissions, University College (1826–9) and the National Gallery (1832–8). University College is approached across a wide and deep courtyard off Gower Street. Broad steps lead up to the main floor and a portico with a spread of ten columns. The capitals are Corinthian but the simple triangular pediment is entirely Greek. The set-back dome peeping over the top of the portico makes little impact from close up, however, and the interior spaces behind the portico are astoundingly cramped. Those who claimed that the columns on the portico were too close together ignored the Schinkel-like effect that they produced. The north and south ranges of the courtyard were built in keeping by Hayter Lewis between 1869 and 1881. Two long frontages of university buildings in Portland stone on Gower Street also achieve a grandeur and purity in the Greek style but they were not completed until 1937.

At the National Gallery, Wilkins was required to use the columns saved from the portico of Carlton House. This made the central portico very low and the galleries followed suit. A series of economies restricted the result in terms of space, design and lighting. This was no Louvre. The compartmentalised frontage, on a seriously constricted site, seems to defer in height and detail to

129   University College, London. The west courtyard. The Neo-Greek style was considered appropriate for a place of learning.

130   University College, London. The Gower Street frontage, completed in 1937 after a long period of gestation, is a very late expression of the Neo-Greek style.

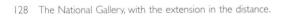

128   The National Gallery, with the extension in the distance.

the church of St Martin-in-the-Fields. It was further diminished by the Nelson Column (1839–42). What Nash's dispersed and inevitably disparate square needed was a powerful northern frontage like the Place de la Concorde's but Wilkins produced a failure. Smirke's British Museum is usually seen as a better performance. Plans to replace the National Gallery with a more worthy building were under discussion for much of the rest of the century, without result.[142]

The best-known building in the new Greek style was St Pancras New Church, built by William and H. W. Inwood between 1822 and 1824, after a competition. This was the first Greek Revival church in London. It

131 St Pancras (new) parish church.

gave in to the London tradition of a tower but its cary-atids (in Coade Stone) were utterly Greek. Charles Porden's St Matthew, Brixton (1822) had a simple but impressive Doric portico. St John, Waterloo Road (1822–4) by Francis Bedford, had a six-column Doric portico and a temple plan, and was about as Greek as they came at this time except for its obligatory spire. The church of St Peter, Eaton Square, by the obscure Henry Hakewill (1824–7) had an Ionic portico of six columns. It was a routine affair.

By 1815 the Greek Revival style was common in London for secular buildings. To show that it was Greek, it was normal to use an order with Ionic or Doric columns, as at Lewis Vulliamy's successful Law Society (1829–32, 1848–50). Without such an order, the Greek character of the design could be lost on the average onlooker. Greek Classical architecture appealed because it embodied simplicity and purity. It could appear to be a return to true Classical principles. However, it had serious structural limitations. The Greeks had developed neither arches nor vaults, and their acme had been the rectangular temple with a flat roof and a colonnade. Their windows were rectangular and their cornices were flat and continuous. In London, Greek Revival buildings often looked awkward and out of place. The style was not versatile enough to be of general application. It was always a scholarly style, difficult to develop and apply because everything had to be at right angles – 'the New Square Style of Mr. Smirke', as Pugin put it.[143] The Greek Revival expressed purity and learning rather than power and wealth. It was hardly ever used in house design, no doubt because the windows would have been the wrong shape. Summerson concluded that the Greek

Revival in England was 'an unsatisfactory interlude'.[144] But did Summerson ever like anything?

SQUARES, LAYOUTS AND LEASEHOLD TENURE

The Palladian style flourished in many of London's new squares and approach streets. Some years ago, Hermione Hobhouse counted about thirty West End squares which had been created by 1800. More recently, Jones and Woodward identified a grand total of 151 squares, many of them in north-east and south London, well away from the fashionable districts.[145] Nearly all were laid out before 1850. Without the square, the Palladian cannot be fully understood.

Some squares, and the planned streets which often led to them, were the work of landowners and their surveyors. The others were undertaken by developers – mainly builders or architects – who usually leased the land rather than bought it outright. Most of the more elegant examples were built on land belonging to the aristocracy and the landowners often secured a high quality of development through the terms of the lease.

The London leasehold system, fully in being by the eighteenth century, was unique. Most aristocratic owner-ships were settled estates, which meant that the owners were not allowed to alienate any of the land, in order to preserve the family inheritance. The land could, how-ever, be leased for a fixed term, as could land owned by commoners. London's earliest building leases appear to date from the early seventeenth century, when the built-up area started to spread into the great estates which the lords had acquired since the Middle Ages in order to be near the Court. Some leasehold building took place in northern and eastern London and south of the Thames but generally on a smaller scale.[146]

The period of the lease was crucial. It was theoreti-cally in the builder's interest to build cheaply so that little or no value was left in his work at the expiry of the lease. The landowner could require certain features and a certain standard of building under the terms of the lease. However, landowners were increasingly aware that the demand for older houses was progressively under-mined by changes in fashion and use, so in many cases they too did not require solid or ornate building. In the seventeenth century leases were very short – initially about thirty-one years, rising to forty-one years by mid-century and to sixty-one years by 1700.[147] In the eigh-teenth they were extended up to ninety-nine years in most cases and this became the London norm. The shorter leases may well have been linked to frequent fires, with builders assuming that their houses would not

survive very long. Even a ninety-nine year lease, however, tended to generate flimsy building. This tradition
lasted until the demanding building regulations of the
late nineteenth century began to raise standards.[148]
Flimsy the building may have been but without the
leasehold system, few of London's great squares and
streets with their elegant, conforming facades would ever
have come into being.

The origins of the London square lie partly in the
series of royal proclamations against new building on the
edge of the City, beginning in 1580.[149] All the monastic
land confiscated by the Crown in 1536 had been used
for building by about 1570 and the uncontrolled development of common land and similar open areas had
begun to cause concern.[150] The City Corporation was
apparently the first body to take advantage of the new
royal policy, preventing building at Moorfields, just to
the north of the City, and laying it out as a rectangular
park by 1607.[151] This was followed by the development
under royal supervision of two areas in which open space
and buildings were combined. These were Lincoln's Inn
Fields and Covent Garden.

At Lincoln's Inn Fields some threatened common land
was surrounded by houses and a church to form a rectangular space of about ten acres in 1638–43. The developer was one William Newton but he was controlled by
the Royal Commission on Buildings, set up in 1618, with
Inigo Jones as a member. Efforts were made to ensure
conformity in the frontages of the houses under the 1618
proclamation and Inigo Jones must have played a big part
in securing classical frontage designs, including his
favourite giant-order pilasters. Lindsey House (c. 1640)
is the sole surviving example. It is often credited to Jones
or a close associate but it looks more like the work of
an artisan builder following a standard frontage approved
by Jones and the Commission on Buildings. Originally
built of brick with stone dressings, it was later covered
with stucco. It would appear that few of these houses
had been built before the Civil War, and after 1660
official efforts to impose coherent frontage designs
lapsed.

Covent Garden, a much smaller, paved space, was
bounded by two rows of houses, a church and the wall
of the Earl of Bedford's garden. All but the wall were
designed by Inigo Jones from 1631 to 1637. The Earl had
obtained a licence to build from the Crown in 1630 at
a cost of £2000 and may have been formally required
to build an ornament to the city. Italian and French
influences can be assumed, though both the concept and
the detail were unique.[152]

Summerson sees much of Palladio and Serlio in the
Jones scheme. The church designed by Jones for the west

132 Lindsey House, Lincoln's Inn Fields, 1640. This is probably based on
a standard frontage by Jones, intended for repetition all round this large
open space. It was originally in brick, later stuccoed, and the detailed design
was probably by an artisan, the central broken pediment, for instance, being
unusual for Jones. It was divided into two houses in 1751–2.

side of the square (1631–3), with its simple Doric portico
and overhanging roof, is in the Tuscan tradition, which
would imply that Jones saw the whole development as
'rural' in the sense defined by Palladio. The elevations of
the two ranges derive from a design by Serlio for a palace
overlooking a square and the arches conform to a type
which Serlio saw as Tuscan.[153] Less is known of a third
development, Southampton Square, Bloomsbury, laid
out for the Earl of Southampton in the 1630s. Like
Covent Garden, it was adjacent to the owner's residence,
Southampton House (1640) (demolished).

In at least one street, development responded to the
new style of the squares. This was Great Queen Street
(c. 1635), which approached Lincoln's Inn Fields from
the west, 'the first regular street in London', according
to Summerson.[154] William Newton was involved in this
street and so, probably, were Inigo Jones and the Com-

mission on Buildings. Some speculation is necessary here but it would appear that in both Lincoln's Inn Fields and Great Queen Street common frontage formulae were developed, with three-storey terraced houses topped by a pediment, block eaves or balustrade and a pitched roof with dormers. Most ambitious of all was the giant order of pilasters stretching up through the first and second storeys.[155]

The creation of squares resumed after the Restoration in 1660. Royal proclamations and intervention continued but the squares were no longer exceptional developments. Bloomsbury Square (Earl of Southampton) and St James's Square (Earl of St Albans) were launched in 1661 and Leicester Square (Earl of Leicester) in 1670. Other fashionable squares were Golden Square (1675), Soho Square (1681), Red Lion Square (1684) and Hanover Square (1717–19). St James's Square, though regularly planned with gated streets approaching the middle of three of its sides, was fronted by houses of different designs, much less grand than the aristocratic mansions originally intended.[156] Most appear to have been demolished by the middle of the eighteenth century, this probably being an early example of the effects of the leasehold system.

Some squares were intended to set off large, aristocratic residences and the new houses built on the squares varied from short, three-storey rows to large, free-stand-

133   Cavendish Square, with these paired houses of 1769–72.

134 (*below*)   Hanover Square, laid out in 1717–19.

135　Bedford Square, laid out in 1776.

ing mansions for the rich. The smaller houses were of plain brick, often with bands separating the storeys, and the eaves or cornices were of wood, like the larger houses in the rebuilt City.[157]

The spread of the Palladian style enhanced many of the new squares. Grosvenor Square, built in 1727–35 by a developer, John Simmons, had seven houses on each side. Colin Campbell made a design for the whole of the east side but this was not used. Instead, Simmons combined the sites to form symmetrical blocks, with tall elements at the centre and at each end. These rows were given a single architectural character by the builders. Only on the north side did some builders refuse to conform.[158] Summerson believes that this was probably the first occasion on which London terraced houses were grouped as though in a single, monumental building or palazzo.[159]

In 1775–80 the Duke of Bedford created Bedford Square as part of his plan to develop his Bloomsbury estate with squares. It was made up of three-storey houses in yellow brick with Coade Stone dressings, with an attic in the roof. The paired houses in the centre of each side were stuccoed with pilasters and triangular pediments. The front doors were topped by semi-circular arches in the style of Adam. It is possible that the original brick was coloured black, with white pointing. The oval gardens in the middle were for use by the residents only.

The architecture of these early squares set a pattern for the West End, especially as builders in adjoining streets, whether or not they leased land from the founders of the squares, tended to conform. Although their designs often varied, their frontages were almost continuous. Most were three storeys tall, though some, as at Hanover Square, were of four storeys. The main building material was brick, grey or brown in colour rather than the red used in the Fire area.[160] Stone dressings added variety without counteracting the overall blank effect of the frontages or the monotony of the fenestration. Because stone trimmings were expensive, much artificial stone was used.

136   This view of north Bloomsbury and beyond (2002) shows how the Bedford Estate shaped this large area of northern London from the 1630s. The large square at the bottom right, with its spreading trees, is Russell Square (1800). The much smaller Tavistock Square (c. 1803) is two blocks above it, with Gordon Square to the left. The leafy Cartwright Gardens (1807), at the extreme right, is one of London's lesser-known crescents. At bottom centre London University (1828–) has spread north of the British Museum, partially using the Bedford layout. This Elysium ends towards the top of the view where Euston Road cuts across from right to left, marked by five recent towers. Euston station covers a broad square towards the top, and the iron vault of St Pancras station can be seen at the extreme right. A very different London of transport and storage, with the homes of railwaymen, cabdrivers and carters, grew up here from the 1840s. Somers Town, between St Pancras and Euston stations, was a slum from the start and the name of one of the new arterial streets, Goods Way, summed up the changes behind the stations. The resulting clearance areas, slab blocks and residential towers visible at the top of the view are typical of most of inner London.

137 Mecklenburgh Square. Building was slow here owing to poor access and this row was not started, by Joseph Kay, until about 1808. The landowner, the Foundling Estate, approved an Adamesque design to attract tenants to an unfashionable area.

In this West End of the squares one curiosity was Seven Dials (1693–1710), a star pattern of seven streets laid out by Thomas Neale, Master of the Mint. This ill-conceived scheme of Baroque inspiration quickly became the home of West End low life and confirmed the square as the developer's ideal.

A new concept in squares came with Brunswick and Mecklenburgh squares, whose east and west sides opened on to the Foundling Hospital (1742–52). Following medical orthodoxy, a large area had been acquired around the hospital and in 1788 the governors discussed laying out the two squares so that their inner spaces could help ventilate the wards. The plan was by the surveyor to the estate, Samuel Pepys Cockerell, the pupil of Sir Robert Taylor. The buildings were the work of Cockerell's pupil Joseph Kay and recalled Adam's Fitzroy Square.[161] Such generous use of land was unusual in London and the paired plan was rarely used except when two squares were laid out on opposite sides of an important thoroughfare.

As the eighteenth century ended, large areas of the West End formed a coherent spatial creation of squares, rectilinear streets, churches, backstreet markets and the occasional secular public building. This was where the aristocracy, the gentry and the upper middle classes lived when they were in London. Behind the greater houses stood the mews where horses and coaches were kept and many of the servants lived. The shops, workshops and homes of tradespeople stood in minor streets which did not disturb the rich.

This impressive townscape took the form of a rough grid, the main streets of which ran from south-east to north-west. The grid was not the product of overall planning, for too many landowners were involved but they had a sense of the main lines and knew that it was in their interests to conform. Meanwhile, an English town was being developed in an almost completely comprehensive way. This was Bath. Here, there was no general grid. Streets, spaces and buildings were established in detail and the principle of the design was not only order and perspective but also the idea of the Picturesque. By 1750 Bath was known throughout Europe and foreign tourists were visiting it in their own version of the Grand Tour. Many were French.

West End buildings were increasingly designed on Picturesque principles but the layout seemed to be fixed in an older mode. It took John Nash, a versatile architect and landscapist, to solve the problem, together with the Prince Regent, later George IV, who was one of those rare rulers who wanted to make his mark on London and for a while had the power to do so.

Nash was an experienced architect who had known varied fortunes. From the age of fifteen he worked in the office of Sir Robert Taylor, the Palladian. At the age of twenty-six he left Taylor, having started to build solid four-storey Palladian houses in London with the support of a rich uncle who gave him £1000, but he went bankrupt in 1783 over some four-storey Neo-Classical houses which he built in Bloomsbury Square. He started again as a country house architect in 1795. In 1806 he was appointed architect to the Commissioners of Woods and Forests, who looked after London's extensive Crown lands. From 1811 to 1830 he worked on the development of Regent's Park and on the creation of Regent Street and related streets and spaces. In the 1820s he worked on plans for Trafalgar Square, which would be laid out in the 1830s and 1840s by Sir Charles Barry. From 1827 to 1833 Nash built impressive terraces on the site of Carlton House, the Prince Regent's London residence, demolished to help finance the new Buckingham Palace,

also designed by Nash. The Regent Street and Regent's Park project, taken as a whole, was the most impressive scheme of architecture, layout and landscape design that Europe had ever seen. Between 1810, when the future George IV became Prince Regent, and the king's death in 1830, Nash was effectively the royal architect. In these two, the West End had its Haussmann and its Napoleon III, half a century earlier.

In 1811 the large, unkempt area of Marylebone Park had reverted to the Crown. The Prince Regent saw potential here for an achievement that would 'quite eclipse Napoleon'.[162] Work on Regent's Park began in 1812. Nash designed the facades for most of the terraces round the park and the *cottages ornés* for Park Village. The

138 (*facing page*)   This view of most of Nash's West End improvements (2002) begins with Oxford Circus at the far left and ends just short of Pall Mall on the right. Until Haussmann's work in Paris in the 1850s and 1860s, London was the city for modernisers to see. The wide street running up from the bottom of the photograph is Piccadilly, and the district to the left of it is St James.

139 (*above*)   Carlton House Terrace (1827–8). This riot of stucco shows Nash at his very best.

140   Nash's Buckingham Palace, the garden front. This can be seen as a modest design, product of restricted funds, or a calm background to the gardens. Stone rather than stucco gives an air of distinction.

141 (*above left*) The County Fire Office, at the southern end of Nash's Quadrant, photographed in 1910. Like the north and courtyard fronts of Somerset House, this was inspired by the Inigo Jones design for the Queen's Gallery, c. 1630.

143 (*above right*) Nash's Regent Street, photographed in 1910, shortly before demolition. Most of these buildings were not the work of Nash but he ensured that they conformed to his scheme for the street. Nash knew better than to interfere with the plans of the commercial lessees whom he needed to attract to his streets.

142 (*below left*) Waterloo Place. This is one of Nash's forum-like layouts, marking a turn on his great drive from Regent's Park to Trafalgar Square and the Strand.

144 (*below right*) Nash's improvements in the Strand, at the east end of his embryonic Trafalgar Square. Nash envisaged an extension of his great drive from here to St Paul's cathedral, mainly using existing streets.

architecture of the whole scheme was divided between picturesque Neo-Classical and fantasy rural. Park Village was a unique collection of fantasy cottages and small villas in a variety of styles, utterly picturesque. The terraces round the park were Palladian with a strong Roman emphasis, using tall, wide porticoes but with varied frontage treatments. The streets leading south from the park were lined mainly by Palladian frontages, all coated in stucco. Nash also built some villas within the park.

Nash presented his first plans for Regent Street in 1810 and a New Street Act was passed in 1813. Nash did not try to impose standard frontage designs but he achieved a coherent, picturesque effect. From 1811 he prepared a plan for the whole of the West End.[163] He intended to locate existing buildings within a general scheme or at least to make them visible. Much care was

145   Regent's Park and surrounding West End development (1973). Most of the lower left of the view was laid out by the Portman Estate from the 1760s, using a rigid grid.

148 Chester Terrace. This is one of the more modest streets behind the park frontages.

146 (*facing page top*) Park Village West, London's first planned 'garden suburb'. Park Village East has almost completely disappeared.

147 (*facing page bottom*) Cumberland Terrace (1827), the last of the Nash terraces facing Regent's Park.

149 Park Crescent (1812). It was intended to be a circus, far bigger than the one in Bath, but the northern semicircle was abandoned.

given to the siting of new buildings, in a period when the Prince Regent encouraged regal architecture using mainly Palladian designs. The quality of architecture improved, and a general Classical style took over. The architectural profession, now more concerted than ever before, was willing to conform.[164]

John Nash remains one of the most admired of London architects. His basic strength was his ability to conceive great urban scenes in which impressive buildings, spaces and greenery combined. Where buildings fronted open spaces, Nash openly designed them as decor. His flair was Romantic and his inspiration was

Roman. His art was the essence of the Picturesque. As one of his biographers put it: 'Nash built in more styles and moods than any other architect before or since his time'.[165] At the same time, Nash's detailing of his many tall, broad facades, was often defective.[166] He also built cheaply, a classic example of London's 'build for a hundred years' approach, and the reconstruction of Regent Street in the 1920s began a long period in which many of his best buildings were under threat. His picturesque but economical reconstruction of Buckingham Palace in 1825–30 harmed the last years of his career when he was accused of financial mismanagement. Finally, Nash was a master of stucco, helping the stucco techniques pioneered by Adam to spread across much of the west of London until the 1860s. Thanks to Nash, Napoleon's Paris had been truly eclipsed – but would it last?

Summerson once wrote in his gloomy way that 'standards of taste are adrift' in London by about 1820.[167] 'Taste began to be eclectic on the one hand, and strictly standardised on the other.'[168] He attributed this change to building for a wave of shopkeepers, artisans, country gentlemen and City residents who moved into the West End from about 1800. We shall see the result in Chapter 4.

CONCLUSION

We have looked at the development of London architecture during the previous three centuries under the influence of the Renaissance. All but a few architects have worked within the Classical tradition. The poorest types of housing may have been the product of a domestic vernacular yet even they are related to the finest West End terraces, no doubt through the moderation of the Building Acts. As we move into the nineteenth century, however, we find the Classical challenged by new styles. Conformity will give way to variety. What will all this mean for London's Augustan tradition?

What is need

Which side,

What is the

ntury London moved into a
a, an era of choice between
resque and the Romantic
late eighteenth century, now
flourished. Even the Classical moved away from rules
and established practice towards more relaxed treatments, culminating in the Italianate. The Palladian
survived but it became just one style among many.
Nearly all the new styles drew on history or on foreign
example. From about 1870 a further increase occurred
in the number of styles available and in eclectic
applications.[1] Finally, the beginnings of a new simplicity
and purity were emerging by 1914, pointing forward to
the Modern architecture of the twentieth century.

As a unique period in London's architectural history,
the nineteenth-century era of choice will secure its
own special treatment here. So many styles and treatments were on display that the reader will be introduced to all of them. Causation and common characteristics are not our prime concern. The child in the
sweetshop expects to see the sweets.

The key to the new cornucopia was the Gothic
Revival. The Gothic was the first radical challenge to
the Classical since the days of Inigo Jones. It had never
completely died out since the seventeenth century and
it was boosted by the State around 1820–40 with the
rebuilding of the Palace of Westminster and parliamentary support for new churches. As a national,
religious, romantic and picturesque style it appealed to
all levels of society. To many, the Classical now appeared
dull and conventional. However, the Gothic never
dominated London building as the Classical had done.
What it did above all was to open the door to other
styles which became available from about 1840 and
especially after 1870.

★   ★   ★

LONDINIUM EKLEKTIKON PANOPTIKON, 1830–1914

The year 1830 is an arbitrary date for the onset of
London's era of 'pick and mix', especially as the Gothic
was as yet being used only for precise purposes and
the Classical was not yet visibly under threat. By 1914,
however, a host of styles had emerged. Architects and
architectural historians usually try to build these styles
into one great movement of Victorian architecture in
which each style has its logical place. This approach
tends to obscure the unique pattern of development
which took over London architecture in the nineteenth
century. It was inventive and creative but it was *not*
logical. Here I present each of the available styles as in
a restaurant menu. Clients, take your pick!

The styles were:

1–7   The Classical styles (Palladian, Wren, English
Baroque, Baroque, Neo-Classical, Greek
Revival, Italianate)

8–10   The Round-arched styles (Romanesque,
Byzantine, Late Roman)

11   Gothic styles

12–16   The Artistic and 'English' Styles (Queen
Anne, Arts and Crafts, Eclectic, Free Style,
Artistic Vernacular)

17–18   French styles (Beaux-Arts Classical, Art
Nouveau)

19–20   Early Modernism (Stripped Classical, Engineers' styles)

The Classical Styles (1–7)

Classical architecture was still in full vigour in London
in 1870, despite the Gothic challenge. With secular
Gothic in decline thereafter, the Classical faced growing
competition from artistic, Modern and vernacular
styles associated mainly with the Arts and Crafts movement but business and state patronage maintained the

Classical in good health. However, the post-1820 growth of the Italianate, a hit-and-miss style with some Classical features, vulgarised the Classical, especially in the newer parts of London.

Palladian (1)

The Palladian declined in popularity after 1830 as other Classical styles expanded. It found it hard to compete with the more ornate and varied effects produced by styles such as the Italianate and the Baroque. Yet it was cheap to build and architects were used to it. The best feature of Sir William Tite's Royal Exchange (1841) was its dominating portico in the Roman style which might have found a place in Palladio's collection of porticoes. The huge Metropolitan Tabernacle (1859–61) at the Elephant and Castle, built by W. W. Pocock for the dynamic Baptist preacher Charles Spurgeon, had an impeccable six-column Corinthian portico. The greatest triumph of the Palladian was Sir Aston Webb's new east front for Buckingham Palace in 1913 which, despite the derision which it has attracted from purists and modernists,

151   Chelsea Vestry Hall by J. M. Brydon (1885–7), in a Wren style.

150   The Royal Free Hospital, Grays Inn Road (1843), now the Eastman Dental Hospital. It was cheaply built and extended, with some sandstone (!) on the frontage, but faithful to Classical principles. The sandstone was not doing very well in 2005.

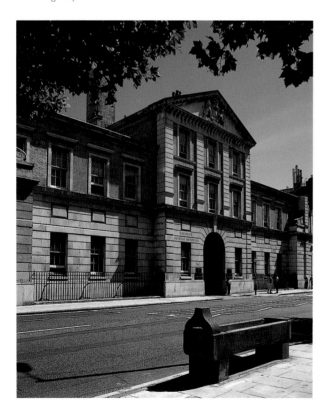

would have secured a place in Campbell's *Vitruvius Britannicus* if it had been around at the time.

Wren (2)

London architects loved to designate their designs as 'Wren' or 'Wrenesque' because the term sounded English and traditional. Examples of 'Wren' occur throughout the century but especially from the 1880s when demand grew for 'English' styles, leading to what Alastair Service designates as 'Imperial Baroque' at the turn of the century.[2] Elements of 'Wren', such as paired columns, could be found in many Classical designs, to which they added credibility.

English Baroque (3)

English Baroque was familiar to most architects because it was descended from Wren. It was seen as part of an English tradition which was especially associated with a powerful and prosperous London. It was also known as Free Classical Revival.

From the late 1880s there was a call for a recognisably English style for large buildings. English Baroque was seen as a candidate and was often described at the time as English Renaissance. It was later known as Edwardian Baroque.[3] Edward Mountford's Old Bailey (1900–06) was an outstanding example. From 1906 opinion turned against English Baroque on the grounds that it was too extravagant. The terms 'Wren' and 'English Baroque' were largely interchangeable at the time, though 'Wren' has gone out of use since the 1940s. This cluster of terms suggests a degree of eclecticism in the Baroque area and this was certainly true of the Edwardian period.

Baroque (4)

The Baroque re-emerged in London after about 1890. It had links to Roman Catholicism, to the developing styles of Richard Norman Shaw, to the Arts and Crafts movement and to English Baroque but its fundamental inspiration came from southern Europe. It received a surprisingly warm welcome in the business world. A Baroque architect could build more decorative detail into the frontage of a mundane office block than had ever been achieved before, though at great cost.

The biggest exercise in the early stages of the Continental Baroque revival was Herbert Gribble's London Oratory, Brompton Road (1880–83). This was the first large new Roman Catholic church to be built in London for nearly four hundred years and was the product of a competition in 1878. The Oratorians specified the Classical style.[4] Great efforts were made to give it the character of an Italian church and it was not immediately emulated. Much more influential was the commercial Baroque which John Belcher and Beresford Pite brought to the City in the 1890s. Their Institute of Chartered Accountants, Moorgate Place, was built in 1890–93 after a competition in 1888, followed by extensions in 1901. Service sees it as an extension of Belcher's Arts and Crafts enthusiasm but Vanbrugh and Italian Baroque are clearly present.[5] It did not symbolise accountancy in any way, except as the home of an expanding profession seeking greater status. In fact, it looked like a rich seminary in Genoa. At the start of his career, in the 1870s, Belcher had built mainly in the Gothic style and his adoption of the Baroque was something of a conversion, connected to his holiday in Italy in 1888. Belcher went on to design a number of Baroque commercial buildings with another Scot, John Joass, in the early 1900s and in 1910–12 he and Joass built the Baroque-inspired Holy Trinity Church in the new Kingsway. City and West End business clients clearly liked the air of opulence, which they were generally not willing to provide inside their

152　The Ministry of Health (Government Offices) in Whitehall by J. M. Brydon (1897–1913). The architect seems to have been aware of the need to conform with Scott's Government Buildings (on the extreme left) but his Classical treatment is more relaxed.

buildings, and some Parisian influence may have been in the air. Service has coined the term 'Arts and Crafts Baroque' for Belcher's version of the Baroque revival but his commercial work with Joass, most of it on steel frames, echoed Charles Holden's Free Classical, particularly at his British Medical Association building (1907–8) in the Strand.[6]

Belcher's triumphant Colchester Town Hall (1897–1902) and the ornate City Hall and Law Courts, Cardiff (1897), by Lanchester, Stewart and Rickards, helped the Baroque acquire a civic role in London. Deptford Town Hall (1902), by Lanchester, Stewart and Rickards, was a rich Baroque building with some ornate references to Continental Baroque. Woolwich Town Hall (1903–6), by A. B. Thomas, was a florid Baroque work on the lines of Colchester Town Hall but lacking a coherent aesthetic. Septimus Warwick's Brixton Town Hall (1908) hit every Classical note available and a few of his own, culminating in a top-heavy Baroque tower, prime candidate for destruction in a Godzilla movie. Sir Ernest George built the Royal Academy of Music on Marylebone Road in 1910–11. Lanchester and Rickards went on to build the Methodist Central Hall, Westminster (1906–10), with Rickards providing a domed structure of French inspiration with detailing reminiscent of the Paris exhibition of 1900.

With civic Baroque doing so well, it was not surprising that it should reach its apogee in Ralph Knott's County Hall (1911–22, 1931–3), the headquarters of the London County Council (founded 1889).[7] With a frontage of 223 metres on the Thames, it rivalled the

153 Methodist Central Hall. The style here is international Baroque, recalling exhibition buildings in Paris and public buildings in Berlin from 1900.

Palace of Westminster and Somerset House. Knott, an assistant in Aston Webb's office at the time of the competition, went for overwhelming mass and gargantuan special features, but avoided the luxuriant sculpture and the tower of Rickards' entry. The most obvious precedent for the steep roof with dormers was Lutyens (including Lutyens's own competition entry). The inset Crescent was a symbolic watergate, possibly derived from some of the other entries. These big features may have been the architect's reaction to standard criticism of Chambers's more cautious handling of Somerset House.

The Baroque did not survive the First World War, perhaps because of its high cost. However, some of its spirit went into war memorials and the official architecture of Lutyens. Traces of it could be found in Neo-Georgian and much more in the London version of the Beaux-Arts.

★ ★ ★

The Neo-Classical style was present throughout the century, though the Gothic and the Italianate left it less room than when it emerged in the second half of the eighteenth century. After about 1890 it spread as the result of a conjunction between expanding London business, new building methods and London traditions of grandeur and history, combined with American influence.

Philip Hardwick's Goldsmiths' Hall (1829–35), Foster Lane, replacing an earlier building, is a fine example of the Neo-Classical, with a giant order of Corinthian columns and pilasters. Pevsner sees it as on the way to 'a Neo-English Baroque'.[8] Fishmongers' Hall (1831–5), London Bridge Approach, a comparable building by Henry Roberts, a pupil of Smirke, used the Ionic order in an elegant Greek Revival composition. The Neo-Classical faded in mid-century but it did very well from the 1890s when it began to serve a new wave of British

154 Fishmongers' Hall from the embankment level.

imperialism. The best example in London is the King Edward VII Galleries (1904–11), a northward extension of the British Museum by the Scot Sir John Burnet, a student of the Ecole des Beaux-Arts from 1874 to 1877. Burnet was selected from a list of twelve candidates provided by the Royal Institute of British Architects (RIBA), having previously done little work outside Scotland. The long frontage of engaged Ionic columns with a powerful pediment and muscular attic has been compared to Schinkel but it is also of its time, with echoes of the commercial frontages of Neo-Classical department stores of American origin such as Selfridge's, the construction of which Burnet supervised from 1907 to 1928. With Daniel Burnham guiding the design, the powerful Selfridge's had a strong whiff of Chicago and was soon recognised as one of London's most impressive buildings. More restrained were the Science Museum (1913), Exhibition Road, by Sir Richard Allison, and the Royal School of Mines (1909–13) by Sir Aston Webb. The interior treatment of the Science Museum, by the Office of Works and Allison, was based on the department store principle and the columns and glazing panels of the main frontage drew on both the King Edward VII Galleries and Selfridge's.[9]

155 Fishmongers' Hall. A fine example of the Neo-Classical with some Greek features, with a creative response to the site's two aspects and two levels. The architect, Henry Roberts, went on to work in model housing.

156 The Science Museum.

157   The Port of London Authority headquarters.

Oxford Circus, rebuilt from 1913 to 1928 by Sir Henry Tanner as part of the Regent Street reconstruction, used impressive concave frontages with a neo-Beaux-Arts roof treatment above the bold cornice. Another striking representative of the Classical revival was the Port of London Authority building (1912–22), by Sir Edwin Cooper, at Trinity Square, near the Tower of London. This was a winning competition entry and its grandiose elevations with a slight Babylonian tinge were topped by a heavy, monumental tower looking like a triumphal arch. Imperial pride shone out here.

Greek Revival (6)

Greek Revival architecture, never firmly established in London during its brief heyday before 1830, faded away thereafter. However, the architects who continued to practise it were good ones. The most striking piece of Greek Revival was the Doric arch at Euston Station by Philip Hardwick, in 1835–7. There may well be something in Summerson's view that the Greek Revival was one step away from the Gothic, in that many of the less able Greek Revival architects moved there. This appears

to have been true of H. W. and W. Inwood, designers of St Pancras church (1819–22), whose Gothic St Mary, Eversholt Street (1824–7), was an utter caricature, though clearly constrained by lack of money.

158   Christ Church, Albany Street, 1838. A late example of the Neo-Greek.

The Italianate (7)

This style rose to prominence from the 1820s when it was first used for West End gentlemen's clubs. Its leading exponent was the versatile Charles Barry, architect of the Palace of Westminster and head of a big office. It is often suggested that the style sprang from a public reaction against the spartan aspects of the Greek Revival and Gothic styles. It spread to banks, office buildings and public houses.[10] It made much use of round-headed windows and deep, decorated cornices modelled on those of sixteenth-century Florence or Roman block eaves. Loosely, the Italianate was a Classical style but it was so easy to use that it was generally degraded, with ideas of proportion utterly disappearing. The Italianate was still in use in 1914, typically for corner shops and branch banks in the East End.

A common product of the Italiante was the palazzo, which could either stand alone or adjoin other houses, as in Renaissance Florence. One of the largest is Bridgewater House, built for Lord Ellesmere in Park Lane in 1845–54 on a large, rectangular site, by Sir Charles Barry. It is a grand palazzo in a High Renaissance style, built in Portland stone. The facades resemble Barry's Reform Club, with the addition of a balustrade over the cornice. It had a large art gallery, open at times to the public, for the Bridgewater art collection. The Saloon, its largest room, is an arcaded marble hall of two storeys. Another palazzo was the pretentious Dorchester House (demolished), built in Park Lane in 1848–63 by Lewis Vulliamy for the millionaire R. S. Holford. It was modelled on the Villa Farnesina in Rome, built by Peruzzi in about 1508, and had a walled and gated front courtyard and impressive frontages. There was a grand staircase hall with an arched colonnade rising from the first-floor landing. Among the smaller palazzi, inspired by the clubs, were Sir James Pennethorne's Museum of Economic Geography in Piccadilly (1847–8) and his Ordnance Office in Pall Mall (1850–51).

The palazzo formula quickly spread to the commercial world as the Italianate developed. C. R. Cockerell designed the London and Westminster Bank in 1837–8 in a very simple Classical style but by 1840–42 he was building the Sun Fire and Life Assurance Offices in Threadneedle Street as a corner palazzo, with engaged columns, balconies, pediments, ironwork and as strong a cornice as the Building Acts would allow. A good corner palazzo was Queen's Assurance and Commercial Chambers at 42–4 Gresham Street, built by Sancton Wood, a pupil of Smirke, in 1850–52 and somewhat altered since. The palazzi were always an inspiration for more modest Italianate buildings, down to the tower pub. They also encouraged the construction of striking commercial buildings in the City which made independent statements in a number of styles, especially the Gothic.

Italianate churches were rare in an era of Gothic but J. W. Wild's Christ Church, Streatham (1840–42) was a great achievement with its Renaissance basilica and bold campanile, all in powerful brick. The City Temple, built in 1874 on the impressive new overpass, Holborn Viaduct, by the Bradford architects Lockwood and Mawson, is an Italianate structure in stone with a tall tower. It has a two-storey portico with columns and a pediment. As the main Methodist church in London, it sought a distinct image. Lockwood and Mawson were influenced by John Ruskin, who had chosen Bradford as his main base in industrial England. Holy Redeemer, Exmouth Market (1887–8 by J. D. Sedding) was built for an Italian community in an early Renaissance style.

Romanesque, Byzantine, Roman (8, 9, 10)

These three related styles were used mainly for churches, though details were used eclectically elsewhere. The most important exception to this rule was the iron-framed, Romanesque Natural History Museum (1868–80) by Alfred Waterhouse, following a competition in 1864. The exterior was in terracotta, of which Waterhouse was a pioneer. No. 60, Mark Lane, by George Aitchison Jr, a block of offices, was built on an iron frame in 1864. This had a Ruskinian flavour, with three floors of Romanesque decorated loggias, a Ruskinian ground floor with stilted arches of the type favoured by Viollet-le-Duc and a line of Wren-like dormers.

London's most important Byzantine building was Westminster Roman Catholic cathedral (1894–1903) by John Francis Bentley. Bentley had already built for the Roman Church, including the Convent of the Sacred Heart, Hammersmith Road, in 1868–88, and was known for his willingness to develop unconventional solutions. The cathedral was commissioned at a time of interest in early Christian styles and both the client, Cardinal Vaughan, and Bentley were interested in these possibilities. No style was specified, however, by the client. Bentley went to look at examples in Italy but was unable to go on to visit Greece and Constantinople. The exterior was encased in red brick and stone, the London atmosphere ruling out marble.[11] The interior, however, has been gradually clad in marble, though most of the vaults and saucer domes were still in grey brick in 2005. The marble helped to lighten the dark interior, the inevitable result of the Byzantine style. Never has London seen so much marble in one place, not even at the Marble Arch. Beresford Pite's Christ Church, Brixton Road (1897–1903), an awkward exercise in Free Style Byzantine, had a plainer interior but its plan, vaults and Diocletian windows set high in the walls recalled Ravenna. At Woodford Green, a Roman basilica, complete with concrete vault and Diocletian windows, was built in 1904 by Charles Harrison Townsend to serve as a Nonconformist church.[12] The church was a striking departure from Townsend's normal Arts and Crafts.

★   ★   ★

159 and 160 Westminster cathedral, showing the tower and the exterior of the nave.

The antecedents of London's Neo-Gothic are to be found in the second half of the eighteenth century but these were mainly details and decorations. A taste for the Picturesque, visible in the work of Nash and others, can be seen as paving the way. A few country retreats in the 'Gothick' style were built near London. In 1814 Nash had built a Gothick dining room in Carlton House. A few Gothic structures of serious intent were built in the 1820s, such as commissioners' churches, John Shaw's hall of Christ's Hospital and Ambrose Poynter's St Katharine's Hospital, Regent's Park, but most secular examples leaned towards the Tudor.[13]

Secular Gothic

Secular Gothic flourished between 1830 and 1870, with Scott's St Pancras Station hotel (1868–76) marking the peak of its influence. It was in decline thereafter except in the new suburbs, where a vulgar dog-Gothic struggled on. Ruskinian or Venetian Gothic, often with two-tone brick borders to the window and door arches, could turn up anywhere. It was often ugly but this was a period in which ugliness was sometimes seen as the equivalent of strength or truth.

A revival of the Gothic clearly needed something more than whim and whimsy or a general leaning towards the Picturesque. This stimulus was provided by the burning of most of the Palace of Westminster in 1834 and a new parliamentary drive to get churches built in the growing towns, beginning with the Act of 1818 and carried on by Bishop Blomfield from 1828. The new churches certainly started architects thinking about the Gothic, as many commissions were available (seventy-eight in the diocese of London in the first ten years) but this alone would probably not have influenced secular architecture, especially as most of the new churches built in the Gothic style in the 1830s and 1840s were of poor quality, with the Gothic often adopted as an economy. What launched the revival of the Gothic as a versatile style with secular application was the reconstruction of the Palace of Westminster.[14]

The main survival of the fire was the huge Westminster Hall. Also surviving was an impressive wing completed by Sir John Soane in the 1820s. This included some important rooms and corridors and an elegant staircase, the Scala Regia, all in a sumptuous Neo-Classical style.[15] The parliamentary commission set up to study the reconstruction of the palace decided in 1835 to hold a competition, with the requirement that either the Gothic or Elizabethan style be used. This decision

161 The Palace of Westminster from Millbank in a painting of 1861 by D. Roberts. The artist has chosen a picturesque view rather than the more familiar but repetitive one from across the Thames.

was based on two points of general agreement, that the Palace of Westminster expressed the strength of a great democratic and national tradition going back to medieval times and that the survival of Westminster Hall merited the reconstruction of conforming buildings. Soane was now eighty-four and no effort was made to find another Neo-Classical architect.

The commission assumed that entrants would be able to design successfully in the required styles but this was a big assumption, given that London still basked in the full strength of Classical architecture. Several architects had produced designs for the rebuilding of the Palace of Westminster in the eighteenth century, most of them on a new, more spacious site, but none had chosen the Gothic or Tudor styles. Few major buildings had been built in either style since 1600. One exception was the work of (Sir) Charles Barry, a versatile and prolific architect of Classical preferences who had travelled abroad in 1817–20 and had built a number of pleasant Gothic churches in the 1820s and the striking, Gothic King Edward's Grammar School in Birmingham in 1833–7. Holy Trinity Church, Cloudesley Street, Islington, was his major London church. In 1835–6 he drew up a design for the Palace of Westminster with A. W. N. Pugin, the great Gothic theorist, and in 1836 it won the competition. It was built between 1840 and about 1865, London's biggest ever building.

The design of 1836 would be much altered but it remained a Gothic building, Perpendicular in character with a hint of Tudor and partly inspired by Henry VII's Chapel. Its planning was Classical, which explains why this huge building could function so well, but Barry's son related that his father would have preferred 'the Italian style'.[16] Its towers and spires added movement to the long river frontage, while Pugin's detail work ensured a degree of authenticity both inside and out, though it was often overwhelming in its effect. However, owing to the huge amount of accommodation that had to be built, the buildings had to push right up to the edges of the site and the resulting screen wall foreshadowed many later government buildings in London. Barry used a strong grid for the facades, producing a

162 Westminster Hall.

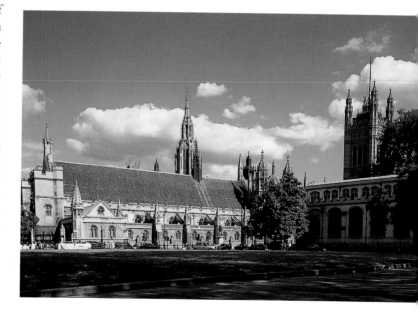

163 The Clock Tower with the Portcullis Building (offices for MPs) on the left.

than the other towers. The interior spaces looked inwards and the continuous Thames frontage precluded open courtyards which would have offered more river views and better direct ventilation.

The Palace of Westminster was nevertheless the greatest architectural event in nineteenth-century London and it is not surprising that—combined with Pugin's national advocacy and prolific churchbuilding—it should have established the Gothic as a major style, capable of challenging even the Classical canon. The victory of the Gothic, however, was complete only in the field of church building. Elsewhere, the Gothic was selected by clients, architects or builders on the basis of individual preference. This produced a great design debate which is often known as the 'battle of the styles' (though this term applies strictly to the contest over the style of the new Foreign Office [Government Buildings] in the 1850s and 1860s). This broader 'battle' was completely new to London, though Lord Burlington's Palladian campaign after 1715 had something in common with it,

164 The Victoria Tower is more utilitarian than artistic, intended for the storage of records.

165 (*facing page*) Westminster Hall, the west front, and St Stephen's Tower, originally built as a ventilation shaft. The cliff-like frontage maximises the floor space but detracts from the overall picturesque effect.

ribbon of repetition which diverged from the Gothic and even the Tudor spirit when used on such a scale. The six pavilion turrets on the river frontage broke it up but in a symmetrical fashion which contrasted with the asymmetrical arrangement of the taller towers and spires standing back from the river. The Clock Tower and the Victoria Tower, while unique skyline features, were blunt instruments in their main task of countering the linearity of the river frontage. Familiarity has obscured their odd appearance and the two towers of Westminster Abbey join in an impressive cluster from some angles. The central St Stephen's Tower began as an exhaust for the ventilation system but it looks more credibly Gothic

as did the campaign for architectural reform launched by Prince Charles in his Mansion House speech of 1984.

Gothic architecture reached the height of its influence in what is often known as the High Gothic, or High Victorian, period from about 1850 to about 1870. The case for the Gothic was put most strongly in these years by Sir George Gilbert Scott, who argued that the style could be used for secular as well as religious buildings, beginning with the publication of his *Remarks on Secular and Domestic Architecture* in 1857. Scott was a fully trained

166 Government Buildings, Main Quadrangle.

167 Government Buildings, south flanking wall.

and experienced architect, recognised as the most distinguished of his day. The other main advocate, John Ruskin, was more learned and poetic than Scott, but as an architect he was a muddled amateur. Pugin had died young, in 1852, though his writings and works were still influential.

The reconstruction of the Palace of Westminster on its old site encouraged the building of offices in nearby Whitehall. Barry, who was now the favoured government architect, built the Board of Trade building in Whitehall in 1845–7. This was an elongated, heavily rusticated palazzo with Venetian features, incorporating engaged Corinthian columns used by Soane in an earlier building, with Barry returning to his favoured Classical. When, in 1856, the massive Government Buildings were commissioned, an open competition was held. The chosen architect was Sir George Gilbert Scott. Scott wanted to build in the Gothic style, partly because he felt that the Palace of Westminster had set the tone for the whole area but mainly because he wanted to demonstrate that his scholarly, medieval Gothic would be suitable for a big London building. The result, however, was a confusing debate involving the national press, many members of London's clubs and, above all, the Prime Minister, Lord Palmerston, who wanted an international style. This, in practice, meant Italianate, which additionally would conform to the established Whitehall Classical tradition since the time of Inigo Jones. The story of the Foreign Office 'battle' could alone fill this book. Fortunately, Ian Toplis's excellent account has already met the need and we can concentrate here on the main issues and the result.[17]

In the end, Scott built the Government Buildings from 1861 to 1875 in a routine Italian Renaissance style –his only work in this mode. Its best feature was the internal Durbar Court, designed as part of the India Office section by the versatile Sir Matthew Digby Wyatt, yet another member of the long-lived architectural dynasty, who had worked in India for the East India Company.[18] Pevsner points out that Scott observed the High Victorian principle of even decoration, producing rows of identical features, though the columns on his Whitehall frontage had a stronger effect.[19] As usual, the government brief required more office space than could easily be fitted in and Scott adopted high circuit walls, as at Barry's Palace of Westminster. However, the facade and roofs facing St James's Park were picturesque, including the one tower that Scott was allowed to build, following a sketch by, again, Wyatt.

In an era of growing parliamentary democracy, architecture was increasingly subject to public debate but the 'battle of the styles' was always likely to lead to

These were needed to avoid monotony in such a large group of buildings. Barry's two huge towers at opposite ends of the Palace of Westminster were always accepted as essential to the design but Scott's smaller towers were deemed expendable. Scott finished the building with a strong sense of disappointment, having had to accept changes large and small over a number of years.[20] The missing statues and uncarved medallion blanks in the Main Quadrangle tell a sad story.

Scott's huge office still had plenty of work in the Gothic style, building mainly churches and related buildings. His painstaking Albert Memorial (1863–76), officially opened (though incomplete) in 1872, allowed him to create a work of pure Gothic art.[21] However, he still wanted to design a big secular Gothic building in London and his chance came when he was asked to enter a limited competition to build the Midland Railway's St Pancras Station Hotel and offices in 1865. He secured the contract and built the hotel in 1868–76. This

168   The Albert Memorial (1867–71).

169   St Pancras Hotel, Clock Tower.

bad architecture rather than good. First, there was a common assumption that the value of a building lay in its exterior, with style seen as a two-dimensional curtain which could be altered at will, the interior treatment being easily adapted. Second, the reduction of architecture to simple elevations meant that even the most ignorant could hold an obdurate and raucous opinion (the 'gentleman's club' effect). Third, each of the contending styles tended to be seen as a symbol or representation of some value or statement. In the case of the Foreign Office, these included internationalism, upper-class culture, English tradition, national honesty, the Empire, religious probity, looking outward, the Palace of Whitehall and its glorious past, the Thames as a vista and symbol of foreign parts, the Liberal Party, the Conservative Party and Queen Victoria.

The result was that architecture became simplified into 'this' or 'that' or 'for' and 'against'. The decision became a political one, which undermined the architecture of the Government Buildings as art. In the end, Scott's switch from his beloved Gothic to Italianate devalued the whole exercise as the architect went back to a style which he had ignored since his student days. He faced a further humiliation when, on grounds of economy, his two main corner towers were deleted.

170   St Pancras Hotel, main front.

171   St Pancras Hotel, west tower.

was Scott's bold High Victorian Gothic in red brick and stone dressings next to the great iron vault of the train shed by the engineers W. H. Barlow and R. M. Ordish (1867). Allowed to work with few constraints other than those of the site and access, Scott produced a building which suggested what he might have done at the Foreign Office without Palmerston's interference. Unlike his scholarly churches, it was strongly eclectic within the Gothic mode, lacking only the Italian content of the Foreign Office design, according to Scott.[22] Scott's remark that the hotel was 'too good for its purpose' suggests that he saw St Pancras as a bravura exercise which would launch a great wave of Gothic building in London. Aware of the danger of tedium on long facades which he had encountered at the Foreign Office, he curved the west end of the building so that it met Euston Road at right angles. He also built towers at each end, probably following Barry's solution at the Palace of Westminster. The eastern tower was a reduced Clock Tower, similar to an early Barry design for Westminster, and the western tower was what Barry might have done with the Victoria Tower if he had thought more about the picturesque and less about floorspace.

Londoners love St Pancras but it has one weakness: it is an extremely ugly building and it looks as though Whitehall, with its Classical aura dating back to the early seventeenth century, was spared an unpleasant intrusion. The Ruskinian side of High Victorianism is very much in the air at St Pancras and the Venetian arches belie Scott's claim that Italian influence was excluded. The North German stepped gables are out of place on a French Gothic building. So is the Purbeck marble on the main frontage. The fenestration, as in other giant London hotels, is repetitive and the crude trefoil heads are out of place in bedroom windows. Scott seems to have plumped for effect in a big building expressing the power of the railway and the clamour of the great metropolis but still struggling to create the maximum of accommodation within a simple envelope. The public rooms were baronial, including more Purbeck marble, with large areas of Puginesque wallpaper.[23] The corridors were long, cramped and airless.

St Pancras suggested that the designing of big Gothic buildings had not changed much since 1836 and also that not much further development could be expected. It thus achieved the reverse of what Scott had intended and secular Gothic went into decline from the 1870s, with most of the specialist Gothic architects no longer in practice by 1890. However, the Gothic had one last triumph.

The most successful of the big Gothic schemes for a public building after St Pancras was George Edmund

172 The Royal Courts of Justice (the Law Courts).

visible until around 1880. With Street dying before completion and his building already looking out of fashion, the Law Courts were more the *nunc dimittis* of secular Gothic than a new stimulus. At least Street showed what scholarship and invention, rather than bravado, could achieve.

Religious Gothic

The debate over the secular Gothic, and some of its curious results, cannot obscure the triumph of the Gothic in the the creation of churches. Here the Gothic was not an opportunity for superficiality, posturing or indiscipline but the equivalent of Burlington's Palladian. It was a serious attempt to recreate or develop a coherent architecture which reflected moral values and Christian tradition and was suitable for worship. For many architects, the enterprise was a scholarly one, resulting in Gothic churches as good as any built in the Middle Ages. For others, the Gothic was an inspiration or a challenge, leading to innovation or rationalisation. Moreover, the nineteenth century was London's greatest age of church building in both slum and suburb.[26] The chancel and nave plan, virtually in abeyance since Wren's time, returned to favour, partly to accommodate growing numbers of worshippers. A growing variety of religious denominations built places of worship and in far greater numbers than in the eighteenth century. London was richer than ever before and getting richer all the time. This meant more spending on churches in a city which remained formally religious until well into the twentieth century.

As in the past, most of the new churches were not designed by specialist architects. They were the work of competent designers but, as was normal at the time, most of these architects could handle a wide range of building types. Without a broad portfolio they could not have made a living. Their church designs were often skimped or conventional but the Gothic style normally kept order. However, sometimes churches were designed by unsuitable architects with puzzling results. One example was St James (1837–8), Chillingworth Road, N7, the work of H. W. Inwood and E. N. Clifton. This looked like a brick warehouse which the architects tried to rescue by an attached Ionic portico and a square tower looking like a giant ventilation shaft.

The most influential church architect in the first part of the century was A. W. N. Pugin. A devout Roman Catholic, he published widely, arguing that the Gothic was the true and only English style, and designed numerous churches and related buildings in England and Ireland, often with limited funds. His buildings rein-

Street's Royal Courts of Justice (the Law Courts) on the Strand, built between 1866 and 1882 to replace premises in Westminster Hall. A restricted competition involving the major architects of the day, including E. M. Barry, Waterhouse and Scott, was held in 1866.[24] There were eleven entries. The judges made no award at first but after much confusion they selected Barry's plan and Street's elevation. In 1868 the contract was given to Street alone.[25] The main frontage was a multi-element stone design in a thirteenth-century French style, eschewing the curtain wall approach. At the rear, a cheaper Gothic facade in brick and stone did the more utilitarian job of fronting large areas of office space. Street's greatest triumph was the great vaulted Gothic hall, reached directly from the entrance. This was like a *salle des pas perdus* in a French palace of justice, used for informal meetings of lawyers and clients and for access to court rooms. It measured 70 by 15 metres and its vault was 25 metres high, much the same as Lincoln cathedral.

Street's original design was altered even more than most government buildings and the result was not clearly

forced his writings and lectures and the Church of England adopted his approach. Pugin did not hesitate to build with cheap materials and this endeared him to many a parish. Most of his churches, schools and vicarages were built of brick. In Ireland he used stone much more but his work there was little known in England. He attached great importance to the spire, which he always tried to incorporate in the body of the church. His influence also led to churches being built with chancels separated from the nave by space under the tower, and processional aisles.

By the 1840s, many distinguished architects had been converted to the Gothic style, at least for churches. A number of churches and church buildings had been built on scholarly Gothic lines, following Pugin's example but sometimes with more impressive and persuasive results. Most were now modelled on the fourteenth century and they used more stone than Pugin had often been allowed to do. George Gilbert Scott was the most admired example, with many of his churches looking more or less like real medieval buildings. Scott had joined the Ecclesiological Society, the main Anglican group calling for a return to purity in the litany and in church buildings, in 1842. Then, in 1844, at the age of thirty-three, came the greatest triumph of his life. This was the commission to build the Nicolai-Kirche, a church of cathedral proportions in the centre of Hamburg.[27]

Scott's early eminence led to his appointment in 1849 as Surveyor of Westminster Abbey. There was more to this than might at first appear, for it made Scott a senior royal servant who was widely consulted and given a wide range of tasks by the Crown and Parliament. Inigo Jones and Christopher Wren had enjoyed similar authority and influence. From 1849 Scott plunged into a series of projects for churches and related buildings in England. Creating what became the biggest office in Britain, he took on project after project, all of which were impeccably completed and on time. Broad Sanctuary, a row of Gothic houses for clerics outside Westminster Abbey (1853), which managed to be gaunt and muscular at the same time, recalled some of the big new college buildings going up at Oxford, no doubt because it had to stand up against the abbey itself, but his Harrow School chapel (1854–7) was a more refined Gothic building. He pursued his studies of medieval Gothic and became an advocate and theorist in the manner of Pugin and he started to call for the use of Gothic for secular buildings.

The High Victorian movement which dominated London from about 1850 to 1870 meant that few non-Gothic churches were built in mid-century. Most were built to serve the spreading suburbs where they were often the only large buildings of architectural distinction. Many were beautiful, scholarly examples designed by distinguished architects like Pearson, and Scott and Street. Others verged on the ugly. A grotesque example was St Stephen, Rosslyn Hill, by the emphatic Samuel

174 (*above*) All Hallows, Shirlock Road, 1889 (James Brooks), 1913 (Sir Giles Gilbert Scott). The wedge-like buttresses have something of a southern French fortified church.

175 (*below*) Union Chapel (Congregational), Upper Street, rebuilt in 1877.

Teulon (1867–76).[28] Here, the sinister brick exterior was matched by brick vaults in the best waterworks style. William Butterfield, the influential follower of Pugin, favoured strong, simple forms which many disliked. His church of All Saints, Margaret Street (1849–59), was in brick with polychromatic bands. Coloured decoration and carving covered the whole of the interior. Hemmed in by other buildings, it was dark inside but the bright decoration countered the gloom. Ruskin and Street thought well of it and Butterfield went on to build St Matthias, Wordsworth Road, Stoke Newington, in 1850–51. This was another High Victorian brick church with stone dressings, long and narrow with a simple tower, similar to many parish churches in northern France.

The prolific John L. Pearson, one of the few architects who specialised in churches, built the huge, High Victorian St Peter Vauxhall, Lambeth, in 1860. It was in a French style and, unusually for its time, was completely vaulted, with stone ribs filled with brick. It had a semicircular apse, which made it look completely un-English but Pearson liked apses. It reflected debates in the Ecclesiological Society in the early 1860s about the proper form for a town church. Pearson's St Augustine, Kilburn Park Road, built in 1870–77 for a High Church rector,

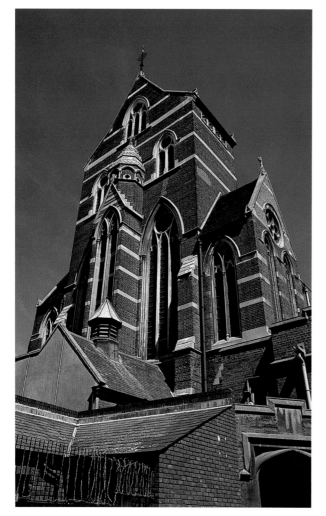

176 (*above*)   This hostel in Limehouse Road, now designated as a mission, dates from 1923. Funding was generous, allowing the architects, T. Daisel and H. Parnacott, to build in this expensive Arts and Crafts, Neo-Gothic style.

177 (*left*)   The Roman Catholic church of St Alban, Grays Inn Road.

with its slender tower and spire added in 1897–8, was another example of French influence, with the structure of the nave and the treatment of the east end and the lancet windows recalling Albi cathedral. Its spacious, intricate interior created some impressive transitions. Again, Pearson vaulted the whole church in stone and brick. Pevsner rates it as one of the best churches in England for its date.[29] Pearson's work was influential, as in James Brooks's St Andrew's Church, Plaistow (1867–70), with its apse and huge tower over the crossing.

After 1870 Gothic churches were still built in large numbers but many treatments became freer. The Arts and Crafts movement began to have an influence. J. D. Sedding's Holy Trinity, Sloane Street, Chelsea (1881–91) broke away from scholarly Gothic and allowed Arts and Crafts to create a much freer design, with ambitious interior decorations. Few Gothic churches were built after 1900.

178 (*facing page*)   Holy Trinity, Sloane Street, London's most impressive Arts and Crafts church. It was built by J. D. Sedding in 1888–90 in a fashionable part of the West End. A variety of committed artists produced the details and decorations.

The Queen Anne was the first of the self-consciously English, artistic styles. It sprang up around 1870 and lasted until the early years of the twentieth century.[30] Its appeal lay largely in its English-domestic character and its combination of rural and small-town images with echoes of an older Dutch and Belgian picturesque. Its characteristic building material was a smooth, bright, red brick which was mass produced in the big Midland brickfields and brought to London by rail, all at low cost. The Queen Anne helped to kill off London's long-running stucco tradition which had reached its apogee in Cubitt's great estates.

The Queen Anne sprang mainly from the work of two pioneers, Philip Webb and Richard Norman Shaw. Philip Webb's Red House (1859) was the main architectural expression of the developing Pre-Raphaelite movement. The idea was conceived in 1858 when William Morris was on a boating holiday on the Seine with Webb and Charles Faulkner, all later members of the Pre-Raphaelite group.[31] Morris commissioned the house, which Webb built in open countryside at Bexley Heath, south-east of Greenwich. Named after its brick walls, it was marked by a series of steep roofs and tall chimneys. Its L shape gave a sense of protection. The fenestration was simple but varied, using small panes.[32] This was no Queen Anne building but it inspired Shaw and many other architects who were attracted by the idea of an urban vernacular. Webb, in his turn, moved towards Shaw when they both started to build large houses in the West End from about 1870.

Webb soon showed how the spirit of his Red House could be applied to a London commercial building when he built a row of business premises in Worship Street, off the City Road, in 1862–3.[33] It is a three-storey building with exaggerated medieval features and a steep roof with huge dormers and large, solid chimneys.[34] His studio house of about 1864–5, now 14 Holland Park Road, is a simple, gabled affair resembling the work of Butterfield. In 1868–70 he built 1 Palace Green, Kensington, for the future Earl of Carlisle. This is a tall, asymmetrical house in brick with a bay and a gable, recalling Shaw's houses of the same period, but more awkward. The interior decoration had much of Morris and the Pre-Raphaelites.

Richard Norman Shaw, a winner of the Royal Academy Gold Medal as a young architect, had spent two years abroad before setting up his own practice in 1862. His impressive Cragside (1870–85) and other country houses leaned towards English vernacular but he preferred his Queen Anne style in towns, where he made a

virtue of using red brick.[35] The domestic potential of the style became clear at the Bedford Park garden suburb, launched as a speculation in 1876, where Shaw was architect between 1877 and 1879. His Tabard Inn and shops there (1879–80), with their gables, jettying, oriels and white rendering, were vernacular inspired but he also built a good number of houses across the estate, using a variety of treatments including the Queen Anne. In its early years, Bedford Park attracted artists and literary figures such as the playwright Arthur Pinero.

When Shaw started to build big West End villas in the early 1870s he developed a characteristic urban style. The main features were tall gables, sometimes 'Dutch' in appearance, tall and broad chimneys, tall, thin windows with glazing bar grilles, bays and oriels, set-backs and loggias, inset porches with impressive front doors and fenestration and a general verticality which carried on the Gothic tradition which had appealed to the young Shaw. He also built a number of studio houses for fashionable artists. This was a new type, with the studio integral to the house.[36] Shaw was acquainted with some of these artists and they probably influenced his designs. The main feature of all his houses, however, was the red brick which linked them to Red House. The resulting 'dark city' spread over much of London until the First World War.[37]

Shaw's influence expanded after he first exhibited in the architecture section of the Royal Academy exhibition in 1873.[38] By this time he had built a brilliant office block, New Zealand Chambers, Leadenhall Street (1873) (demolished).[39] Using Jacobean oriel windows, inspired by Sparrowe's House in Ipswich (c. 1680), and an arrangement of offices which allowed a great density of floorspace combined with generous interior lighting, this was a revolutionary office building with a beautiful facade on Queen Anne and Arts and Crafts lines, including a concave, overhanging cornice and dormers. The charming oriels were adopted by so many architects that they became the late-Victorian equivalent of the Serlian window. However, New Zealand Chambers did not have much influence in the City, perhaps because few of the architects who built there had the necessary virtuosity.

Shaw also designed and influenced a generation of large, terraced houses in the Knightsbridge area which have come to be known as 'Pont Street Dutch'. This manner can be traced back to his 196 Queen's Gate, sw7, built in 1875. Later he built tall brick houses in rows, with gables, as in the four houses he built in Cadogan Square in 1877–9.[40] Ernest George and Harold Peto built 'Dutch' houses on an even more grandiose scale in Harrington Gardens and Collingham Gardens in 1880–83.[41] On a more limited site, J. Dunn built the comparable

Surrey House in Surrey Street, Strand, in about 1895. This was a five-storey building including the gabled roof (demolished).

One of the great strengths of Shaw's architecture was that it could be applied to very large buildings. His Swan House (1876), at 17, Chelsea Embankment, was an early four-storey house with huge dormers. Albert Hall Mansions (1879–86), his biggest project till then, was a sweeping group of balconied apartment buildings in red brick, reaching up as far as nine storeys including the roof. It embraced the Albert Hall in a carefully planned, sloping layout and its utilitarian style was enlivened by 'Dutch' gables and some of London's rare loggias. His Alliance Assurance Office (1881–3), St James's Street and Pall Mall, was a five-storey corner structure with tall gables and roof, a ground-floor loggia and a corner turret rising through the whole height of the building. The elevations were of pink brick, with bands of Portland stone. This banded style was carried on to Shaw's baronial-eclectic New Scotland Yard, Victoria Embankment (1886–1906), another huge structure.

I have discussed the Queen Anne and its derivatives at length partly because Richard Norman Shaw was the most creative and versatile architect to emerge in London between the Great Exhibition in 1851 and the outbreak of the First World War but partly also because of their pervasive influence in the spreading railway suburbs between 1870 and 1914 and even until 1939. There they helped shape a multitude of quite small, terraced houses whose gables and bays created something of a Gothic effect; they were also often used for institutional buildings such as public libraries, institutes and

180 'Pont Street Dutch' houses in Sloane Court.

179 Houses in Sloane Gardens.

meeting halls. The Queen Anne was much used for the elementary schools of the London School Board when E. R. Robson was its architect from 1871 to 1889. These schools were technically up to date in aspects such as ventilation, lighting, furniture and play space and they reflected the latest thinking on teaching methods and theory.[42] The Queen Anne also figured in early LCC housing estates between 1889 and 1914, notably in the Boundary Street estate (1897–1900) in Shoreditch, where Shaw and Webb influenced the young municipal

architects of the day. Despite its seventeenth-century origins, the Queen Anne was welcomed as a modern style which replaced secular Gothic after 1870 and met the requirements of even the largest and most complex buildings until 1914. It also helped give body to the Arts and Crafts style.

181 Albert Hall Mansions, Kensington Gore (1879–86), by Richard Norman Shaw. He studied Parisian flats before designing this impressive scheme.

183 (*above right*) Gable roof of hospital, Queen Street, in the style of Shaw.

182 Albert Court forms a huge part of the cluster of mansion flats around the Albert Hall.

Arts and Crafts (13)

This style was inspired by John Ruskin and guided by William Morris. It was linked to a social philosophy based on handicrafts, which affected education and politics as well as art. Its influence on building can be traced back to Philip Webb's Red House of 1859. Arts and Crafts began to affect London architecture more widely in the 1890s. Buildings in this style were expensive and often had some kind of educational or admonitory function. Most were schools, institutes, churches and the houses of rich adherents. Charles Robert Ashbee built a varied collection of houses in Chelsea, most of them on Cheyne Walk, between 1894 and 1913. They emphasised height and many had tall windows, steep roofs and gables. Many were occupied by artists. Alan Crawford sees much of the Queen Anne in them but he also points to Ashbee's determination to produce a complete townscape drawing on the past, not unlike the efforts of Geddes in Edinburgh.[43] No. 38, a studio house for the artist C. L. Christran, was a fully developed and decorated Arts and Crafts design. The Bishopsgate Institute (1892–4), Bishopsgate, by Charles Harrison Townsend, was the Arts and Crafts product of a competition. It was clad in beige faience and had some Art Nouveau decoration. Its large, round-arched doorway was influenced by the American fundamentalist architect H. H.

Richardson. The Whitechapel Art Gallery (1899–1901), also by Townsend, was in Arts and Crafts, veering on Art Nouveau. Townsend designed the Horniman Museum (1896–1901), London Road, Forest Hill, in the same combination. Arts and Crafts details such as door handles were often used in house building about 1900 and 1920. However, complete Arts and Crafts buildings were rare, probably because they required a high artistic approach with committed architects and expensive materials and treatments. Even the Whitechapel Art Gallery ran out of money and was never completed.

Perhaps the best of all, well worth a visit by the stroller or tourist, is The Black Friar (c.1905), Blackfriars. This is a small public house, remodelled in about 1905 around a monkish theme by H. Fuller Clark in a combination of Art Nouveau and Arts and Crafts. Its burnished interior is unparallelled in London, though there are similar pubs in Liverpool.

Eclectic (14)

Most of the buildings erected in London after 1870 were eclectic to some degree but architectural historians have seen the Eclectic as a distinct style. Sir Aston Webb's extension of the Victoria and Albert Museum (1899–1909) followed a competition in 1891 and was in his early eclectic manner. It was intended to symbolise design and handicraft but it also had an imperial flavour. Thomas Collcutt's Imperial Institute, built nearby off Exhibition Road in 1887–93 (demolished apart from its impressive, Californian tower), had much of Charles Foster Kane's Xanadu. Making a big effort, the viewer can discern an overall Baroque and Jacobean character and detailed influences from Shaw and Webb. Gables, turrets and loggias abound, with some Moorish features and a generally Hispanic air. It was built to honour the British Empire and a few years later would probably have been built in Edwardian Baroque.

Collings B. Young's Savoy Hotel of 1889 included a river frontage with ornate balconies on every floor, separated by paired columns. Indian influence may have figured here though the interior detailing was mainly Renaissance.[44] C. Fitzroy Doll built two eclectic hotels, the huge brick and terracotta Hotel Russell (1898), Russell Square, in Arts and Crafts Italianate, and the nearby Imperial Hotel (1905–11) (demolished). Harrod's department store (1901–4), by Stevens and Munt, was in eclectic terracotta, as was Fitzroy Doll's bookshop block in Torrington Place (1907). The towering Royal

184 (*above right*) The tower of Collcutt's Imperial Institute.

185 (*right*) Hotel Russell, 1898. The specialist hotel architect, Fitzroy Doll, used an eclectic, imperial style to break up his towering facades.

Academy of Music (1910–11), Marylebone Road, by Sir Ernest George, was in a Wren-Shaw-Louis XIV style which stood, perhaps remotely, for imperial values. The Court of Honour of the White City (demolished), created for the Franco-British Exhibition of 1908, was an Indian extravaganza.

By 1900 much of London's eclectic work was linked to Britain's imperial might and the exotic composition of the Empire's populations.[45] There was also a strong link between the Eclectic and terracotta, favoured by Waterhouse from the 1860s as an easy, self-cleaning means of creating a panorama of symbols and ideas, as at the Natural History Museum. Waterhouse's University College Hospital (1896–1906) was a visibly functional building, tall and dense, using cruciform axes and extensively clad in terracotta. His King's Weigh House Chapel, Duke Street (1889–1891), with its flanking buildings, was another powerful building albeit on a smaller scale. Waterhouse was probably the main influence on the selection of Collcutt's design for the Imperial Institute. It is impossible to do full justice here to Collcutt's work in terracotta, though its festooning effects are not to everyone's taste.

Free Style (15)

The Free Style made its mark on London between about 1890 and 1914. It is difficult to define except through its links with the Arts and Crafts movement. Free Style buildings tried to break away from the formal styles of the day but they often used stylistic features from them. They often sought an English identity.[46] One of the best, Mary Ward Settlement, as it is now known, was built in Tavistock Place in 1895–8, after a competition assessed by Shaw. The architects were Dunbar Smith and William Cecil Brewer. At first sight it brings the work of Charles Rennie Mackintosh to mind. There is also a flavour of German Jugendstil and there are links with Townsend's Bishopsgate Institute. The Serlian windows added to the artistry of the building and the diagonal arrangement of the staircase windows broke away from the 'windows in line' which were still a feature of London architecture. The variety of window shapes was greater than on any other building of this size in London. The office building by H. Fuller Clark at 59 Riding House Street (1903) also uses varied fenestration though the floor levels are standard.

Alastair Service, who is fascinated by the Free Style, dates its origins back to about 1870 in the work of Gothic, Queen Anne, Arts and Crafts, Art Nouveau and Baroque architects.[47] The Arts Workers' Guild, founded in Bloomsbury in 1884 as part of the Arts and Crafts

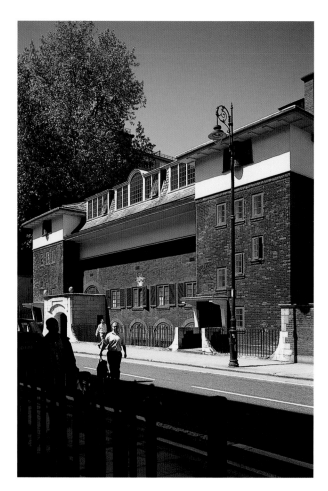

186   Mary Ward House, 1895–8.

187   Mary Ward House, entrance.

188   Free Style building in Grays Inn Road.

Towards the end of the century, most of London's new housing was built in the spreading suburbs served by public transport. Densities were lower than in the past and the three to five storeys of Cubitt's day were replaced mainly by two-storey houses with individual gardens. Many of these houses stood back from the street. In some cases trees were planted on the verges. Terraced layouts remained predominant but sites were longer.

Higher incomes and lower densities had implications for the developers and builders. Most houses and house types were designed by architects but on the whole they were local men who were not required to show much originality. Designs featured in builders' publications could spread all round the suburbs, with elevations popping up miles away from their place of first use. However, architects of standing influenced suburban design when they were commissioned to build housing of quality. Among the first to set an example was Shaw. The big houses he designed in the 1870s were for rich clients but their red-brick walls and gables could be reduced in dimensions and combined in terraces. Stefan Muthesius has detected the Shaw style filtering down into cheaper middle-class housing as early as 1880, as at Riverdale Road, N5, where three-storey terraced houses dating from about 1880 have token gables and bright red brick.[53]

Shaw also seems to have influenced the terraced, two-storey 'villa' with a projecting bay and gable and a garden wing at the back which spread through outer London's railway suburbs between about 1870 and 1914. Built of brick and slate, most of these houses stood in rectilinear streets on estates planned by developers. An early example, probably influential, was the Queen's Park Estate, NW6, built by a model housing company, the Artisans', Labourers' and General Dwellings Company, in 1875–83. These houses varied in size but the design concept remained the same.

C. F. A. Voysey, a follower of the Arts and Crafts movement, designed houses in both country and town which merged with the landscape through their use of materials and their horizontal form. He was also an interior designer, especially of furniture, wallpaper and carpets.[54] In London his clients were often artists, as many of Shaw's had been. Mainly of two rendered storeys, with gables and low, strip windows, the houses were highly individual but cumulatively they had a suburban character. Voysey built only five houses in London but these and his similar country houses were highly influential. Overhanging eaves and battered (leaning inwards) buttresses came to be applied to many small, suburban

movement, attracted architects who started to develop Free Style designs.[48] Styles and features were often taken from different periods and places, and forms were created for their own value. Some Free Style architects reacted to the turbulent waves of variety by calling for pure design. They especially admired Shaw and William Morris.[49] Many LCC fire stations were built in a Free Style development of the Arts and Crafts, under the direction of the LCC Architect W. E. Riley. The station on the north side of Euston Road (1901–2), by Charles Winmill, is a good example, making inventive use of its corner site.[50]

The Free Style was not widely adopted in London, and faded away after 1900, but one example was St Peter's Church, Mount Park Road, Ealing, built by Henry Wilson in 1892. Another was the Public Library (1891), Ladbroke Grove, also by Henry Wilson. Beresford Pite built 37 Harley Street in 1899 in a mixture of Free Style and Baroque.[51] Treadwell and Martin built Free Style offices and public houses in the West End.[52] Some would claim that the Free Style heralded the Modern but the connection is tenuous.

★   ★   ★

189 Sanderson's wallpaper factory by Voysey, Barley Mow Passage, off Chiswick High Road, 1902.

houses. At 14 South Parade, Bedford Park, w4, his Studio House (1891) was of three storeys in an intriguing but awkward Arts and Crafts style, perhaps influenced by his artist client. At Annesley Lodge, Platts Lane, NW3, Voysey built a house for his father in 1896. With two wings set at right angles under a tiled roof in a garden, this had many of the features of the suburban house as it developed into the 1930s. With Voysey and also Lutyens, gradually the country came to town and the twentieth-century suburb was born.

Beaux-Arts (Parisian) (17)

With so many styles in circulation, the French Classical style had a better chance in London than ever before. It did especially well in luxury hotels with an international clientele, after the arrival of the railways. This new gen-

eration of hotels tried to be and to look luxurious. They were also open to foreign influence, especially from France. Their most striking feature was usually the tall, decorated mansard roof, a vulgarisation of the more tasteful, restrained Parisian version which had been adopted in the early 1850s.[55] The first was the Great Western Hotel at Paddington Station, built by Philip Charles Hardwick, the son of Philip Hardwick, in 1851–3. It was a rusticated Classical design recalling Cubitt, stuccoed and with big towers, a little French in its feel. The Grosvenor Hotel, built in 1860 by James Knowles, Jr, next to Victoria Station, on one of the Paris lines, was a good example of the 'Second Empire' style, with a mansard roof, a deep, decorated cornice and horizontal bands at every floor. Only the Venetian windows, set in the cornice, and the intricate decoration of the cornice itself, came from another source, that of Ruskin. However, every feature was heavily emphasised and the building lacked the subtlety of even the most ornate Parisian hotels and apartment houses. This crude English version of Parisian architecture may well reflect the architect's efforts to overcome London gloom and fog. Although vulgar, the Grosvenor oozed luxury inside and out and it would have been appreciated by Continental visitors not accustomed to the London standard. The French, especially, must have enjoyed the armchairs, considered too vulgar at home.

The Langham Hotel, built at the south end of John Nash's Portland Place in 1864–6 on the site of Robert Adam's Foley House, was designed by John Giles and G. Murray. This was a riot of round-headed windows and a bold water tower and a more cautious mansard roof.

190 The Langham Hotel.

191 The Grosvenor Hotel.

Appropriately, the exiled Napoleon III stayed there for a while. Its eight-storey brick mass clashed heavily with Adam's Portland Place.[56] De Keyser's (demolished), a 400-bedroom hotel near Blackfriars Bridge, established by a Belgian former waiter in 1874, was also in the London version of the Second Empire style.

Around 1901 a modernised French Beaux-Arts architecture began to find favour in London. This was the elegant, refined, decorated architecture, the Paris Luxury Style, which grew up in the French capital from about 1895.[57] Used mainly for luxury hotels, museums, rich apartment houses and railway stations, it was Classical in the Louis-Quinze tradition. Most of it carried great quantities of carving which merged with the facades. Parisian limestone, easy to work yet durable, now came into its own more than at any other time in history. In London, its air dirtier than ever, rich carving was out of the question and the Beaux-Arts style had to be expressed mainly in mass and forms. It was used mainly for hotels and clubs, expressing wealth and leisure as in Paris.

The Ritz Hotel (1903–6), by Mewès and Davis, is the best-known example. Charles Mewès was a French hotel specialist who had built the Ritz in Paris. Davis had studied at the Ecole des Beaux-Arts from 1894 to 1900 and Mewès made him his London partner in that year.[58] The Ritz was London's first entirely steel-framed building, partly clad in Norwegian granite, but its straight lines and angular forms weakened the Parisian effect. Even the arcade at ground level, presumably based on the Rue de Rivoli by Percier and Fontaine, lacked the elegance of its Parisian predecessor. The Waldorf Hotel (1908), Aldwych, by A. Marshall and A. G. R. Mackenzie (an architect who had studied at the Ecole des Beaux-Arts), was much more Parisian, even down to the casement windows.

When the Entente Cordiale was formalised in 1904, French architecture came into even more favour. The new boulevard-like improvements, Kingsway and the Aldwych, were influenced by Paris. Sir Reginald Blomfield's reconstruction of Piccadilly Circus, launched in 1913, used an eclectic Baroque style with much of the Parisian about it. Service sees his work as that of a French Classicist, which he had brought to London in 1906 and

192　Building in the Beaux-Arts style in Petty France.

193　The RAC Club in Pall Mall.

which was appropriate to a *rond point*. The Royal Automobile Club (1908–11), in Pall Mall, by Mewès and Davis, was in a grand and luxurious Parisian style. Its underground, Doric swimming pool was the epitome of luxury.

London's most convincing Parisian clone was Inveresk House, Aldwych (now One Aldwych with its roof raised to the heavens, its dormers replaced by an extra storey and its beautiful *grands boulevards* cupola replaced by an extension of the roof), built in 1907 by Mewès and Davis. This was a steel frame building and its facing in Norwegian granite was ambitious for its day. It was built to house a newspaper, *The Morning Post,* but was converted into a hotel in 1998. The carving, integral to the stone blocks of the elevations, emulated the best work of the Paris Luxury Style.

Art Nouveau (including Jugendstil) (18)

Art Nouveau, which had a superficial resemblance to Arts and Crafts, was another exercise in high art which never got beyond the curiosity stage in London. In the 1890s a group of Belgian architects led by Victor Horta developed a completely new style inspired by sinuous natural forms. They promoted it as a modern style and it spread to France. In London it was often combined with Arts and Crafts design. Very little pure Art Nouveau was built in London and its use was mainly limited to decorative panels and interior features, especially in places of entertainment. When Parisian taste suddenly turned against Art Nouveau in 1905 it faded in London.

The German and Austrian equivalent, Jugendstil, was virtually ignored in London. Charles Rennie Mackintosh, the Glasgow genius who was much admired in Germany and who adopted much of the Jugendstil, might have established the link but London architects virtually ignored his work until the First World War. Mackintosh exhibited only once in London, at the Arts and Crafts Exhibition in 1896, but his work was rejected as decorative Art Nouveau.[59] By the time he moved to London in 1915 or thereabouts his self-destructive lifestyle (drink) had weakened his powers and he achieved little. Two able Scottish architects—James MacLaren and Arthur MacMurdo—worked in London at the end of the century within the Shaw tradition and they provided a link with Glasgow modernism and asymmetry, as in MacLaren's houses at Palace Court, Bayswater. A hint of Jugendstil can be detected in London Free Style but the Free Style is full of hints.

Stripped Classical (19)

In the early 1900s the larger buildings, especially those using steel frames, were sometimes given a compromise cladding which linked them with the Palladian past. Normally, their frontages were shaped by rows of vertical, non-load-bearing components which recalled the orders but which lacked trappings such as capitals and fluting. A few were curved in section but most were flat, projecting a short distance beyond the glazing which was usually set in vertical, metal frames. Sir John Burnet's Kodak House in Kingsway (1911) developed this style as far as the beginnings of the Modern but as London's finest Neo-Classical architect Burnet retained a link with the past after the war and Kodak House probably reflects the modernistic preference of the client. The Stripped Classical would come to be more widely used after the First World War.

Engineers' Styles (20)

Engineers made a bigger mark on London architecture in the nineteenth century than ever before. They are best known for their metal roofs and vaults over railway stations, markets and interior spaces. Iron and glass had become much cheaper from the second half of the eighteenth century. With buildings becoming taller, and covering a larger area, the potential of lighting them from above became clearer. Some of these glazed spaces, like top-lit staircases and conservatories, were small and an architect could design them himself. Top-lit shops and restaurants spread after 1875—such as Rule's, Covent Garden, founded in the 1890s—and did not require an engineer.[60]

Railway station roofs and vaults were almost always built by engineers. The railway companies were generally perceptive in predicting the number of tracks they would need, and this meant building very wide stations right from the start. All favoured a high, wide span or spans, to allow the steam and smoke to disperse in calm air well above the heads of the passengers and to exit through louvres in the roof. Beginning with King's Cross in 1850, one or more iron vaults became the usual covering for the larger stations. Architects generally designed the offices and waiting areas but sometimes engineers designed the frontage buildings as well.

194   King's Cross Station.

195   Paddington Station, c. 1890.

121

For instance, George Berkeley, an engineer, built Fenchurch Street Station in 1853. As well as the roof and side walls, he designed the frontage in a window-rich Italianate style topped by a shallow arch with the same outline as the train shed roof. This was not an innovative formula but Berkeley's work helps confirm that the Italianate was easy to do. In 1865 William Baker, chief engineer of the London and North Western Railway, built Broad Street Station in an astoundingly eclectic style with borrowings from French railway stations. It is easy to make fun of engineers' architecture but it was at least as good as, say, much hotel architecture.

The Great Exhibition of 1851 led to a whole generation of engineers' architecture. It was the subject of an international competition which attracted 245 entries but the Building Committee, composed of leading architects and engineers, decided to produce its own design. The domed basilica was a complete 'camel' and, in the nick of time, Joseph Paxton, the eminent landscape architect and glasshouse designer, was asked to take over.[61] His proposal moved entirely away from the

196   The Crystal Palace, Sydenham, c. 1890. The longitudinal vault and the towers were added after the move from Hyde Park.

masonry approach which had dogged most of the other schemes. Its iron, glass and wood structure was based wholly on engineering principles but it did not launch an architectural movement in London, except in aspects of museum design. For example, its revolutionary interior colour scheme by Owen Jones, using primary colours following discoveries in Greek archaeology and stressing the building's horizontals with red banners and balustrades, had no influence outside the exhibition area (except possibly at the Victoria and Albert Museum).

The exhibition left its mark, however, on the district of scientific and cultural buildings to the south of the Crystal Palace site, between Kensington Gore and the Cromwell Road. This area of 87 acres, purchased with some of the profits of the Great Exhibition, was intended to become the great centre of science and the arts envisaged by Prince Albert as the permanent product of the exhibition. It was laid out on a geometrical network of streets. Started in 1859, it became the finest cultural centre in Europe and a superb example of planning, even though it has never had much recognition. The layout and several of the buildings were designed by military engineers on account of their experience in planning and in building covered spaces. However, the Crystal Palace had no influence on the International Exhibition building which went up on Cromwell Road in 1861-2. This was a return to masonry, iron vaults and domes by Captain Francis Fowke of the Royal Engineers, the architect and engineer to the Department of Science and Art at South Kensington.[62] It had a conventional glazed vault, reminiscent of the cheap solution adopted at King's Cross Station, and an Italianate exterior. Fowke's building was pulled down after the first disappointing exhibition in 1862, to be replaced by Waterhouse's Natural History Museum in 1873-81 (though Fowke posthumously played a much bigger part in the Waterhouse design than is usually acknowledged). Fowke's galleries of the Horticultural Society (1861) survived. Parts were rebuilt in 1873 as the Alexandra Palace, Muswell Hill, but this burned down only sixteen days after opening.

The Royal Albert Hall (1867-71) stood at the head of the Exhibition Road precinct and was the work of two military engineers. Fowke designed the building and Lieutenant-Colonel Henry Scott built it after Fowke's death. Fowke's design was influenced by the Dresden opera house of Gottfried Semper (1838-41), whom Prince Albert had asked to draw up plans for the hall when the architect was in London in 1853. The Albert Hall—a tall, oval amphitheatre—is a reduced version of the Colosseum and the world's first domed arena, now holding some 7000 spectators close to the action, though many of them are seated well above it. It was intended for displays and scientific gatherings, so the unique acoustics were only an occasional problem until the Sir Henry Wood Promenade Concerts moved there in 1941 after the Queen's Hall was bombed. The brick and terracotta exterior, with its decorated frieze, was modestly effective in masking the simplicity of the concept. The semi-circular arches of the elevation reflected the oval plan.

The irony of the Albert Hall is that military engineers, who studied architecture as part of their training because

197 (*above*) The Albert Hall.

198 (*right*) The Henry Cole Building.

they might have to build barracks, forts and offices in the Empire, were by no means inferior to the average London architect. In fact, they probably received more formal training in architecture than most architects. For instance, Henry Scott's School of Naval Architects (now known as the Henry Cole Building; 1870–71) on Exhibition Road is a mature building, a tall Italianate structure using much the same decorative combination of brick and terracotta as the Albert Hall. The two long loggias, one at the entrance level and the other projected forward at the attic level, are unusual and the overall effect is a bit like a tropical hospital but Scott knew what he was doing. So did the engineers, including Fowke, who worked on the nearby Victoria and Albert Museum under the guidance of its first director, Sir Henry Cole, from 1856. Fowke built the earliest surviving gallery, the Sheepshanks (1857–8), in what Pevsner identifies as a Lombard Early Renaissance style, and Scott was responsible for the huge East Court (1868–73). Fowke's quad-

199 (*top*)   The main court of the Victoria and Albert Museum in an early Renaissance style by Fowke and Scott. The style reflects the museum's dedication to art and craftsmanship as a permanent expression of the ideals of the Great Exhibition.

200 (*above*)   Pediment of the main court at the Victoria and Albert Museum.

rangle (1859–72), completed by Scott, was also in a Renaissance style. The early courts were utilitarian structures but they were decorated later by some of the most exotic painters of the realm, including Lord Leighton.[63] This was a completely new approach to architecture, emphasising light, circulation, display and flexible use, ignored by most architectural historians but owing much to the Crystal Palace.

201 (*left*) Interior of the Coal Exchange, Thames Street, 1849.

The engineers did not sweep all before them, however. Engineers often contributed to steel-framed buildings but the architects took most or all of the credit. Buildings for water and sewage pumping engines, most of them built by the Metropolitan Board of Works, always involved an engineer. An architect often took part but the results generally used every cliché in the book, though sometimes hitting a sublime note. One of the biggest was Abbey Mills Pumping Station, Stratford, built by London's most distinguished sanitary engineer, Joseph Bazalgette, and the Board architect, E. Cooper, in 1865–8. This 'Cathedral of Sewage' was mainly Venetian Gothic in the Ruskinian manner but it had mansard roofs, two chimneys disguised as minarets (demolished in 1940 as a potential Luftwaffe landmark) and a central tower which could have graced the Kremlin. The interior had several levels of ornate but practical ironwork.[64] Most of London's new pumping stations were Gothic or Romanesque in style, or a mixture, like the Cross Ness Pumping Station, Belvedere Road, Erith, of 1865, also by Bazalgette.

While engineers could produce distinctive architecture, many architects could make good use of the new materials of the Industrial Revolution. A novel use of iron was the Coal Exchange (1846–8), built by J. B. Bunning, the City Corporation's prolific and versatile architect. It was an ordinary stone Italianate building on the outside but the circular dealing floor was topped by an iron drum with stairs giving access to the merchants' offices and roofed in iron and glass. The piers of the drum were highly decorated in cast iron. In 1845–7 the landscape architect Decimus Burton and Richard Turner, an engineer, built the Palm House in Kew Gardens. Both wrought and cast iron were used here. F. Peck's Agricultural Hall, Islington (1861–2) is a huge display hall (117 × 66 metres) under a light and elegant vault in iron and glass, 46 metres high. It had engineer support. The hall stands behind a central entrance arch flanked by two powerful Italianate towers topped by Baroque cupolas. It looks very much like the Thames frontage of Cannon Street station (1865–6) before the glazed vault was removed.

The Public Record Office, Chancery Lane (1851–8), by Sir James Pennethorne, Edward Blore's successor as Crown Architect, had something of the Palace of

202 (*left*) Iron building in Great Eastern Street. A rare example of a type of building which was common in New York.

203 and 204   The Public Record Office, 1851–66 and 1891–6. Its iron structure was intended to stop the spread of fire, and to allow large volumes of documents to be stored in a limited space. The stone facades to Fetter Lane and, later, to Chancery Lane, are military in appearance.

Westminster. Iron framed and fireproof, it used a repetitive Gothic style on a long frontage, with pavilions and a central tower. The deeply inset windows and the segmental arches over the bays gave it a prison-like effect, as though to discourage casual access.

THE DYNAMICS OF ARCHITECTURE AND LAYOUT

This plethora of London styles was without equivalent in the world, except perhaps in New York after about 1870. But how did the styles relate to one another and to the layouts of streets and sites within which they were set? We shall take some examples: the City of London, the 'clubland' of St James's, Roumieu's atrocious archi-

tecture, Imperial London, housing, the architecture of private wealth, prisons, markets, public houses and theatres. We begin with the City of London, where the 'battle of the styles' was hardest fought.

The City of London

During the nineteenth century the City of London was almost completely rebuilt as an office district. It was London's biggest 'battlefield of the styles' where most sites were redeveloped individually, without reference to a coherent street plan like the West End's or to neighbouring structures.

Until the end of the eighteenth century most of the City's business and manufacturing was carried on from buildings which, at least on the street frontage, looked like ordinary houses. Public buildings were nearly all in a Classical style and Wren's churches still dotted the City. All this began to change from the early 1800s. The population fell from 128,000 in 1801 to 27,000 a century later. Dedicated commercial buildings multiplied and they grew higher, encouraged by the Building Act of

205 View of the City from Bow church, c. 1895. The height ceiling imposed by the Building Acts has produced this visual wasteland.

1774 which had abolished maximum heights on existing streets. After about 1830 the Classical styles were joined by a growing number of alternatives. Exotic and eclectic styles multiplied. Some of this building was carried out in an ignorant or crude way but much inventive design had appeared by the end of the century. City builders and architects enjoyed a much greater freedom than in the West End, for outright competition was encouraged and nowhere in the world, except perhaps in Manhattan, did they have an equivalent district to emulate. Most building conformed to the Classical styles, with the Palladian doing well because it looked good and was cheap. However, Pevsner detects the rise of the Italianate which had become the common design language of the City by the 1850s.[65] The Gothic attracted many clients and architects in both its pure forms and the dog-Gothic (mainly debased or exaggerated Ruskinian) which made its mark in the City, more than any-

where in London, in the 1850s and 1860s.[66] The Italianate carried on until 1914, mainly in degraded forms drawing on a wide variety of British and foreign examples. As we have seen, the Italianate was the easiest Classical style to adopt: there were no rules and architects could copy an Italianate building in the next street.

Many of the offices and banks built in the City after 1830 followed national design fashions and were designed by well-known architects. Many more, the products of less famous architects including M. E. Collins, who did a lot of work in the City, were routine buildings, sometimes pretentious or lacking in finesse. New warehouses were built by such architects, sometimes with curious stylistic effects. Many of the streets in the City retained very narrow frontages dating from the Middle Ages and architects could build high, even in narrow lanes. This produced some striking effects, especially when the Gothic was used. Pevsner points out that the City's varied facades hid interiors of little interest, composed of warrens of offices, stores or workshops. This contrasted with the West End, where many beautiful interiors were hidden by ordinary facades.

206 The Stock Exchange, Old Broad Street, c. 1890. This was a new building, the work of J. J. Cole.

207 Holborn Viaduct, c. 1890. These commercial buildings probably date from the late 1860s and stand on tall arches on either side of the bridge, visible in the foreground.

Sir William Tite's Royal Exchange (1841–4), the highlight of City architecture in the nineteenth century, was built to replace Edward Jerman's post-Fire structure (1667–71), burned down in 1838. It hit a Roman note with its big, eight-column portico and tall, triangular pediment, though the rest of it is normally judged to be eclectic, with its many round-headed arches and a tower. Owing to confusion arising from the competition and its assessment, Cockerell's Neo-Classical/Baroque entry, clearly superior to Tite's as architecture, was not favoured. This outcome is often presented as a major scandal.[67] However, Cockerell's design would clearly have exceeded the Treasury limit of £150,000 without

the imposition of swingeing economies, while Tite's bluff portico was much more in the City tradition than Cockerell's artistic entrance facade. Above all, Tite's design was more like the previous Exchange than was Cockerell's and tradition was clearly important to the clients.

Cockerell had to be content with building some City banks in a more restrained style. C. O. Parnell put up a striking building for the Westminster Bank (demolished) in Lombard Street in 1861, with an extension in 1874. This displayed a wealth of Classical features and styles, a little like English Baroque but more Palladian than anything else.[68] The building's exuberance, which recalled an ornate tower pub, would have been too costly to reproduce in most City structures. An ornate, Italianate corner block was built at 39–40, Lombard Street in 1866–8 by F. and F. J. Francis. The ornate, projecting cornice and the two heavily decorated upper floors draw the eye upwards. Business premises at 6–7, St Mary-at-Hill (1873), by Ernest George and Thomas Vaughan had decorative, semi-Ruskinian, arched brickwork over three windows and a bas-relief in Coade Stone, together with a stone ground floor, but otherwise was a plain brick building. Looked at more closely, its rectangular, divided window openings and strong, no-nonsense facade were reminiscent of New York. A big example of a Ruskinian office block was Albert Buildings at 49–53 Queen Victoria Street, by F. J. Ward, built in 1871 on a triangular site. In 1844–5 Edward l'Anson and Son built the Royal Exchange Buildings in Freemen's Place. This was one of London's first office buildings designed to be let by the floor and the result was predictably repetitive. The

208 The interior of the Royal Exchange in Charles Cockerell's submission, 1840. However brilliant on paper, this expensive project would always have been financially impossible.

209   The Royal Exchange, c. 1895.

210   The Royal Exchange in a brief interval of sunlight in 2004. Ancient Rome could not have offered a finer sight.

National Provincial Bank of England, on Bishopsgate, by John Gibson, was built in 1865 in the Baroque style. The National Provident Institution Building in Gracechurch Street was built in 1863 by Robert Kerr, the author of *The Gentleman's House.* It was a strongly Italianate building, with semi-circular arches and a loggia.[69]

Some of the most impressive office buildings were in the Strand, just outside the City boundary. Cockerell's Westminster Insurance Office, at 429 the Strand, was built in 1831–2. It was a massive Doric structure. In 1852, H. R. Abraham built a block of shops with four floors above at 188–92 the Strand. This was in the Classical style, with modified Serlian windows on the first two floors.[70] In 1868 the City Offices Co. built a large block at the corner of Lombard Street and Gracechurch Street. This was a carefully detailed four-storey stone building with an attic, strongly Italianate and looking like a government building in Rome.

The strongest statement made by an office block was the Prudential Assurance building in Holborn, opposite Staple Inn. This was built in two stages by Alfred and Paul Waterhouse in 1879 (rebuilt in 1932) and then in 1899–1906. This huge structure in shiny terracotta, with tall roofs and towers, was the St Pancras of commerce. Anti-pollution defence was a feature here, with self-cleaning materials and a fiery red colour which could penetrate the gloomy winter days. One of the most powerful buildings was 46–7 Cheapside, which replaced two buildings destroyed by fire in 1881. Here Sir Ernest George and Peto combined the two sites and built a Gothic office building in cast iron and red brick. Its tall gables recalled Bruges or Lubeck.[71]

211   A palazzo in the City. D'Arcy House (1867–9, by E. I'Anson), 146, Queen Victoria Street, originally the home of the British and Foreign Bible Society. It could be in Rome.

212   Palazzo-style bank at 15, Bishopsgate, by John Gibson (1864–5), hailed by Pevsner as the best Victorian bank in the City.

213   Palazzo commercial building at the corner of Gracechurch Street and Lombard Street by the Francis brothers in 1866–8. Italianate design is very strong here.

Clubs

The cluster of gentlemen's and professional clubs in and around Pall Mall was linked to the royal and aristocratic area of St James and to Nash's Regent Street scheme. Pall Mall crossed Regent Street at its lower end, and ran from St James's Palace to the emerging Trafalgar Square.

Clubs had originated in St James's Street from the 1760s, with Boodle's, a brick building in the style of Robert Adam by John Crunden, in 1765, followed by Henry Holland's Palladian Brooks's in 1777–8, built in white brick, and James Wyatt's White's in 1787–8, altered in 1852. There followed Benjamin Dean Wyatt's Devonshire Club, St James Street (1827), and the Oriental Club, Hanover Square (1827–8).

Nash planned two great clubs facing each other across Waterloo Place, south of Pall Mall. He built one of these, the Palladian United Services Club, in 1827. Decimus Burton, who had an interest in the Greek Revival, built the other, the Athenaeum, in 1828–30. Nash's building was remodelled by Burton in 1842, producing a hybrid structure looking forward to the Italianate. The Athenaeum's statue of Pallas Athene, the Doric columns

214 (*above*)   The Prudential Assurance building, High Holborn, lit by a low, western sun.

215 (*below*)   The Neo-Classical Brooks's Club (1777–8) by Adam's rival, Henry Holland, an admirer of Ledoux. White brick and 'tuck pointing' produce smooth walls which at first sight resemble ashlar. However, this was a very expensive method of enhancing brick and Adam's success with his new stucco recipes meant that it was not widely used after the 1770s.

216 (*top*)   The United Services Club.

217 (*above*)   The Athenaeum. These two clubs formed part of Nash's ambitious layout on Pall Mall and the architects were happy to adopt conforming designs.

on its porch, the Grecian entrance hall, the attic and the bas-relief cornice were explicitly Greek features reflecting its association with knowledge. The design had some similarities to the work of Schinkel in Berlin, where Greek Classical influences had taken hold more strongly than in London.

Clubs now spread along Pall Mall. They served the professions and civil servants rather than the rich, who had West End houses of their own (though they would also have been members of one or more clubs). They allowed gentlemen, civil servants and professionals to hold informal meetings or read the newspapers in the mornings, to buy a steamy lunch of meat and vegetables served from tureens and to rent a room for the night if

necessary. Evenings could be spent playing billiards or cards, or reading. The Classical architecture of the clubs represented this pattern of existence very well. Barry built the Travellers' Club in 1828–32. Though a palazzo, it was adjoined on both sides and made its statement through its facade. It was a simple, even modest, building with Classical features but its cornice maintained the line of Decimus Burton's Athenaeum while adopting an Italianate rather than a Grecian treatment. Its colonnaded interior hall was ordered and impressive. The Italianate garden facade had a charming, rustic treatment.

Barry went on to build the Reform Club next door in 1837–41. This, with three storeys, was the tallest club so far and its height made it much more clearly an Italian palazzo than its predecessors. Two strong horizontal lines divided the tall facade and a heavy, projecting cornice clearly referred to Renaissance Florence. Barry built a top-lit, colonnaded atrium (saloon) rising through two storeys. The Oxford and Cambridge Club (1835–8), built by Smirke, was the last club in the Classical tradition, before the onset of the Italianate.

The Army and Navy Club (demolished) was built in 1848–51 by C. O. Parnell and Alfred Smith. This was a palazzo, modelled on a Venetian example, with rustication on the ground floor and round-headed windows above. A similar frontage was provided by Sydney Smirke when he rebuilt the Carlton Club in 1847, with pilasters on each of the two floors. The whole effect was that of a large branch bank. Smirke's choice of Caen stone proved disastrous when decay began ten years later and the building had to be refaced in 1923–4.[72] Also resembling a bank was the Conservative Club, St James's Street, built by George Basevi and Sydney Smirke in 1843–4. The style here was a heavy Palladian with something of the palazzo. Most of these clubs were topped by balustrades, even when there was a powerful Italianate cornice, presumably to hide the shallow pitched roofs behind. After about 1860 fewer clubs were built and they diverged from the Classical style. For instance, the National Liberal Club, Whitehall Place (1885–7), an impressive Gothic building on a corner site, by Alfred Waterhouse, stood outside the main club area.

London's clubland, built on a rectilinear network of broad streets enhanced by Nash as part of his great West End plan, was a brilliant example of the voluntary application of Classical design. This was how they did it in Paris. And this was how they did not do it in the City of London. No wonder foreign visitors were confused.

★   ★   ★

Outright Bad Design:
The Example of R. L. Roumieu

This free-for-all in the City was bound to generate bad architecture as well as good. One architect and developer, R. L. Roumieu, the McGonagall of London design, will represent, in what follows, an anonymous army of incompetents.

Roumieu with his partner until 1848, A. D. Gough, was a busy architect and developer from inner London whose work suggests at first sight that he had no architectural training, taste or visual sense. He also seems to have been impervious to the influence of other architects, current or past, good or bad. However, he was the grandson of an architect of Huguenot origins and had studied with Benjamin Wyatt. Everything he built was as solid as a rock and probably more solid than it needed to be. Gough had a bit of a reputation up Islington way as a church architect. He was moved to name his son after Roumieu. The son became an architect and his warehouse work in Bristol would be very much in the family tradition.

In 1837 the firm put up the box-like Literary Institute in Almeida Street, Islington. Pevsner detects a whiff of the Grecian in this simple building but this must be in the absence of any other style. Roumieu's De Beau-

219 The Almeida Institute (1837), now a lively arts centre. Just a box, but strong as an air raid shelter.

218 Milner Square, looking east in late afternoon.

voir Square, N1, and adjacent streets (1838), were a development of semi-detached houses with gables and some crude Tudor detailing, resembling Richard Carpenter's more respected Lonsdale Square, Islington (also 1838). It formed part of a large suburban development, De Beauvoir Town, off Kingsland Road. The weedy buttresses ending at the top of the first floor were of neither use nor ornament. The crude window surrounds do not even merit the description of Mannerist.

The contrasting Milner Square, near the Angel, was built by Roumieu and Gough in yellow brick in 1841–3. This was a startlingly narrow version of a West End square. The chunky, four-storey frontages had the standard Palladian horizontal division but the fenestration and the broad, sunken pilaster-like divisions between the openings, together with the round-arched attic windows, looked like nothing on earth. The reader can be spared Summerson's assessment, for once. However, the oddities of the design were outweighed by the quality of the construction, still solid early in the twenty-first century, and by the intimate, protected environment produced by the long, narrow rectangle of the plan and the lush, wooded garden strip in the middle, more obviously

221   Roumieu's Vinegar Warehouses, Eastcheap.

220   The old parish church of St Pancras, as 'restored' by Roumieu and Gough.

a children's playground than most London squares of its time. The north–south orientation provided a generous distribution of sunlight. There is something about Milner Square and many, including this author, find themselves drawn to it.

A number of talentless architects were given ecclesiastical commissions in the early 1800s and Roumieu and Gough were no exception. In 1842–3 they enlarged St Peter in St Peter's Street, Islington, apparently with the approval of Sir Charles Barry who had built the cheap original in 1834–5. Their new, brick front was like a Pugin caricature of an early Commissioners' church.[73] Indeed, apart from its disturbingly thin spire, a Gough trademark, it recalled St Mary's, Somers Town, the ultra-cardboard effort by the Inwoods in 1822–4. Gough was noted for forgetting nothing and learning nothing and his was no doubt the guiding hand here and not just for the spire. In 1848 the partnership restored and extended Old St Pancras church, an eleventh-century building. Little remained of the original church when Roumieu

134

and Gough got at it and almost nothing was left when they had finished. Their Norman windows and tower were in the best waterworks style.[74]

In 1865 Roumieu built the barely competent brick French Hospital, Victoria Park Road, with dark brick diapering and a central tower. Pevsner sees it as Franco-Flemish but Roumieu would have been flattered. On a broad frontage at 33–5 Eastcheap Roumieu built the Vinegar Warehouses in 1868. This was a grotesque Gothic building with two tall bays separated by a narrow section of facade.[75] David Gentleman was drawn to it and did a striking sketch.[76] Roumieu liked powerful facades but this one was brutal. However, Jones and Woodward are impressed by the way the building has resisted the passage of time.[77] In 1874 Roumieu replaced two adjacent seventeenth-century houses at 48 and 49 Cheapside.[78] These are six-storey buildings with attics. They stand on the original medieval sites so that their height is completely out of proportion to their width. One building incorporates a huge, integral Gothic arch. The other does not. These two facades would not have disgraced a 'Batman' film set. At least Roumieu had learned that Gothic arches were pointed. He also saw the potential of glazing and transoms set within large, structural arches, which makes him somewhat of a pioneer. Maybe he was influenced (for once) by Skilbeck's Warehouse at 46 Upper Thames Street, remodelled by the inventive medievalist William Burges in 1865–6. This was five storeys high on a narrow site, with part of the frontage set back to allow winching. The cowls covering the top of the hoists were Gothic in spirit if not in style. This combination of striking art and commercial convenience was widely admired by the architects of the day.[79]

The Roumieu saga shows how a mediocre but hard-working architect, noted for structural solidity and no doubt for completion on time, could build up a large portfolio of commissions in the City and the East End. It also suggests that many clients did not require stylistic purity or aesthetic integrity. Here lies the secret of most London architecture in the nineteenth century and here are the origins of the contrast with Paris where most architects and clients expected a higher standard.

Imperial London

At the end of the nineteenth century there was new progress towards a London of grandeur and imperial might, the first since Nash. It began in the 1890s when the newly founded London County Council (1889), the Crown Estate and the Office of Works jointly recognised the potential of a great imperial way running from Buckingham Palace to St Paul's cathedral via Trafalgar Square. Several improvements were planned, all of them Classical in inspiration. Buckingham Palace and its surroundings were to play a big part.

The story of royal palaces in western London had been one of modesty ever since William III acquired what became Kensington Palace as a private residence in 1689. Wren, Hawksmoor and Kent worked there but it emerged in 1702 as little more than a simple, brick country house, a shadow of Easton Neston, Northamptonshire, built by Hawksmoor at much the same time. Only the Orangery, probably built by Hawksmoor with some changes by Vanbrugh (1704–5), is a work of art. Buckingham Palace, too, began life as a noble residence, and a modest one. George III acquired it as a private residence in 1761 but the monarchs were mainly dependent on parliamentary funding of works there, via the Office of Works, and they were constantly disappointed.

In 1825 John Nash started to convert it to a palace for his friend George IV but his Neo-Classical, Napoleonic concept in Bath stone, with one central and two projecting porticoes round the forecourt, and a pleasant garden front, looked modest even though the king demolished his exorbitant London residence, Carlton House, to contribute to the cost and provide furniture and decorations.[80] The triumphal arch designed for the forecourt by Nash in 1828, and built of the best Carrara white marble, was the highlight but shortage of funds did not allow its decorations to be completed as Nash had intended and the arch was moved to its present site in Hyde Park in 1851. Now known as Marble Arch, its once brilliant surfaces have been dulled by the London atmosphere. A bigger arch, Constitution Arch, built by Decimus Burton in 1827–8, was intended to mark the northern entrance to the palace grounds, but in 1883 it was moved to the top of Constitution Hill, north-west of the palace.

Victoria and Albert, deciding to make Buckingham Palace their London home, sought to extend the building but they too were denied the money that they needed. Perhaps the magnificence of Windsor Castle, lately improved by Sir Jeffry Wyatville in 1824–40, reduced Parliament's sympathy for further expense. They also had to work with the embarrassingly under-achieving Edward Blore, whose reputation as a cheap architect had reached Westminster when he was appointed by the Office of Works to succeed the disgraced Nash in 1832.[81] Blore was best at exotic, historicist buildings, including Alupka (1837–40), a palace in the Ottoman style in the Crimea, and two buildings in the Tudor/Jacobean style, Ramsey Abbey (1838–9) and Worsley Hall, Eccles

222 Buckingham Palace (1991) in the familiar form created by Sir Aston Webb's east front of 1913. The work of Nash and Blore lies behind it. The Nash portico is visible in the courtyard.

(1840–45). Classical design was never his forte, which was bad news for Buckingham Palace. Blore had to complete (1832–7) and then expand Nash's curiously emaciated solution for the front of the palace. First he completed Nash's two portico wing fronts but he then had to meet requests from Victoria and Albert for more space, including extra bedrooms for the royal children. He decided to move Nash's triumphal arch and erect an eastern range between the ends of Nash's two wings (1847–50). The task was hideously beyond him and he was given very little money, resulting among many other weaknesses in the ill-fated use of Caen stone and Coade Stone dressings and carvings. Even this modest solution had to

223   Blore's frontage of Buckingham Palace, already going black in c. 1860. In Germany and Austria they would have called this style 'Biedermeier' and we may wonder if Albert influenced it.

be financed in part by the sale of the Brighton Pavilion to the Brighton Corporation. Hermione Hobhouse's judgement on the design – 'a rather bad form of Franco-Italianate baroque' – is just.[82] Worse, the Caen stone started to deteriorate immediately and went black within a few decades. To Blore's credit, he refused the knighthood which would normally have been his due when the work was completed and pursued his real labour of love as an antiquary to the end of his life in 1879 at the age of 91. As for Victoria, she rarely came to the palace after her bereavement in 1861, preferring Windsor when she needed to be in the metropolis.[83] Meanwhile, what remains of Blore's Caen stone has been protected by a thick coat of stone paint.[84]

Sir Aston Webb, who had the biggest practice in London and who could build in any style, became the main servant of Buckingham Palace and its surroundings in 1901. His idea was to link the palace via an enhanced Mall to Nash's Trafalgar Square, its buildings increasingly Classical since its designation as London's great representative *place* in 1835. Landscaping and additional buildings would produce a great Baroque perspective. Webb started by building the Queen Victoria memorial *rond-point* in front of the palace in 1900–1. His Admiralty Arch dates from 1910 and his new, broader Mall was completed in 1911. In 1913 he gave a great new Palladian facade to the palace itself, covering the frumpish, decaying Blore frontage of the 1840s with Portland stone.[85] Webb's office could certainly deliver when necessary: the work cost only £60,000 and took a mere thirteen weeks, allowing George V to return from his summer break without tripping over the builders. Delighted, the king put on a dinner for all the building workers. Meanwhile, the theatre architect Frank T. Verity, a product of the Ecole des Beaux-Arts and known for his ornate Baroque interiors, had completed the redecoration of some of the rooms.[86] London now had a palace which ranked with Europe's greatest royal and imperial palaces, thanks mainly to its Palladian frontage.

The biggest expression of the Neo-Classical was the LCC's Kingsway–Aldwych improvement scheme. The roadways were ready by 1905 but it took longer to finish the buildings on the cleared sites, with the last going up long after the war. These tall frontages, together with some monumental buildings on the Aldwych island, prompted a number of Classical and Neo-Classical solutions.[87] Some architects seem to have been inspired by recent additions to Trafalgar Square and by new buildings in the Exhibition Road area.

224   Kingsway office buildings, with a variety of efforts to achieve maximum height under the 1894 Building Act. Paris would have done it much better.

The choice of the Classical for big urban layouts was confirmed by the reconstruction of Regent Street, first mooted in the early 1900s and completed in the 1920s. The large stone buildings of the new Regent Street would influence most commercial rebuilding in the West End until the Modern took over in the 1930s. Looking pompous and expensive, most of them added nothing to London's creative portfolio but consumed large quantities of Portland stone.

This great surge of the Classical created the concept of the 'Grand Manner', which was more suited to London as imperial metropolis than it was to the provinces. With competitions multiplying for major schemes, the growing number of students on formal courses and other young architects let rip, most of them favouring the Classical which they could apply more easily than other styles. In schemes carried out, however, the Baroque predominated as at London County Hall.

Housing

Historians have detected Londoners moving into the nearby countryside as early as the Middle Ages but the small country villa and the suburb first stand out around 1800. The aesthetic of the Picturesque had become popular in the second half of the eighteenth century and growing personal wealth allowed more Londoners to aspire to life in sylvan environments. Horace Walpole's Gothic Strawberry Hill (1749–76) at Twickenham was one of many Picturesque houses built upstream from London in both the Classical and the Gothic styles. However, most of London's new housing was built on the edge of the built-up area and bijou villages and suburbs were the exception.

Despite the rise of the Picturesque, London housing was not greatly affected by the Gothic style. The windows were the wrong shape, for one thing. Pointed sash window frames were too much trouble. It was possible to make rectangular frames rising behind pointed arches but the result looked false from the inside. Tudor designs did not raise the same problems but they also were rare. The occasional housing scheme diverged from the Classical style, as in the work of Carpenter and of

225   James Wyld's New Plan of London in 1866. The east–west emphasis is achieved by excluding part of the northern suburbs.

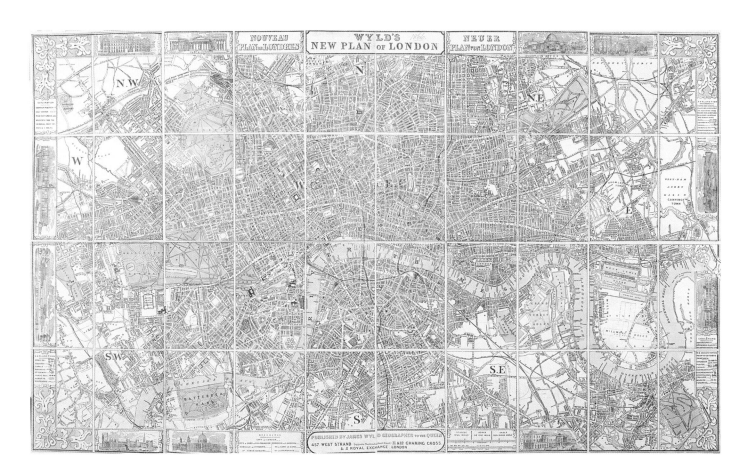

Roumieu, mentioned above. Housing developments on estates to the north and north-east of the City, generally modest in scale, mainly clung to the Classical, often in a crude or debased form. Percy Circus (c. 1819), off King's Cross Road, was surrounded by modest but elegant three-storey brick terraced houses with four-storey houses on the street corners. They were pleasantly Georgian in style but had no great distinction. Two-storey brick terraces designed to look like villas or semi-detached houses could be found at Croston Street, Hackney, Lloyd Square off King's Cross Road, Barnsbury Park (1830s) and other estates.[88] They had a modicum of Classical features, such as pediments and cornices. Suburban villas became more common from the 1840s. Albion Square (1846–9), a few metres from Roumieu's De Beauvoir Square, was designed by J. C.

226, 227 and 228 (*below and right*) The Lloyd Baker estate in Finsbury was developed for middle-class residents shortly after the French wars. Great Percy Street and Percy Circus are shown here. This estate and its neighbour, the New River estate, generated a variety of houses and layouts, but all were in the Classical style. Demand was probably local (doctors, schoolmasters, etc.) rather than commuters. Strollers who are tempted to visit this area will be rewarded.

Loudon, the landscape architect. These semi-detached brick villas had stucco trimmings. There was nothing new about them as architecture but their deep front gardens gave them a sylvan effect. Their slate roofs had become normal by this time, using the Welsh slate which had been brought to London since the 1760s.[89]

In the west the Palladian continued, together with stucco, until the 1870s. A standard housing style for the upper and middle classes developed after 1820, concentrated on the West End and Belgravia, and spreading outwards from there. The style was a bland Classical derived from the Palladian, with a bit of Adam and Nash, but also influenced from 1804 by Percier and Fontaine's rows of houses along the Rue de Rivoli in Paris. There was an emphasis on horizontal lines, though the houses were high, often reaching four storeys or more.

Stucco coatings were almost universal, often with artificial rustication on the ground floor. The main hori-

229 Terraced houses disguised as villas in Lloyd Square. There was clearly a movement in the 1820s towards suburban layouts but builders were reluctant to make a complete break from the terrace.

231 (*right, centre*) The New Cut, off Waterloo Bridge Road, in about 1895. These houses must date from the early nineteenth century. They look in good condition but utterly nondescript. The South Bank was never very special, in contrast to Paris where the Left Bank was not noticeably inferior to the Right Bank.

zontal line passed under the first floor, and under the attic floor there was a strong cornice. Window openings, especially on the lower floors, were often decorated with triangular or curved pediments in stucco. The corners were sometimes trimmed in rusticated stone but usually moulded stucco achieved this effect. Balconies were often placed at the level of the first floor and some were topped by light, trellis-work verandahs. These tall houses, which were almost always built in rows of common height, contributed to perspective and vista effects which owners and tenants appreciated.

After 1830 architects gradually withdrew from development, and builders took their place. Builders could work on the bigger scale that the faster growth of London demanded and they continued to use architects, sometimes full time, as did Thomas Cubitt, James Burton and other big builders.[90] Cubitt, whose work in specu-

230 Piccadilly, c. 1895. Frankly, this is a pretty nondescript scene, with the shored-up houses on the left suggesting flimsy building under the leasehold system.

232 Prince's Gate, Kensington, c. 1890, at the south-west end of Hyde Park. These are the houses of rich people, or perhaps *nouveaux riches* would be a better term.

233 Houses in Gower Street, built about 1790. The symmetry is impressive here, though these are not expensive houses.

lative building and development had started around 1805, was the main influence on London housing after 1830. His huge housing estates, most of them in Belgravia, Pimlico and north Bloomsbury, were under construction between about 1820 and 1850. Cubitt used the Palladian style on a bigger scale than had previously been normal in the West End, as at Tavistock Square (1806–26) and Eccleston Square (1835), though his designs conformed to the rates defined in the Building Act of 1774. There was normally a basement for the use of servants and storage, with access directly from the street via a depressed front courtyard known as the area. Access to the front door was via a bridge or steps over the area. This access was often covered by a Classical porch with columns and a pediment. The area occupied land off the street line which would normally have formed part of the area of the house, and this made it desirable to increase the height of the house, which could rise to five

234 (*right, top*) The west side of Tavistock Square, 1820–26, by Thomas Cubitt. The groups of four pilasters add strength to this very long row, recalling the Adelphi but without Adam's careful spacing.

235 (*right, centre*) Endsleigh Street, part of the Tavistock Square layout, c. 1824. Here, two groups of four pilasters terminate the ends of the row, leaving the central bays without decoration. The effect is either Neo-Greek or brutal, depending on the observer's taste.

236 (*right, bottom*) Backs of houses in the Tavistock Square area. Here the effect is brutal, whatever the observer's taste, and the London box house reigns in a new glory.

237 (*above left*) Montpelier Square, with houses built c. 1840–45. Laid out by new owners in 1826, the area developed slowly owing mainly to poor access and crowding by other estates. The best houses were in the square.

239 (*above right*) Another side of Montpelier Square, facing north and without stucco and pediments.

238 (*left*) Smaller and cheaper houses on Montpelier Street. The developers have secured the general design formula of Montpelier Square while tolerating much smaller and cheaper houses. On balance, the developers did very well here over a period of twenty years, though the houses in the street are less well built than those in the square.

storeys, often with attic rooms in the roof above. The horizontal divisions were not always present or consistent in the taller houses. Cubitt coated his houses in stucco, following the example of Adam and Nash, and used stucco features such as pilasters to articulate his long facades. He built well. His taller houses, in particular, had to be very solid structures and most survive today. No. 11, Eaton Square was for sale in 2002 at an asking price of £20 million after previous ownerships by Soraya Khashoggi, the arms millionairess and racehorse owner, Lord Andrew Lloyd-Webber, the theatrical entrepreneur, and Viktor Kozeny, the international businessman, whose

attempts to make it bullet- and bug-proof had reduced it to a shell.[91]

Matthew Wyatt, a member of the great architectural and artistic dynasty, was a major developer in Pimlico and Paddington. His stuccoed houses were influenced, he claimed, by Nash's West Strand improvements, and in his four-storeyed Victoria Square (1838–40), near Buckingham Palace, he made some use of the corner bows and domes ('pepperpots') used by Nash at Charing Cross. He went on to develop a number of stuccoed streets in the Paddington area, where his output was second only to Thomas Cubitt's.[92] Corner bows and turrets were also used by Robert Cantwell in a big, four-storey, stuccoed scheme round Royal Crescent, Holland Park (1837–46).

Much of the new housing to the north and the north-east was a reduced version of Cubitt, without the stucco. The yellow London stock brick was the main building

of genteel aspirations such as teachers, doctors and solicitors who appreciated a superior environment. Squares were rare in the East End, east of Shoreditch High Street and Kingsland Road, and down by the Docks, suggesting that the genteel element was smaller there. Instead, a distinct East End environment based on the brown-brick cottage row and the narrow street in the Docks area begin to emerge from about 1800, as the docks spread down the Thames from the Pool of London.[94] These very small houses were of two storeys, often with a parapet on the street frontage. A shallow roof or roofs were normally at right-angles to the street.[95] Described

242   This unusually sturdy East End row stands just off Commercial Road, Limehouse. The parapet is typical of the East End but its exaggerated height indicates large sites and tall roofs.

240 (*top*)   Belgrave Road, SW1. Typical houses in Belgravia, a large area developed by Cubitt on the Grosvenor estate from 1826. Here, as in Bloomsbury and Marylebone, Cubitt set out to create the maximum volume of accommodation in simple boxes. In Belgrave Square and other squares built here by George Basevi and Cubitt's other architects, the frontages were broken up by columnar features and setbacks, but in Belgravia's very long streets the frontages were utterly repetitive, enhanced only by white stuccoing and long vistas.

241 (*above*)   Oxford Street, looking east, c. 1895. Quality architecture is clearly absent.

material. It resisted smoke damage well but went black quickly. Developers made much use of squares but they were more widely dispersed, smaller and set in less ambitious street networks.[93] They showed that among those working in the north and north-east there were people

by Walter Besant as 'the City of Dreadful Monotony', the East End offered almost nothing of architectural interest except for the occasional church or school.[96]

In the 1850s builders began to experiment with blocks of apartments for the well-off, beginning in Victoria Street and later in Pimlico.[97] Over a long period of development from the first example in 1853, much the same style was used and most blocks were of brick, six storeys high, with an attic.[98] Hydraulic lifts began to allow greater heights from the 1860s. Shaw's Albert Hall Mansions, already mentioned, and the nearby Albert Court, in Prince Consort Road (c. 1890), are outstanding examples of tall flats taking full advantage of large and prestigious sites, reaching as high as nine floors in places. Between the Building Acts of 1774 and 1894, and in contrast to Paris, no absolute height ceiling was imposed on residential buildings in London. Although other constraints normally prevented excess, some very tall apartments were built in open locations before 1894. The highest was the fourteen-storey Queen Anne Mansions (1874), which overlooked the gardens of Buckingham Palace. The longest rows of flats were in Victoria Street which became, by the end of the century, London's biggest concentration of what were known as mansion flats. Apart from Shaw's Albert Hall Mansions, few of these blocks had any visual distinction.

At much the same time, block housing was developed for the working classes, to counter the effects of over-crowding in inner London.[99] These blocks were mostly the work of charities, housing reform bodies and private companies. The objective was almost always to house skilled workers and small tradespeople, not the very poor, and much of this accommodation was of a good standard despite the gloomy exteriors. Nearly all were designed by architects, Henry Roberts and Henry Darbishire being among the most distinguished. After 1889 the newly founded LCC built large numbers of flatted homes before it branched out into suburban cottage estates at the turn of the century.[100] Most of its designs were the work of its own Architect's Department under W. E. Riley. The creation of the Housing of the Working Classes Branch in 1893 led to efforts to break away from the generally dour architecture of London workers' blocks. The Branch's main inspiration was Richard Norman Shaw but it made frequent sallies into Free Style with touches of Arts and Crafts, Art Nouveau and even Jugendstil, possibly including Charles Rennie Mackintosh.[101]

The LCC's low-density initiative followed the example of private builders who started to develop suburban

243 (*below left*) Model Homes for Families, 1849. One of the first model tenement blocks, this gave priority to air and light, as in this access way. The architect was Henry Roberts.

244 (*below right*) Derby Lodge, Britannia Street, Kings Cross. One of the many blocks of model tenements built near the Metropolitan Railway, c. 1863. It uses H. A. Darbishire's modular formula of flats reached from an open stairway and short balcony.

245 (*above*) Peabody Buildings on the Mint Estate, a clearance area of the 1880s.

247 (*below*) Sandringham Buildings, Charing Cross Road, built by the Improved Industrial Dwellings Co. in 1884.

246 East End Dwellings Co. tenements just south of St Pancras station, 1892. This company catered especially for Jewish immigrants and its uniquely low rents were partly the product of shared facilities. The sash window lived on in cheap, high-density housing to promote ventilation and lighting.

248 (*above left*) Part of the LCC's Boundary Street Estate. The influences here come mainly from Richard Norman Shaw and the Arts and Crafts movement.

250 (*above right*) Houses in The Highway, near the docks, c. 1900. This is a commercial street and most of the houses are three storeys high.

251 (*right*) The Old Oak Estate, Acton. This was the last of the LCC's cottage estates to be built before 1914.

249 and 252 (*below*) Builders of suburban houses could be quite creative by 1900. These examples are in Elwood Road and Avenell Road, Highbury, across from the Arsenal football ground.

estates of terraced houses after about 1870. Most of these were two-storey brick houses for the middle and lower middle classes. The taller, stuccoed houses lapsed after 1870, except in rich districts on the fringes of the West End. Railway commuting grew apace and these suburbs spread for distances of up to eight miles from the centre of London.[102] H. J. Dyos, the authority on London suburbs, detected a noticeable 'suburban trend' from the 1860s and an even more marked trend from the 1880s.[103] The architectural interest of these suburbs was limited but they provided a great, dull backcloth for the works of competent London architects, such as schools and churches. A. A. Jackson, another suburban specialist, has detected two types. One was the two-storey row of

253 Terraced houses for the lower middle classes at Kensal Rise, pictured in 1921. This type, with angled bays, turrets and large back additions, could be found all round the suburbs as builders adopted a winning formula between about 1890 and 1910. Some have detected the influence of Richard Norman Shaw in this design. Noel Coward's *This Happy Breed* (1944) is set in a similar house in Clapham, on the other side of London.

narrow, dark houses with back additions housing the scullery, toilet and an upstairs bedroom. These continued to be built until 1914. The other was a detached or semi-detached house of lighter construction and rectangular plan. These houses, which looked forward to the inter-war years, started to come on the scene around 1900 and Jackson detects Voysey's design influence.[104] Architects played their part in these developments but Susie Barson's detection of a 'Victorian vernacular' followed by an 'Edwardian vernacular' in houses whose builders

254 Middle-class houses near a suburban station in Woodford, c. 1910. They look detached at first sight but form a row with the service rooms set back, in the long London tradition. The elevations look American but they may be merely mature Arts and Crafts.

sought a modest element of distinction using pattern books and industrially produced decorations is entirely persuasive.[105]

The idea of housing Londoners at lower densities generated the possibility that the suburbs could be planned comprehensively to encourage even more to move out. Open spaces and private gardens were seen as essential. Bedford Park (1876–), though not built for the working class, was an early step.[106] Hampstead Garden Suburb, laid out by Raymond Unwin and Barry Parker from 1905, incorporated Hampstead Heath while private gardens and street planting produced lush green effects.

255 Sir Raymond Unwin's mature domestic style at Hampstead Garden Suburb.

It was intended to cater for a mixture of social classes. Unwin had started out as an Arts and Crafts architect and his buildings at Hampstead Garden Suburb had a cottage-like character recalling Voysey's ground-hugging work. The LCC, turning to suburban cottage estates after the turn of the century, drew heavily on Unwin's example. Private builders continued to create dense, terraced suburbs but most houses were of two storeys only. By 1914 outer London was moving towards the green tapestry dotted with detached or semi-detached houses which still lives on as the ideal of most Londoners.

The Architecture of Private Wealth

The rich still wanted houses in central London and they could afford them. It was the middle classes who moved to the suburbs. As clients, the rich looked for the same standards as they had enjoyed in the eighteenth century but growing numbers of *nouveaux riches* from the business and legal worlds often had different values and employed architects who were more prepared to serve their tastes or the lack of them. As before, these rich owners usually maintained country estates and they would often employ the same architect in *urbe* as well as *rure*. Sometimes the architect was not capable of the versatility that was required, while the client was not capable of noticing the difference.

The most distinguished houses were to be found in the St James area, which had grown up round St James's Palace ever since Henry VIII had built it for his own residence in the 1530s. In 1825–7 John Nash built Clarence House for the Duke of Clarence and Benjamin Dean Wyatt remodelled Londonderry House (c. 1765) in Park Lane (1825–8) (demolished). It had a huge, top-lit, gilded Corinthian picture gallery in the Louis-Quatorze style which Wyatt is said to have introduced to London, with his favourite engaged columns. This was a heavy composition and a Louis-Quinze treatment would surely have have been a better choice. In 1825–7 Benjamin Dean Wyatt built Lancaster House for the Duke of York. This is a classic example of a plain, Palladian exterior in Bath stone, though with three two-storey porticoes and an ornate interior. Outstanding was the wide Classical entrance hall with twin staircases rising to a first-floor landing with Corinthian colonnades. There were numerous, mainly French, influences, including elements of Wyatt's ornate Louis-Quatorze style, and the overall effect was one of grandiose opulence which foreshadowed the Second Empire style and marked a departure from strict Classicism, perhaps inspired by Carlton House and court preferences under George IV. The Corinthian columns ran riot here. However, other architects, including Charles Barry, worked on this house until the 1840s, enhancing the opulence in some cases.[107] Benjamin Dean Wyatt went on to work on the Duke of Wellington's Apsley House, an externally modest home which Robert Adam had built in 1771–8 for Baron Apsley. Wyatt added a Corinthian portico and an extension and covered the brick walls with Bath stone, in 1828–9. His interior decoration had much of his Louis-Quatorze, while retaining two of Adam's rooms.[108]

Nouveau riche influence started to come on the scene after about 1850. J. Mordaunt Crook judges that the great phase of building for *nouveaux riches* lasted from the 1870s to the 1920s, while large fortunes were being made from finance.[109] These people lived mainly in Piccadilly, Park Lane, Grosvenor Square, Kensington Palace Gardens and St James's Square.[110] The Grosvenor Estate, which owned huge areas of land to the east of Park Lane, had a policy of locating big family houses there and the *nouveaux riches* could then compete with the aristocracy for these prime sites. Mordaunt Crook detects a *nouveau riche* style in the Edwardian period and calls it 'a type of Anglo-American Beaux-Arts'.[111] A vulgarity competition would be hard to judge but Baron Albert Grant's towering Kensington House, designed in a French style by James Knowles of Clapham (a district not noted for distinguished architects) and completed in 1875, would have been a strong contender had it not been demolished for its materials in 1881 owing to the owner's chronic financial problems.[112] Sir Matthew Digby Wyatt built Alford House (demolished), Ennismore Gardens, in 1871. This was a solid, rectangular, decorated design with a mansard roof and a French character.[113] It showed no sign of the revolution which Philip Webb would generate in the next few years. Nor did Brooke House, Park Lane, built in 1870 by T. H. Wyatt. This was a pretentious, eclectic building, with four storeys and dormers and an ugly projecting cornice under the roof.[114] Aldford House (1897) (demolished), Park Lane, was built by Eustace Balfour and Thackeray Turner for Sir Alfred Beit, the South African diamond millionaire. It was eclectic but with a hint of Jacobean.

The arrival of new wealth had affected house architecture over a wide range by the end of the century. Mordaunt Crook has selected some of the most tasteless and indeed styleless houses ever to be built in London, including 5 Hamilton Place, built in 1879–91 by W. R. Rogers for the gambler and racegoer Leopold de Rothschild.[115] Its style is difficult to classify; Italianate/Rococo might be one approach but given the amount of overhanging carving, 'dripping in wealth' might do it more justice. In 1895 T. H. Smith and Charles E. Sayer built an overblown eclectic mansion for Barney Barnato, the diamond speculator and fraudster at 45 Park Lane (demolished). Viscount Windsor's 54 Mount Street (1896–9) by Fairfax B. Wade, was an inflated building, far too big for its Queen Anne style. E. M. Barry's Temple Gardens, an extension of the Temple towards the Thames in 1878–9, pushed the opulent, Loire-chateau style to its very limits. This was in Portland stone with plenty of carving and must have cost a mint of money. Designed as chambers for lawyers, it had much of a luxury hotel about it. The backs of houses on Park Street backing on to Park Lane epitomised this process. They were a motley collection of random extensions and glazing.[116]

★   ★   ★

256 Temple Gardens, an extension of the Inner Temple. The opulent, French style seems completely out of place here. Lawyers normally try to look poor.

257 Pentonville Prison from the air (1972), showing the Panopticon plan, with the cleared site of the Caledonian Market in the middle of the picture. The author did not dare photograph the prison at a time of great tension.

Prisons

The demand for new prisons rocketed in the mid-nineteenth century as the City prisons were closed. Pentonville Prison was built on the Panopticon principle in 1840–42 by Major Jebb, the first Surveyor General of Prisons, within a big outer wall. It was the most admired prison of its time and expressed the ordered, mechanical life of the prisoner which was favoured in its day.[117] The five radiating wings looked logical but the fortress-like entrance block was threatening. Holloway Prison,

Parkhurst Road (1849–52) (demolished), by J. B. Bunning, the City's architect, was a stone and brick castle from the outside but the cell blocks followed the Panopticon model and used the metal interior framing developed by Bunning at the Coal Exchange. Its tall ventilation tower was inspired by Warwick Castle. Bunning followed Jebb's separate system, which kept many of the prisoners in isolation for most of the day and night. Wormwood Scrubs (1874–90) abandoned the radiating wings of the Panopticon in favour of four parallel blocks designed to ensure lighting and ventilation for every cell.

The big exterior walls hid the reality of the prison from most Londoners. Architects designed entrances which implied security with a degree of the Picturesque. Cell blocks used metal frames and glazed roofs. The latest ventilation techniques were essential and the prisoners must have been very cold in winter. Architects who built prisons, including the governors themselves, were a select group and 'the battle of the styles' certainly did not apply to them.

Markets

Most London markets were roofed, or re-roofed, in the nineteenth century. This brought in the engineer or the architect who could handle iron supports and glazing. However, the results were less striking than the railway termini and such markets as Leadenhall and Smithfield will not figure here. There is one market, however, unforgettable for those who visit what is left of it, which deserves attention. This is the Metropolitan Cattle Market (Caledonian Market) on the Caledonian Road, or 'Cally' as they call the area, just a step away from the site of Katie Johnson's house in *The Ladykillers*. J. B. Bunning built this huge, square, livestock market, close to Pentonville prison, in 1850–55. This was the City of London keeping animals well away, as well as felons. The market was overlooked by a tall, central tower in a top-heavy Italianate style, designed to tell the time throughout the market and to act as an outlook point for the movement of livestock through the surrounding streets and through a series of pens, weighbridges and check buildings. Its broad base housed bank offices and a telegraph house. Bunning also designed four almost identical public houses sited at each corner of the market, designated for various types of drover, market worker and buyer, according to the specialism of each quarter of the market area. The pubs were of the tower type and their style is a spartan, symmetrical Italianate, impressive and reassuring.[118] The market is now a pleasant park, but there is something eerie about this area, close to Jebb's Pentonville Prison and not far from Bunning's Holloway.

258   The Clock Tower at the former Caledonian Market (Metropolitan Cattle Market). The threatening sky emerged mysteriously when this picture was developed.

We can be confident that the latest techniques were used for handling both thieves and sheep.

Bunning also rebuilt the Billingsgate fish market in 1850–52 and Sir Horace Jones roofed Smithfield meat market in 1851–66. Dead fish and meat were clearly no threat to the City.

Public Houses

Architects were involved in the construction of even the most ordinary buildings. The inn or public house was one of these. Early in the nineteenth century most pubs were small places which merged with the houses on either side. Their style, if they had been designed for their purpose, was standard residential Classical but some were converted from existing houses. After the Beer Act of 1830 brewers became more competitive and the comfort and style of their drinking premises were seen as important to their patronage. The building of more ornate pubs accelerated in the 1850s and the style was usually Ital-

259 The Caledonian Market in 1928. Three tower pubs stand at the corners and two large hotels and a chapel stand on the nearest side.

ianate.[119] The result was often grotesque, with much use of manufactured components and prefabricated brick and stone from the builders' yards. One result was the 'gin palace', a luxurious hostelry which owed its name to the fact that the working-class establishments encouraged by the Act were not allowed to serve spirits.[120] In theory, the gin palace attracted a better class of customer

and many of these places looked good from the moment the stroller sighted the huge, tapering, glass lantern hanging over the entrance. These lanterns have lived on and are so frequently used in pub restorations that few people notice them.

In the middle of the century the larger brewers started to employ their own architects, for whom the interiors alone created plenty of work. The distinct London phenomenon of the 'tower pub' emerged. The example may have been set by Thomas Cubitt, who sometimes liked to mark the corners of his streets by Classical buildings

260 (*above*) 'The Gin Palace', Market Road, Caledonian Market. The tower pub in its pure form.

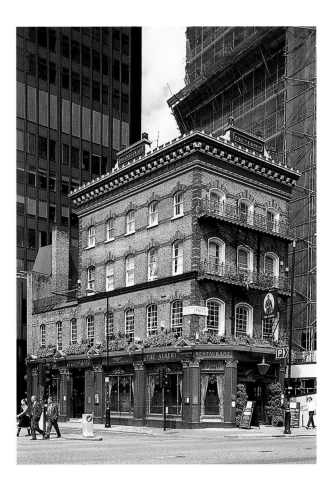

261 (*left*) The Albert, Victoria Street. Dating from the 1850s, The Albert is a short walk from Petty France and may have attracted civil servants. It had a restaurant on the first floor. The style is mildly Italianate. It is a tower pub rather than a palazzo but the cornice would have been admired in Renaissance Florence.

on a square plan, rising to between three and five storeys, with a heavy cornice or eaves. The Hudson Mansion, Albert Gate, is an early and striking example dating from 1845.[121] The brewers soon began to build similar structures, preferably on street corners where they always preferred to site their pubs, and they became so common that they could be set in street frontages where necessary. The earliest tower pubs were in the expanding areas of the West End where Cubitt and others were creating their stuccoed world of Classicism but they soon spread across inner and suburban London, switching to London yellow brick as soon as they moved out of the stucco zone.

The Gloucester Arms (c. 1852), Gloucester Terrace, Paddington, was in central 'stuccoland'. It had only three storeys but this was normal in the west. The Albert, 52 Victoria Street, rebuilt in 1862 as a tower pub, was designed by J. Carter Woods, an experienced architect. Its distinguished design included a palazzo-type cornice and wrought-iron balconies. As the Victoria Street area was being developed with brick, not stucco, the Albert had conforming, best-quality twin-coloured brickwork. In a carefully designed tower pub, rich and poor could equally be catered for as long as they were kept separate.[122] Osbert Lancaster identified a variant pub style which he called the 'South Kensington Italianate'. This could be used for tower pubs or for smaller examples. It was generally three storeys tall, in stucco. It had a parapet or balustrade at roof level and a large lantern over the door.[123]

Pub interiors were ornate and fairly dark, with a lot of dark, polished wood. Decorated glass and mirrors were used in profusion from mid-century. In the larger pubs booths were common, partly to allow different social classes to use the same pub in confidence. Many pubs had shuttered bars for the same reason. Embossed wallpapers were developed in the 1870s.[124] By the end of the century ornate pub interiors, with heavily decorated exteriors, were very common. This trend reached its peak in the 1890s when there was a boom in building pubs but the subsequent slump of 1899 hit private owners especially hard.[125] These ornate pubs became the model of the London pub from the 1960s when a wave of restorations set in.

262 (*above left*)   The Red Lion, Soho. A typical tower pub, dating from the middle of the nineteenth century, when many new pubs resembled houses on new estates by Cubitt and others.

263 (*above right*)   The Ship, Hart Street, a City pub designed by M. Caritas in a Neo-Jacobean style in 1887.

Theatres

The building of theatres and music halls followed a course similar to the pubs except that they did not usually secure corner sites. Most of today's forty or so London theatres were built in the nineteenth century and most date from after 1880 when the fire hazard was at last contained. They were cramped, even pokey places, with ornate decoration making up for their many limitations. They were, however, usually the work of competent, specialist architects and were logical and coherent.[126] Frank Matcham, who was active throughout the country from 1882 to 1931, worked on twenty-four theatres in London.[127] Normally built on narrow sites, their frontages grew increasingly ornate. They were

usually Classical in style, with E. M. Barry's rebuilt Royal Opera House, Covent Garden (1858), reaching the peak of grandeur. Eclectic designs grew more common after 1880. Victor Glasstone sees the years 1837–1914 as one of the 'summits of achievement' in the history of theatre design.[128]

At the end of the nineteenth century there was heavy investment in theatres, as in pubs. Thomas Collcutt's Palace Theatre, Cambridge Circus, completed in 1890, was the biggest of its day, being originally planned as a D'Oyly Carte opera house. For all this, its circulation spaces are horribly cramped even by London standards. Its towering, eclectic elevations and turrets, built of red brick with faience inserts, with much of Collcutt's favourite Moorish detail, and filling every inch of the site, look like a giant bordello. Much better theatres were already being built in New York at this time.[129]

★   ★   ★

154

CONCLUSION

In 1914 no end was in sight for the great proliferation of styles which had begun around 1830. The Gothic had declined after 1870, except in the building of churches. There were signs of the emergence of a Modern style, often using 'industrial' materials, but it was not clearly defined and was used only for certain types of building. There was an interest in national styles, of which there were two main examples. One was based on rural and pre-industrial traditions and the other was an imperial style which drew on the Palladian, the Baroque and exotic symbols from the colonies. Architects were beginning to receive a full training. Then came the war, ending for ever the architectural festival of Victoria's reign.

264   The main entrance to the Hoover Building at Perivale. The detail draws on the American 'Miami style'.

5 The Modern Breaks Through, 1914–1939

The First World War was the biggest turning point in London architecture since the fire at the Palace of Westminster in 1834. Function began to play a bigger role in design and the Victorian styles soon began to look artificial, self-indulgent, out of date or just plain ugly. Decoration was greatly restrained though aesthetics could determine some of the result, as in Art Deco and Streamline Moderne. In the rapidly spreading suburbs, design followed received views of English tradition. Public housing aped the English cottage row and private housing adopted the form of the reduced villa, especially in the uniquely English semi-detached pair.[1]

THE NEW CONTEXT OF LONDON ARCHITECTURE

More large architectural practices were at work than before the war. The sheer size and number of projects for office blocks, town halls, power stations, housing estates and flats were partly responsible. Buildings tended to become bigger, partly thanks to framed construction in steel and, increasingly, in reinforced concrete. Work could be delegated to middle-ranking architects in these firms, though this could lead to conformism and repetition. Structural engineers played a growing part as consultants or as employees in the big architectural practices. Although their contribution was generally hidden or implicit behind the architects' facades, they were often a strong influence. Sir Owen Williams was the most important of these, especially in his assumed role of 'architect-engineer' between 1929 and 1939.[2]

Styles still survived but there were fewer than before 1914 as the Modern created a new stylistic order. Available were the Classical styles (Palladian, Neo-Classical, Stripped Classical, Neo-Georgian, Lutyens Monumental); the Modern styles (Art Deco, Modern, Moderne, Streamline Moderne). There were also two approaches which were more than just styles and are better seen as design philosophies: the Modern Movement and English Traditional Domestic.

This list includes more imports from abroad than the list in Chapter 4. There was a contribution to the Modern from the Low Countries but the results were limited. The striking brick style used for large office buildings in Holland was tried in London but very little came of it. H. P. Berlage's Holland House, Bury Street (1914–16), commissioned by a Dutch shipping company, drew on pre-war Amsterdam but it was an awkward, even ugly, building. Charles Rowan House, a block of flats on Merlin Street, Islington, was a caricature of the Dutch red-brick style. De Stijl (the Dutch version of the Modern Movement) made almost no impact in London but a number of successful buildings were inspired by W. Marimus Dudok's simple, rectangular brick style. The Moderne and Streamline Moderne styles were heavily influenced by French, American and German practice. The influence of American commercial and industrial architecture could be seen throughout the City and the West End and on the Great West Road. Art Deco, which came from France in the 1920s and later in a more striking form from the US, mainly affected interiors and merged with the Moderne and the Streamline Moderne after 1930. The Modern Movement was acknowledged by its supporters as originating in Continental Europe and it produced some outstanding buildings when supported by enlightened clients. These innovations gave London architecture a strong impulse towards modernism and internationalism.

In the suburbs, rising incomes, better public transport, a wide range of electrical equipment for the home and a growing number of motor cars reduced densities. Before 1914, most new suburban housing had been in terraces but after the war even public housing stood back from the street and the rows were divided into shorter lengths. The private housing boom of the 1930s produced many houses in the semi-detached form which some villa builders had begun to use in the nineteenth century. However, this new generation of the semi-detached was more lightly built, with a move towards cottage styles. Town planning powers under the 1909 and later Acts produced looser layouts but they had little effect on the architecture. These new houses had little architectural distinction but most of them conformed to the English Traditional Domestic (cottage) style as modernised by Lutyens and Voysey and promoted in the public sector by Raymond Unwin and Barry Parker.[3] Tudor treatments with fake timbering were popular in the private sector.

THE PALLADIAN LIVES ON

The survival of the Palladian after 1918 reflected the extraordinary strength of this London tradition, by then three hundred years old. None of the Palladian architecture in this period had any great distinction but it looked clean and fairly modern, seemed to provide grandeur and was an easy external solution for blocks of offices on steel frames. It also allowed cheap steel window frames to be used *ad infinitum*. The result was 'windows in line' with a vengeance, sometimes with little reference to interior arrangements. The cladding was often in Portland stone, using thin slabs, though bricks were often used 'round the back' or away from prestige locations. In many cases the Palladian merged with the Neo-Classical, the Stripped Classical and the Neo-Georgian but there were plenty of examples where the undying Palladian strode on, perhaps benefiting from the complete demise of the Italianate.

The Palladian had a strong connection with education and especially higher education. The Ionic order was the norm here, with Greek features still a symbol of knowledge and purity. The Wellcome Building in Euston Road, built in 1931 by Septimus Warwick, is a solid, conventional Palladian building, its elevations dominated by a scholarly four-column portico with a modest, Greek, pediment. The nearby Camden Town Hall, Judd Street, by A. J. Thomas (1937), Palladian with a bit of Baroque, is an awkward building which is not rescued by its engaged porticoes. South Africa House, in Trafalgar Square, built by Sir Herbert Baker in 1935, is a Palladian building with two porticoes on a triangular site, intended to add more porticoes to Nash's Trafalgar Square scheme.

THE NEO-CLASSICAL

The Neo-Classical continued for a while on pre-war lines, fading a little in the late 1920s but contributing to

the Modern and the Moderne in the 1930s. Sir Edwin Cooper's Westminster Council House (1914–21) and Public Library (1939) on Marylebone Road, linked by a high masonry bridge, mark a clear evolution within the Neo-Classical over twenty years. Many commercial buildings in this style retained a Chicagoan flavour, with the completion of buildings on Kingsway and Aldwych encouraging continuity. The huge Bush House (1925–35) at the southern end of Kingsway, looking like a state courthouse out of a Perry Mason drama, was the work of American architects, Helmle and Corbett.[4]

Just north of Kingsway, on Southampton Row, C. W. Long built Victoria House, the head office of the Liverpool and Victoria Friendly Society, in about 1925–

35. Described on completion by Harold Clunn as a credit to London, it is a huge Neo-Classical building with Ionic columns separated by glazing with metal transoms, occupying an entire block on Selfridge's lines.[5] Its steel frame allowed Long to give this massive structure a light appearance so that it merged with its surroundings on its main street frontage and appeared to float when seen through the trees of Bloomsbury Square at the rear. Its four elevations were almost identical, following American practice. The interior, however, was a solid mass of offices, with a cramped entrance hall which would have been a disgrace in America.

Sir Herbert Baker's new Bank of England (1921–37) had the problem of surmounting the distinguished stone screen round the island site and the result was more fussy and pompous than grand. Baker had worked with Lutyens on the great New Delhi buildings so was used to building on a large scale. However, he could have done much more to retain Soane's unique interiors and a serious loss to London architecture occurred here. J. Lomax-Simpson built the Neo-Classical Unilever House, New Bridge Street, on the Embankment in 1930–31, with Sir John Burnet, Tait and Lorne. This had a tall, curving frontage with a long colonnade masking

268   The Bank of England, showing the new building by Sir Herbert Baker, 1921–37. Baker demolished, or allowed to be demolished, all Soane's banking halls and other work within the curtain wall. As the architect of South Africa House, to boot, Baker has had a poor press. However, Soane's Bank Stock Office (1793) was recreated in 1988 as part of the Bank's new museum. Meanwhile, Baker's slightly sinister elevations and roof no longer look out of place in the Post-Modern and Neo-Modern City.

the upper floors. The stone-clad Cumberland Hotel of 1933 at Marble Arch, by F. J. Wills, was also Neo-Classical.

The biggest piece of Neo-Classicism in London is also the most mysterious. This is Freemasons' Hall (1927–33) in Great Queen Street. Designed by Ashley and Newman, it is like a closed-up Bush House. It is dominated by an exuberant columnar structure, like the Port of London Authority, with Neo-Classical features on its main frontage. Anyone suspicious of Freemasonry would have their fears confirmed by this building.

In the 1920s many motor garages were built on semiclassical lines with a triangular pediment hiding the pitched, glazed roof over the work area. Macy's Garage

(1926), Balderton Street, by Wimperis and Simpson, was one of the more distinguished, together with the Bluebird Garage (1924), in the King's Road.[6] The classical treatment was probably derived from petrol stations in the US and may have reflected the conservatism of the car-buying classes and of the motor manufacturers.

Mewès and Davis, departing from their usual French style, looked to the Italian Renaissance when they built the National Westminster Bank at 51–2 Threadneedle Street in 1920–31 and 1936. The dominating frontage was based on Peruzzi's Palazzo Massimi (1535) in Rome, with overall rustication and a projecting cornice.[7] Although very different from most Neo-Classical office blocks of the time, this one showed how much scope the style still offered when tackled by creative architects.

STRIPPED CLASSICAL

Stripped Classical was more the product of changing building techniques than of artistic evolution. It had been foreshadowed before the war, for instance in Burnet's Kodak House. After the war it was much used

269 The Masonic Hall would not be out of place on Kingsway, if it had more windows.

door, was designed by Bernard George in 1933. It too was Stripped Classical but with Moderne interior fittings.

To present Lutyens as a distinct architectural style is a deliberate tribute to England's new Wren. He was a national artistic figure of similar stature to Edward Elgar, a master of his craft who represented the finest qualities of the nation. Both men received the rare award of the Order of Merit. Lutyens's funeral in 1944 was in Westminster Abbey and his ashes were placed in the crypt of St Paul's, where Wren was buried. Lutyens had developed two impressive styles before 1914, a vernacular style for small houses which had much in common with Shaw and Voysey and a highly personal Neo-Georgian architecture which he sometimes called 'Wrenaissance' and often used in London, for instance at the *Country Life* offices (1904), 2–10 Tavistock Street, where he drew on Wren's Hampton Court. After 1918 he developed his own Neo-Classical style which I have termed Lutyens Monumental, in preference to 'Lutyensian Classic' and 'Elemental' as coined by one of his biographers.[9] After the war he was much sought after for monumental work. This was as much the result of the commissions offered to him as of the natural development of his art and some critics have detected a degree of artificiality in his post-1918 work.

Above all, he made no concessions to Modernism. He became the consultant for a number of business firms, including the Midland Bank, and for the Grosvenor

for public buildings and commercial premises. Alastair Service believes that it represents a reaction against some of the overblown architecture of the Edwardian period but it was also much cheaper and conformed to the growing use of steel frames and concrete rendering.[8] The common use of commercial frontages combining glazing panels and steel transoms, separated by tall columns or piers, could produce a Stripped Classical effect even when one was not intended. It often merged with the Modern and the Moderne, as for instance at Barker's department store in Kensington High Street, remodelled by Bernard George in 1937–8. The metal-framed glazing recalled pre-1914 trends while the two streamlined frontage towers with the zigzag cornices might have been called Art Deco were we not already firmly in the era of the Streamline Moderne. Derry and Toms, next

270 Barker's Department Store, Kensington High Street, completed in 1938 by Bernard George. Some architects believe that Albert Speer selected it for his London headquarters.

271 The Midland Bank headquarters, by Edwin Lutyens.

but it defies standard classifications.[13] It stands for City, Empire, the Renaissance and Rome, with an overall spirit of English Baroque. Lutyens provided generous circulation spaces, unusual in an English office block of the day, including a circular atrium in a Roman style. The second of the buildings was the Midland Bank headquarters (1924–39), Poultry. Its extensive rustication and many small windows made it look like a fortress or strongbox. English Baroque springs to mind as an inspiration, with Vanbrugh's ghost flitting about the facade.

Lutyens soon became a master of effects, not unlike Hawksmoor. He has been criticised for his move from art to business but he created some influential treatments of large office blocks. Modern architects dismissed him too easily after 1945, for he was the great English formgiver of the twentieth century. Maxwell Fry used to relate that when Le Corbusier's Chandigarh team visited New Delhi, the great French architect said of Lutyens's work there: 'Ça, c'est quelque chose!' Few modern architects ever received such praise from the leader of the Modern Movement.

NEO-GEORGIAN

One of the most widespread styles was the Neo-Georgian, though it often merged with the London version of the Modern. In inner London, many municipal flats were built in this style and it was standard for General Post Office (GPO) telephone exchanges. Banks, office blocks and hotels often used it, some of which were very large. John Gloag complained that they distorted the proportions beyond what the Georgian could bear and used the terms 'Gigantic Georgian' and 'Bankers' Classic' to describe the results.[14] The cartoonist, Osbert Lancaster coined the term 'Bankers' Georgian'. This style was often influenced by Lutyens who did so much work that even his own office buildings sometimes sank into routine Georgian, like his neo-Georgian Young Women's Christian Association (YWCA) Hostel at 16 Great Russell Street (1930–32). Here, however, a tapering of the upper part of the building via smaller windows and a steeply pitched roof, responded to the great ceiling height of the lower two floors.

ART DECO

So far we have been looking at the survival of the Classical spirit after 1914. This was an English tradition. The parallel rise of Modernism came mainly from abroad.

Estate. Roderick Gradidge concludes that he did so in order to secure an adequate income for his family in the uncertain post-war climate. He moved from the often rough texture of his pre-war buildings to the smooth, white surfaces of official, grandiose buildings in Portland stone but in many cases he designed only the exterior, while the interior – and the steel frame where there was one – were entrusted to others chosen by the client.[10] His office became highly productive; between 1919 and 1930 it completed some 180 schemes, including his many war memorials but excluding his continuing triumphant work on government buildings in New Delhi. One of his biographers, Christopher Hussey, compares him with Wren in terms of output and maintains that he, like Wren, took responsibility for even the smallest details.[11]

His first major commission in the new style was the Cenotaph (1919–20) in Whitehall, a monument to those killed in the First World War. Although an abstract design, it was Greek in inspiration. From this point on, Lutyens often drew on Classical inspiration and Classical features. There was also an imperial character in his work which prolonged Sir Aston Webb's London and was reinforced by his experiences in New Delhi. Indeed, his intimate correspondence suggests that Lutyens was a committed imperialist of the 'white man's burden' type.[12] Two early buildings set the pattern. He built Britannic House (1921–5), in Finsbury Circus, for the Anglo-Persian Oil Company. Its concave frontage, drawing on the English crescent tradition, was an utterly individual design. Pevsner relates it to 'North Italian Mannerism'

France continued to make a contribution in luxury design. Art Deco sprang from the world of the Paris rich in the early 1920s. It was a response to the rigours of the First World War and a celebration of French victory. Its first big triumph was at the Exposition Internationale des Arts Décoratifs in Paris in 1925. In London it was applied mainly to the interiors of hotels and restaurants, to add the ultimate touch of luxury. Factories, cinemas and garages were also affected in the 1920s. The Jazz Age foyer (1927) at the Park Lane Hotel in Piccadilly was designed by Kenneth Anns and Henry Tanner.[15] This was the first London hotel in which every bedroom had its own private bathroom.[16] The huge Regal cinema at Marble Arch, built in 1929 by Clifford Aish, had an imposing Classical-Modern exterior in Portland stone and an ornate Roman-inspired interior by Charles Muggeridge.[17] In 1929 Oliver Bernard, Britain's greatest architectural decorator, designed the new interiors of the Strand Palace Hotel. Claridge's was equipped with new Art Deco public areas by Basil Ionides and Oswald Milne in the late 1920s.[18]

Exterior Art Deco was generally applied rather than integral. One of the best examples was Palladium House (originally Ideal House), Argyll Street, designed by Raymond Hood and Gordon Jeeves in 1928. Hood was the noted New York skyscraper architect who had won the *Chicago Tribune* tower competition with a fantasy Gothic cathedral termination in 1922–3, while Jeeves was a London architect who probably ran the office. The building was clad in polished black granite, with a cornice and upper-floor treatment of oriental character, including decoration in enamel on bronze by the Birmingham Guild of Handicraft.[19] This design had much of the Babylonian and Egyptian craze which had a good run in the US in the late 1920s.

London acquired a suite of striking, modernistic factories in the 1920s and 1930s. Many were branches of American companies and were built principally in the west and north of London where they had good access to high-speed roads and the newly extended Underground lines. The first was the Wrigley chewing gum factory in north Wembley, opened in 1927. In the 1920s these factories were mainly built in a hesitant Art Deco but they merged with the Moderne and the Streamline Moderne in the 1930s. The best were designed by Wallis, Gilbert and Partners, whose first was the Firestone factory (demolished) in Brentford, built in 1929 for the American motor tyre company.[20] It was a long, low building of two floors hugging a sloping site. The white elevations contrasted with the dark interiors showing through the metallic fenestration. Its inspiration was loosely Egyptian. Pyrene (1930), also in Brentford, was a

272   The Hoover Building at Perivale (1931–5).

glass factory. The Cox's Building in Watford (1937), by Fuller, Hall and Foulsham, was classified by Bayer as Moderne.[21] Sir Banister F. Fletcher's Gillette factory (1936) had a long frontage on two floors. It was built of brick with expanses of metal glazing and a tall tower topped by a giant clock. The plan and style were Palladian but there is no sign that Fletcher's inspiration sprang from his noted work as an architectural historian. One of the best was the Streamline Moderne Hoover factory in Perivale (1932–7), by Wallis, Gilbert and Partners. Many of these factories had gigantic entrances decorated in shiny or metallic primary colours. The detailing often had an Egyptian tinge, as at the Arcadia Works, the Carreras cigarette factory in Camden Town (1926). Their facades, normally painted white, were among the first in Britain to be floodlit.[22] Joseph Emberton's long, horizontal facade for the Olympia Exhibition Hall, Hammersmith Road (1930), an impressive exercise in Streamline Moderne, brought some of this factory style to fashionable London. Many of these buildings were encouraged by the Board of Trade's Council for Art and Industry, which fostered modern design.

Battersea Power Station (1930–34, 1945–53) makes an interesting comparison with these American-influenced buildings. It was the work of an architect, Sir Giles Gilbert Scott, who had made his name as a designer of big interior spaces with his Liverpool Cathedral (1903–), and an engineer, James Halliday. The whole concept reflected the engineering realities of building two huge, parallel turbine halls in succession as demand for electricity built up. The effect was *sui generis* with a Baby-

Ionian tinge at the corners but as the largest brick building in Europe it may owe something to Dudok as well as to American industrial building. Scott built Bankside power station just after the Second World War on similar lines.[23] Both were built close to their water supply in the Thames and Scott was clearly aiming to create sweeping riverscapes in the heart of London. Like the new factories to the west, Scott's power stations were works of massive horizontality with heavily stressed vertical features verging on the Expressionistic.

MODERN

With new types of building generating new forms and design treatments, more general tendencies are hard to perceive. One strand stood out, however, which I shall refer to here as the Modern. Appropriately, the RIBA commissioned an excellent example of the Modern for its headquarters on Nash's majestic Portland Place in 1932–4. The architect was Grey Wornum, the designer of municipal flats. Its Portland stone facing and rectangular form established its Modern credentials but Wornum's varied fenestration and asymmetrical balcony treatment stayed well clear of the Palladian trap. The interior was fitted out with the finest materials and the staircase core had a different design at every level, with an open plan which led freely into the rest of the building. This was building of the highest quality in a clear London tradition.

Some of the best examples of London's Modern arose with architects who tried to show creativity when handling big commercial contracts. An outstanding example was Sir John Burnet, the Paris-trained Glasgow architect discussed in Chapter 4.[24] Burnet was creative, reliable and versatile. He had set up a London office under the care of Thomas Tait in 1905.[25] In 1910–11 he had abandoned the Baroque treatments which had once been his hallmark and after study tours in Germany, Austria and the US he turned towards the Modern. Adelaide House, on the northern approach to London Bridge, was built by Sir John Burnet and Tait in 1921–5, with engineer support. At eleven storeys high (45 metres), it could not adopt the Stripped Classical used by Burnet for Kodak House; instead he used tall panels of identical windows with decorated transoms. It was London's tallest commercial building when completed and among the first to depart from the Classical spirit. The cornice has a touch of the neo-Egyptian and Pevsner detects the possible influence of Frank Lloyd Wright.[26] However, the grouping of the windows and the medallions in the transoms recall Otto Wagner.

In 1929–33 Sir John Burnet, Tait and Lorne built the Royal Masonic Hospital at Ravenscourt Park. This is a simple, monumental building in red brick, probably inspired by Dudok. However, the huge, curved balconies at the end of the wings, used by patients in warm weather, were probably influenced by the work of Erich Mendelsohn in 1920s Germany. This was Burnet's last building before retirement and the design was probably in other hands. The giant Mount Royal Hotel, Oxford Street, was built in 1932–3 by Sir John Burnet, Tait and Partners.[27] Jones and Woodward detect Beaux-Arts planning (including lightwells), Dutch elevation styling and the influence of Erich Mendelsohn here, though the general effect was Streamline Moderne.[28]

Dudok's influence continued into the 1930s. Hornsey Town Hall (1934–5), at The Broadway, Crouch End, by R. H. Uren, Slater and Mobberley, was inspired by Dudok's Hilversum Town Hall of 1928–30. It is a rectangular, brick composition with a simple, striking tower, rather like a firemen's practice tower.[29] Greenwich Town Hall (1939), by E. C. Culpin and Bowers, is even more impressive, with a simple, dominating 'Outlook Tower' unlike any previously built in London. Hilversum Town Hall was again the inspiration here.

One of London's most admired Modern architects was Charles Holden, the senior member of Adams, Holden, and Pearson. Holden's commissions for the Law Society and the British Medical Association before the

274 (*facing page*)   The Royal Institute of British Architects, Portland Place, by George Grey Wornum, 1932–4. A 'British Modern' is apparently sought here, though there may be some Swedish influence.

273 (*below*)   Adelaide House. Again, the effect could be called 'British Modern'.

275 (*above*) The tower of the former Greenwich Town Hall. That the council agreed to pay for this 'outlook tower' reflects the prestige that Modern architecture, and foreign example enjoyed in the later 1930s.

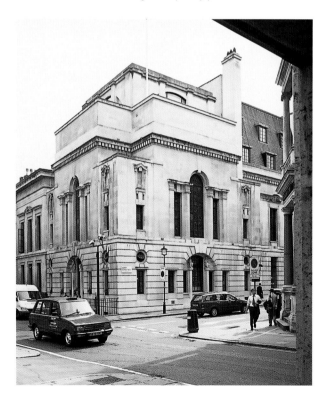

276 (*left*) Extension of the Law Society building by Charles Holden, 1902. This was the architect's first major exercise in Stripped Classical.

war had looked forward to the Modern while retaining a grip on the Neo-Classical. Holden was also fascinated by vertical clustering as he had shown early in his Free Style Belgrave Hospital for Children, Clapham Road (1900–3). He secured a number of commissions for new Underground stations in the 1920s and 1930s, most of which used vertical symbols reflecting the shafts underneath. He normally chose between glazed drums and Portland stone-clad monoliths. His stations favoured geometrical forms, especially rectangles and circles, recalling Boullée and the French Neo-Classicists of the late eighteenth century, but probably drawing more directly on Swedish and Dutch modern architecture by such as Asplund and Dudok. The first station was a two-storey Portland stone structure at Clapham South (1925–6). This was Stripped Classical with a hint of Egyptian, with two columns topped by capitals shaped like three-dimensional Underground logos and three large Underground logos on the facade. He went on to design Arnos Grove (1930–32), Sudbury Town (1931), Bounds Green (1932), Southgate (1933), Boston Manor, Morden (1932), Osterley and Park Royal.[30]

Among the biggest Modern buildings was Charles Holden's London Passenger Transport Board headquarters (1926–9) at 55 Broadway. Holden was commissioned by Frank Pick, head of the London Underground. The building had a steel frame clad in Portland stone, with a two-storey podium and setbacks above the seventh storey, culminating in a monumental tower. It looks like a creative struggle between the architect and the height regulations, with space conceded lower down the building in order to achieve a height of about fifty-three metres. The rows of windows recall some of the Palladian offices of the time but Holden was now London's monolith specialist and the windows went with the concept. Holden's characteristic cruciform plan, used for the first time in an office building, worked well even on this cramped site. Still a friend of the leading artists of the day, Holden commissioned external sculpture from Jacob Epstein, Henry Moore and Eric Gill. The inset pieces of underground symbolism played a useful part in the building but some of Epstein's prominent compositions were not obviously related to mass transport. The juvenile penis in his 'Day' had to be smoothed down, recalling the adjustments required by the British Medical Association to Epstein's 'obscene' sculptures at their Holden-designed headquarters in 1908.

277 Southgate Underground station, by Charles Holden (1933). The author's tendency to detect arcane symbolism in Holden's work reaches its peak at Southgate where he sees a Tibetan prayer wheel on the roof of the station. His Modernist friends tell him that this is total nonsense.

278 Chiswick Park Underground station, in the style of Charles Holden.

279 'Day', by Jacob Epstein at 55 Broadway. Epstein was an utter liability when working for public buildings.

280 Holden's Senate House. They kept Epstein away from this one.

Holden went on to his greatest monolith success at the Senate House of the University of London (1932–7). The Senate House was the biggest of a group of university buildings planned from 1928 by a consultant, H. V. Lanchester.[31] This urban campus, and the Senate House above all, were intended to provide a focus for a widely dispersed university. The idea of a tall tower was present right from 1928, inspired in part no doubt by the towers of big American campuses. German inspiration – Taut's 'Stadtkrone' or Lang's 'Metropolis' – does not seem to have played a part.[32]

Holden was selected as architect in 1931. He quickly prepared an axial plan for the entire Bloomsbury campus but his responsibility was soon reduced to the Senate House alone.[33] Urged by the client to express modernity, he designed simple elevations with Portland stone

cladding. Richard Simpson suggests that he strove to create the lasting qualities of modernism rather than to emulate the latest fashions in America and on the Continent.[34] Simpson also reveals the constant involvement of Frank Pick, a founder of the Design Industries Association in 1915, even in detailed aspects of the design. The tapering, 64-metre tower was impressive in mass and dimensions but the simple elevations probably reflected Holden's underlying interest in monoliths.[35] His plans for sculpture by his friend Epstein and other modernists were ignored by the university, perhaps remembering the controversies at the BMA and 55 Broadway.[36] The reception areas and the grandiose staircase to the main lecture theatres were transitional between Art Deco and Moderne, with a Greek tinge suggestive of knowledge.

Broadcasting House (1930–32), by G. Val Myers, was an enhanced version of the Holden style.[37] It was loaded with more modernistic symbolism than any other building of its time in London. Myers used the curve of Nash's Portland Place to create a great liner sailing south towards Oxford Circus. Masts and aerials, with a symbolic clock and statue of Prospero and Ariel, and two tiers of railings gave an effect of great strength and modernity. Some of the most distinguished Modern architects of the day, including Modern Movement representatives, contributed to the interior. Predictably, the whole structure was clad in Portland stone but it was camouflaged in battleship grey during the war.

The *Daily Telegraph* Building (1928) in Fleet Street is best classified as a Modern building, though it had much in common with Long's Neo-Classical. The architects were Elcock and Sutcliffe, with Tait (Burnet's associate). The fenestration was divided by huge, modernistic columns and set within a rectangular masonry frame. There was a set-back attic level. Jones and Woodward see it as one of London's rare examples of Jazz Modern, especially in the entrance hall, but it is really not quite so focused.[38]

A big Modern building using a curved facade but with a costly bronze curtain wall rather than stone cladding was W. Crabtree's Peter Jones department store at Sloane Square. Dating from 1936–8, it was inspired by Eric Mendelsohn's Schocken store in Stuttgart but quickly qualified as a classic London building, pointing

281 (*top*) The School of Hygiene and Tropical Medicine, 1926–8, by Morely Horder and Vernon Rees. This anticipated Holden's Senate House.

282 (*left*) The *Daily Telegraph* headquarters, Fleet Street, 1928. Looks like Kingsway, again.

283 (*facing page*) No. 55 Broadway, by Charles Holden.

284 The Peter Jones department store, 1936–8, by W. Crabtree. One half expects one of those long Berlin double-deckers to roll past. Peter Jones looks forward to the elegant 1940s Modernism that the war denied us.

continued after the war. Instead, architects played safe with brick construction in subdued hues, rectangular windows in portrait mode and metal window frames.

Dolphin Square (1937), designed by Gordon Jeeves, was a massive example. To put 1236 flats on a 3.1 hectare site by the Thames – once Thomas Cubitt's builder's yard – was an achievement in density which surpassed any local authority scheme. The flats are arranged in a rectangle round a central area with facilities, retaining some of the ideal of the middle-class service flat of the 1920s to which Raymond Unwin had contributed. Most of the elevations are tedious Neo-Georgian, with row upon row of identical windows. The upper floor is decorated with horizontal bands of light-coloured brick, perhaps following Dutch examples, but in this case probably reflecting Hood's influence on Jeeves at Ideal House. Dense car parking surrounds the blocks and there is an underground car park. There is easy road access to Westminster along the Thames, which may account for the location of this huge but surprisingly restrained scheme.

The Modern reached its peak in the tall blocks of flats for the rich which sprang up in the 1930s on the fringes of the West End and in the exclusive western suburbs and here there was some building of distinction. Dorset House (1935), Gloucester Place, by T. P. Bennett with Joseph Emberton, was a striking arrangement of jettied wings with curved corners and setback upper levels. Viceroy Court (1937), a suave block of brick flats in Prince Albert Road, was by Marshall and Tweedy. One of a number of luxury blocks in the locality, its semicircular window bays were elegantly Moderne. Flats at 59–63 Princes Gate, SW7, by Adie, Button and Partners, had balconies, wraparound metal windows and tapered upper floors reminiscent of New York. (Sir) Owen Williams's Dorchester Hotel (1929–30) on Park Lane, though completed with alterations by a more conventional architect, W. Curtis Green, spread its narrow wings across an entire block, providing light and air across the whole interior.[39] R. Atkinson's The White House (1936), a nine-storey block of service flats on

the way to a civilised modernity of the future. It also represented the smooth London prosperity of the 1930s, the mirror image of the depressed regions further north.

In the 1930s the Modern was often used for the many blocks of private flats. It sometimes resembled the Neo-Georgian of public sector flats. Builders of flats often tried to create an attractive style which combined tradition, style, health and an impression of modernity linked to efficiency. Experiments, fashion (which might go out of date), quirkiness, excessive foreign influence, genius and similarity to pre-1914 mansion flats were not required. If London, like Paris, had had a popular tradition of flat design before 1914 that tradition might have

285 (*facing page top left*) Dolphin Square flats.

286 (*facing page top right*) The White House, built as service flats by R. Atkinson in 1938. It resembles the original Dorchester Hotel design of the engineer-architect, Sir Owen Williams. Tony Hancock, Britain's most famous comic actor, lived here in the 1950s.

287 (*facing page bottom*) Parliament Court, Parliament Hill, Hampstead. Modernism makes a virtue of this simple block of brick flats (c. 1935). This formula would go on from strength to strength, especially on private estates, after the war.

Albany Street, NW1, was very similar to the revolutionary Williams example.[40]

Reinforced concrete engineering now began to alter the face of London. Concrete was used in big projects with an engineering character, some of which incorporated architectural design. As in the nineteenth century, some of the engineers proved to be very good architects. Unfortunately, this could not be said of Wembley Stadium (demolished), which was built in 1921–4 for the British Empire exhibition of 1924–5. The design was by Maxwell Ayrton and John Simpson. It was a simple structure in reinforced concrete, a larger version of the Olympic stadium at White City (1908), with concrete beams supporting the terraces. The minimal roofing inside the stadium looked like an enlarged grandstand from a Victorian racecourse. The main entrance was a crude effort. Michael Hebbert has rightly drawn attention to its echoes of the British Raj, which had partly inspired the White City exhibition buildings of 1908, but it still looked like third prize in a Lego competition.[41] (Sir) Owen Williams was the consulting engineer but in a rushed job he did little more than convert Ayrton's ideas into concrete.[42] The nearby Empire Pool, built by Sir Owen Williams in 1933–4, without the help of architects, achieved an impressive cantilevered span of seventy-three metres with unique hanging buttresses outside but was not recognised as architecture.

The Royal Horticultural Hall (1927–9) marked a big step forward in the British use of reinforced concrete. It was built by (Sir) John Murray Easton and Howard Robertson and drew on French methods.[43] Robertson trained at the Ecole des Beaux-Arts in 1908–12 and Easton had worked in France before the First World War. Its huge catenary-shaped arches and reinforcing purlins allowed unique, tiered daylighting along the whole building. The Royal Horticultural Hall never achieved the respect as architecture which it deserved. It is now famous as one of the BBC's 'all red' interludes (the reverse rope trick), though only gardeners would recognise it.

By the 1930s the growth of leisure produced a much greater recognition of the new places of entertainment as architecture. The new Arsenal East Stand of 1934 with its partial cantilevering, and the second stand built in 1939, both designed by Claude Ferrier, provided London with the most advanced sports stadium in Europe (the new Olympic stadium in Berlin was not roofed). The East Stand, with its Modern interior, is now a listed building.[44] Earl's Court (1937), by C. Howard Crane and Partners, made much use of reinforced concrete and at that time was the largest reinforced concrete building in Europe, with a main span of seventy-six metres.

288   The East Stand of the Arsenal Stadium at Highbury, now one of Britain's few listed sports grounds.

Private builders made the occasional foray into the Modern in the late 1930s when they built rows or groups of houses with flat roofs, rendered walls and metal window frames. Few were of architectural interest and the flat roofs tended to leak. These houses normally stood on large estates of traditional houses to provide a minority alternative for purchasers and they did not affect the planning of the estate.

★   ★   ★

MODERNE AND STREAMLINE MODERNE

The Moderne is often seen as an extension of Art Deco.[45] Its development in the 1930s was a distinct style, however, especially in its Streamline Moderne variant used for many places of entertainment. One of the earliest examples, unique in its day, was the New Victoria cinema (1930), near Victoria Station, by E. Walmsley Lewis. Its facade, divided into horizontal bands and strips, eschewed the classical styling of many new West End cinemas and was inspired by recent work in Holland and Germany, looking forward to Burnet's Mount Royal Hotel. P. Morton Shand welcomed it as an 'excellent, if somewhat Germanic facade'.[46]

Cinemas were built all over London in the 1930s, the largest being known as 'supers'. At the end of the silent era in the 1920s, a few Art Deco cinemas were still being built, such as George Coles's Carlton (1930) in Essex Road, an Egyptian fantasy.[47] In the 1930s most of the exteriors were Streamline Moderne but their interior decoration was often Art Deco or ornately historicist. A few large, 'atmospheric' cinemas (with exotic interiors and ceiling lighting simulating the night sky) were built around 1930. The Granada Cinema, Tooting, built in 1937 by Masey and Uren, had London's richest historicist interior by Theodore Komosarjevsky, in the style of a Gothic cathedral. A deep, illuminated canopy over the entrance gave protection from the rain though long queues still got wet. Lettering on the fascia of the canopy announced the films on show.

The first Odeons, an especially striking variety, were launched in 1933. There was a national design team of Harry Weedon and Cecil Clavering, later joined by George Coles, Andrew Mather and Robert Bullivant, but the best in London were built by George Coles.[48] Odeons used cream faience, curved corners, finned towers and crisp lines in Streamline Moderne compositions which normally extended to their interiors. In London they included Muswell Hill (1936), Leicester Square (1937), Woolwich (1937) and Balham (1938).[49] Many of these cinemas had striking, or tall, towers.[50] Like the towers of new London factories, they were probably inspired by American skyscrapers with a whiff of German Expressionism. Walmsley Lewis, a talented architect, had studied in Germany and France and had worked in the US. Much of his inspiration came from Germany.[51]

290 The Daimler Car Hire garage (1931), off Russell Square. A riot of Crittall windows and ramps.

Streamline Moderne public houses were built all over the country, especially as roadhouses, but London saw very little of the style. However, buildings connected with motors were obvious candidates for Streamline Moderne treatment. One example was the Daimler Car Hire Garage (1931) at Herbrand Street, by Wallis Gilbert and Partners, with its curving ramp.

The best expression of Streamline Moderne in office design was a City block, Ibex House, in The Minories, built by Fuller, Hall and Foulsham in 1935–7. The *Daily Express* Building (1929–31) in Fleet Street was shaped mainly by the engineer, (Sir) Owen Williams, with architects Ellis and Clarke handling the exterior detailing and

Robert Atkinson designing the interior. The entrance, staircase and lift hall were in lush Art Deco by Atkinson. Its concrete frame and the sparse elevations clad with glass and black Vitrolite were Streamline Moderne, however. Hotels, some of them larger than ever, continued to seek an international, modern character, with Burnet's Mount Royal Hotel already mentioned. One of the last Moderne buildings was the Imperial Airways Building (1939) by Albert Lakeman.

THE MODERN MOVEMENT

The British branch of the Modern Movement was mainly London-based.[52] It achieved far more than is generally acknowledged. In the 1920s De Stijl and the Bauhaus had little influence in Britain but after the foundation of the Congrès Internationaux d'Architecture Moderne (CIAM) in 1928 the Modern Movement

291 The BOAC (Imperial Airways) headquarters, 1939, by Albert Lakeman. One of many combinations of Moderne, Neo-Classical and symbolic that sprouted in London in the 1930s.

292 Ibex House, The Minories.

293 The former headquarters of the *Daily Express*, Fleet Street.

attracted more British architects and it was reinforced in the 1930s by architects from the Continent who settled in Britain, mainly as refugees from Fascism.[53] The Modern Movement was strongly didactic and in 1933 its leading British members set up the MARS Group. The initials stood for Modern Architectural Research Society. This was one of many national organisations set up by supporters of CIAM, which had issued the Athens Charter in 1933. The national organisations were expected to promote CIAM principles but they were also encouraged to develop examples of modern architecture appropriate to their own countries. In 1938 the MARS Group held an exhibition in London to draw

attention to its achievements and to publicise what it could do in the future.[54] This was an influential exhibition which pointed the way to much of the design and planning which would become normal after 1945.

Most Modern Movement buildings in London were residential but the roll call of high-quality designs is extremely impressive. Wells Coates, the co-ordinator of MARS, built the Isokon Flats in Lawn Road, Hampstead, in 1933. This was one of the experiments in communal middle-class living which were popular between the wars and several modern architects lived there, including Gropius.[55] This building had a smooth, white, rendered exterior but its emphatic access balconies linked it to London tenement traditions. At 10 Palace Gate, w8 (1938), Coates built a much more adventurous block of flats with direct quotations from Le Corbusier. Harding and the Tecton group built Six Pillars, Crescent Wood Road, Dulwich, in 1933–5. This was an attractive Modern Movement house built out onto pilotis (the thin, white columns favoured by Le Corbusier). Berthold Lubetkin (who had arrived from Paris in 1930) and Tecton built Highpoint One, North Hill, Highgate, in 1933–5, with engineering support from Ove Arup, followed by Highpoint Two in 1938. Highpoint One was a white, rendered block of flats of up to eight storeys with maximum privacy and sunlighting which conformed to the key features of the Modern Movement, including pilotis. Lubetkin and Goldfinger lived there for a while and other tenants were involved with modern architecture.

The Penguin Pool (1933–4), London Zoo, by Tecton, created unprecedented forms in reinforced concrete, influenced by Russian Constructivist sculpture.[56] In 1932–3 Maxwell Fry (with Elizabeth Denby) built Sassoon House, a five-storey block of flats at Belfort Road, Peckham. This was associated with the modernist Pioneer Health Centre which Sir Owen Williams built nearby, in 1933–5. This exercise in air, light and space did more with reinforced concrete than any Modern Movement building constructed in London up to that time, without ever looking like a Modern Movement building. The Finsbury Health Centre (1938–9) was designed by Lubetkin and Tecton on pure Modern Movement lines but with an efficient Beaux-Arts plan and advanced technical features. Frederick Gibberd built a block of white, balconied flats at Pullman Court, Streatham, in 1934. Fry followed it with 65 Ladbroke Grove, w11, a high-quality five-storey block of flats. Fry went on to build Sun House, 9 Frognal Way, Hampstead, in 1935 for a rich client. This echoed many buildings at the Stuttgart Weissenhof Siedlung exhibition and was built of concrete. It was the equal of the best German work of the early 1930s, which is not surprising because the RIBA required immigrant architects to form partnerships with RIBA members before they could practise. Gropius and Fry, and Mendelsohn and Chermayeff, two examples of these partnerships, built adjoining houses in Old Church Street, Chelsea, in 1936. Lubetkin, meanwhile, had built a row of four Modern Movement houses at Genesta Road, Plumstead, in 1933–4. In 1936–8 Fry and associates built the Kensal House Estate, in Ladbrove Grove. Denys Lasdun, who began as the employee of Wells Coates, built a Modern Movement house at 32 Newton Road, w2, in 1938. Again, the pilotis reveal the link with Le Corbusier but the whole house was inspired from the same source. Simpson's Department Store, Piccadilly, was built in 1935 by Joseph Emberton, by now the architect of the Blackpool Pleasure Beach, in collaboration with Felix Samuely, engineer and member of the MARS Group. It had much of the Modern Movement, with its facade similar to Le Corbusier's apartment house at the Rue Nungesser-et-Coli in Paris and to the Berlin work of Eric Mendelsohn, by then in England. Its welded steel frame by Samuely, the first in the UK, followed Samuely's structure for Mendelsohn's and Chermayeff's De La Warr Pavilion in Bexhill, in 1934. The interior design by Laszlo Moholy-Nagy also recalled the Modern Movement, as did Emberton's membership of the MARS Group.

This array of riches makes a point that is often ignored. Towards the end of the 1930s London was moving into an era of creative modernity which, without the war, would have established a completely new architectural and design world by the late 1940s. The inter-war years are often seen as an insignificant period in the history of London architecture. In fact, they were an exciting era of experiment and change. Victorian excesses were a thing of the past. Modernism was already on the scene. National tradition shaped much of what was built. Summerson summed it up in 1941 in a lecture at the Architectural Association when he said, 'Soon it will not be modern architecture any longer. It will just be architecture.'[57]

6 London in the Age of Modern Architecture, 1939–2000

From 1940 to 1951 almost nothing was built in London. There was no precedent for such a hiatus. The concentration of resources on the war explains the lack of building until 1945. Thereafter it was owing to the need to pay for war debts, which required an increase in exports, and the creation of the Welfare State. Public housing got under way but slowly. The New Towns programme (1946) provided housing for Londoners but outside London's new Green Belt. This was the first effort to reduce congestion in London by moving employment and workers and their families well outside the built-up area and it slowed down building in London itself.

THE TRIUMPH OF THE MODERN

Architects struggled on by doing maintenance and repairs.[1] Until 1946 and even 1947, many young architects were still in the Forces. When they returned, they added to the employment problem. Some tried to move into town planning and surveying. Others worked on local authority housing schemes.[2] The profession encouraged competitions to sustain enthusiasm. Politically, London architects moved to the Left. The Architectural Association School of Architecture, whose students had welcomed the Modern Movement in the 1930s, produced shoals of innovating and radical architects in the late 1940s. All the schools were crammed with students and short of staff, so new ideas spread quickly even though much teaching remained conservative.[3] The need to innovate to meet the public housing shortage between 1945 and 1954 made architects open to new building and planning techniques which appeared capable of creating a more equal society. The Modern Movement and its proposals for a completely new environment came to the fore; Le Corbusier replaced Gropius and Mies van der Rohe as the main inspiration for British modernists.

294   The bombed area round St Paul's after the Blitz.

The war produced a new debate over architecture, as in other fields. Modern architecture did not sweep all before it in the journals, with the *Architectural Review* favouring English tradition and regional methods, but a major change in opinion was clearly taking place from as early as 1940.[4] There was a general agreement, extending far beyond the architects themselves, that Britain should be rebuilt using a new architecture which would abandon the styles in favour of an efficient, aesthetic mode of design appropriate to the better world of the future.

★   ★   ★

British architects had their first big chance to reveal the new architecture when they were called to design the Festival of Britain on the South Bank in 1951. All the new buildings were temporary apart from the Festival Hall (1948–51), formally accredited to the LCC, Leslie Martin and Peter Moro, which was Britain's outstanding modern building of the early post-war years. It was the work of a large team under Robert Matthew, who had been appointed Architect to the LCC in 1948. Among the many appointments which Matthew made in much haste, the most important was Leslie Martin, whose work for the London Midland and Scottish (LMS) railway company had revealed a rare skill for linking engineering and design. Holden, no less, had already designed a stripped classical concert hall for the site with the senior LCC architect Edwin Williams, as part of his short-lived post-war plan for the South Bank, commissioned by the LCC.[5] The final brief greatly surpassed Holden's, partly because of the need to exclude noise from the adjacent railway bridge, and the 'floating' solution adopted for the auditorium, on Martin's advice, required a fresh start. Matthew and his team welcomed the chance to design a practical but prestigious building which would take account of the recent debates within the Modern Movement but the design was an amalgam of practical and aesthetic decisions which went beyond CIAM principles while drawing at times on Le Corbusier.[6] The large design and technical team recalled the group which Charles Garnier brought together to build the Paris Opéra in the 1870s. Public and profession were equally enthusiastic about the Festival Hall and it launched British modern architecture into the 1950s.[7]

THE MODERN FREE STYLE

After a Conservative government took power in 1951 restrictions on house building were reduced, first in the public sector and then, from 1954, in the private sector. Office and industrial building were freed from materials restrictions. There was now plenty of work for architects again. The older architects could still remember a time before the war when a choice of styles was available. In the mid-1950s there was only one. This was generally known as 'modern architecture'. Much of it used steel and concrete frames, simple, repetitive elevations, flat roofs, curtain walls and metal windows. There was some development into reinforced concrete in the 1960s, especially in high-rise housing and offices.

Universal town planning, confirmed by the Town and Country Planning Act of 1947, also affected architecture. All building after 1947 required planning permission under the terms of a local plan or interim arrangements. In theory, statutory planning did not include architecture but many architects had to conform to broader requirements. Working for local authorities and big developers, many awoke from their wartime dream as heroic creators of a new Britain. Housing estates, slum clearance, commercial redevelopment and roads generated layout and planning solutions which restricted the architect's creative freedom.

The conventional trappings of Modernism could clad the buildings easily enough. White, vertical, rendered or concrete surfaces were the norm, though the more expensive brick could be a cosy alternative. By the end of the 1950s, however, the new architecture had begun to pall. In the main areas of production – housing estates, factories, office blocks and schools – it was increasingly seen by the public as routine design of little distinction. It was, in fact, just a style. 'Modern Free Style' is the term I shall use henceforth.[8] Meanwhile, however, an elite of Modern architects remained true to the ideals of the Modern Movement and to the founders of the 1930s. It is their work that will dominate what follows.

HOUSING

Much of London's post-war architecture was public housing. In 1946 the LCC Valuer was made responsible for housing but his unimaginative building was criticised and the LCC Housing Division took over in 1949. The LCC built large areas of public housing, much of it in slum clearance schemes. There were many flats. Architecture and planning were brought closely together in this work. Land for new estates inside the LCC boundary was in short supply. Some 'out-county' estates, such as Debden in Essex, were built near Underground stations but these were mostly low-density cottage estates, using traditional building methods. More adventurous were the estates built on cleared land, or other available sites, which included flats. Edward D. Mills's 'Brett Manor' flats, in Brett Road, Hackney (1947–8), though built on a small site under great difficulties, made good use of their concrete frame to provide a visible and harmonious cellular structure with inset balconies and a touch of Tecton and of Goldfinger's Willow Road houses of 1937–9.[9]

The LCC was happy to put some of the bigger of these schemes out to competition and the winners, often very young architects, acquired considerable influence.

In inner London, where Sir Patrick Abercrombie's plan of 1943 had called for a density of 136 people per acre, the slab blocks recommended by Abercrombie were at first widely adopted, as at Tecton's Rosebery Avenue slabs for the Borough of Finsbury in 1946–50.[10] In 1946 Philip Powell (aged 30) and Hidalgo Moya (aged 26) won a competition for the Churchill Gardens housing estate in Pimlico, which was partially completed by 1950, with further additions until 1962. The architects had been in their final year at the Architectural Association (AA) School of Architecture at the time of the competition. Planned as the initial phase of a neighbourhood unit, this was a large area of 'mixed development' with ten-storey slab blocks, maisonettes and houses, most of them parallel or nearly parallel and oriented towards the south in the layout known in pre-war Germany as *Zeilenbau*. Carefully planned, the blocks were clean and simple. The estate was much praised at the time and continues to be so, with materials wearing well, careful maintenance and order kept throughout.[11] Many of the higher flats have sunny Thames views towards the south and the power-ful silhouette of Battersea Power Station. Churchill Gardens is Abercrombie in action and a great monument of planning history.

Another early example, the Lansbury Neighbourhood (1950–) in the East End, was partly finished in time for the Festival of Britain. The buildings were conventional but Lansbury was a convincing example of mixed development, with houses, maisonettes and flats, a pedestrian network and a popular market area. Also much admired was the Golden Lane Estate, built on a bombed area north of St Paul's by Chamberlin, Powell, and Bon, who won the competition in 1952. The residential density here was 200 per acre, Abercrombie's target for central London, and the architects followed Churchill Gardens in using tall slabs. The geometrical plan was centred on a tall tower and strong design features gave character to the estate, stressing its urbanity.

The Woodberry Down Estate in Finsbury (1946) was an early LCC scheme. Most of the flats were five-storey brick blocks with long brick balconies and hipped roofs, similar to those built before the war. However, the Valuer also built four eight-storey blocks with concrete slabs, lifts and flat roofs.[12] Stalingrad would have had nothing finer to show at the time, except that there would have

295   A scene in Churchill Gardens.

296 Battersea Power Station in 1992 under partial demolition for use as an entertainments centre. The Churchill Gardens estate is visible top right. The first half of the building featured in Hitchcock's *Sabotage* (1936). The partially demolished structure was a location for *Richard III* (1995). Many cameramen used the flat roof for panning or zoom shots, as in *This Happy Breed* (1944).

been no lifts and the rooms would have been much smaller. The LCC Ackroydon Estate (1950–53) at Wimbledon had a high standard of design and included ten-storey tower blocks, among the first in Britain and influenced by Sweden.[13] This mixed-development estate was the work of the Housing Division of the LCC, which went on to set its mark on public housing in London until the 1970s. Darbourne and Darke built the Lillington Gardens housing estate (1961–72) on Vauxhall Bridge Road, after winning a competition. This garnered immediate praise and came to be known as an example of the 'new vernacular', part of the growing reaction against tower blocks, with large family units housed at ground level with private gardens, an emphasis on individual access and the creation of dwelling 'identity'. Balconies and decks, with complicated brick elevations and lush planting, were intended to counter the effects of high densities. Darbourne and Darke were soon in demand and built the Marquess Road Estate, N1, in 1970. Elsewhere, many dense and complex 'urban villages' followed their example.[14]

On the fringe of London, at Roehampton, the LCC built two high-rise estates, Alton East and Alton West, in 1952–9. These tested some of Le Corbusier's ideas on mass housing, and the Swedish example which had been much discussed during and after the war. Alton East (1952–5), which looked to Sweden, had point (tower) blocks of eleven storeys, terraced maisonettes and houses set among mature trees on Swedish lines. It was soon praised, by Pevsner among others, for reflecting picturesque traditions of design and layout.[15] Alton West (1955–9) was designed by a younger team which valued the ideas of the Modern Movement and sought to create a Corbusian cityscape in a British context. It was the product of enthusiastic efforts by young followers of the Modern Movement in the LCC Architect's Department and the influence of the Smithsons (see below). The five slabs on pilotis looked like reduced versions of the *unité d'habitation* and the point blocks and maisonettes were designed on Corbusian lines. Using an existing, undulating landscape, these two schemes – especially the Corbusian element – were much admired at the time, though nothing of Le Corbusier's planned new social system was created and the slab blocks were much too small to recreate the effect of Le Corbusier's iconic *unité d'habitation* at Marseilles. Yet they looked very good indeed – for a time.

Le Corbusier's influence reached a peak in London in the 1950s. William and Gillian Howell and Stanley Amis built a row of six three-storey houses on a slope at 80–90 South Hill Park, Hampstead, in 1956 while they were in the LCC Architect's Department, working on Alton West. The use of Modulor dimensions and internal planning features, derived directly from the *unité d'habitation* at Marseilles, bore witness to a powerful commitment to Le Corbusier. The frontages were only 3.6 metres wide but the houses were unusually deep, most of them having double-height living rooms and gallery bedrooms. Full-width balconies and garden rooms under the main accommodation added to the space. This was Le Corbusier via the Smithsons, adapted to the English tradition of the terraced house and with the inevitable internal lighting problems tackled by downlighters.[16] 'What they wouldn't let us do at Alton West' could be the right name for this row.

297 Nos 80–90, South Hill Park, NW3.

During the 1950s much new London public housing was high-rise and this meant that Modern Movement ideas, particularly those of Le Corbusier, had considerable currency. Denys Lasdun had been a leading figure in the conversion of the Continental Modern Movement into a distinctive English Modernism from the 1930s, when he worked with Wells Coates and then Tecton. From 1951 to 1959 he was joint architect of the Hallfield Housing Estate, Bishop's Bridge Road, Paddington, including the Hallfield Junior and Infants' School, Porchester Road (1951–4). The estate's fifteen large slabs and related social buildings had a Corbusian flavour but the school was sensitive and flexible. Lasdun built two blocks of maisonettes at Usk Street and Claredale Street (1952–8), Bethnal Green, as part of mixed-development housing schemes. The use of central service cores here was novel and Lasdun's term 'cluster block' was generally adopted. The aim, especially in the later and taller block, Keeling House, was to provide 'houses in the sky' with front doors and kitchen balconies allowing conversations between neighbours.[17] Lasdun played an important part in the housing debate of the 1950s, which sought to recreate working-class communities in high-rise redevelopment. Nothing much would come of it but no one knew that at the time.

London also fostered a number of linear schemes stressing horizontality. In 1958 James Stirling and James Gowan built the Langham House development at Ham Common, a linear combination of three-storey brick flats and houses on an extremely narrow site with external homage to Le Corbusier's Maisons Jaoul.[18] The most adventurous was the shopping and flats precinct of the Brunswick Centre (1965–73), in Bloomsbury, by Patrick Hodgkinson. This was the closest Hodgkinson ever came to creating the ideal, medium-rise city block which he had begun to study under Sir Leslie Martin at the Cambridge School of Architecture early in the 1960s.[19] A bigger but less-noted scheme was at Alexandra Road, NW8, in 1969–79. It was designed by Neave Brown for the Architects' Department of the London Borough of Camden. It was the last of the big schemes of comprehensive redevelopment which had originated in the 1950s.

298   The west front of the Brunswick Centre.

The abolition of rent controls in 1957 encouraged some developers to build housing for rent, at any rate for middle-class tenants and businessmen seeking a pied-à-terre. Many of these schemes were linked to shops and offices at high densities. Centre Heights (1961) is a high-rise scheme of shops, offices and houses on the Finchley Road. Designed by Douglas Stephen and Panos Koulermos, it is an impressive structure with some New York parallels. In the suburbs, many large residential sites, often fronting main roads, were developed with simple, three-storey blocks in brick, sometimes with timber or tile cladding.

THE UPS AND DOWNS OF THE MODERN MOVEMENT

The MARS Group grew even more active during and after the war and for a while the work of the CIAM was centred on Britain, as potentially the most important European source of a new architecture.[20] The sixth CIAM meeting was held at Bridgewater in 1947. Le Corbusier, Gropius and Mies van der Rohe remained, however, the leading international figures. Building flourished in the US and the main example for commercial and industrial building came from there. Since Britain's leading architects were heavily involved in public housing they failed to set a British example which would be noted within the CIAM. On the contrary, many British architects looked to the Swedish example in housing, which had not been interrupted by the war. Le Corbusier had many admirers but his revolutionary approach was decried by others. He built nothing in Britain and his visits, influential in South America, were rare, perhaps because he had little English. The AA students, to their great credit, invited him to speak at the AA centenary celebrations in 1948 and he came to receive his RIBA Gold Medal in 1957.[21] Yet while even a casual visitor to Brazil will notice the many public buildings – hospitals, town halls, hospitals, universities – on *unité* lines, Corbusian influence is much less obvious in Britain apart from the occasional use of pilotis. David Aberdeen's Trades Union Congress (TUC) headquarters, Congress House (1953–7), Great Russell Street, won an important competition in 1948. Although there was little chance of its being built at that time, the competition was intended to attract the best modern architects. Aberdeen's solution, which had open circulation spaces in the foyer and powerful supporting columns inside the frontage, was much admired by the profession. Clearly influenced by Le Corbusier, its completion was delayed until 1957 and it was symbolic of the postponement of the introduction of modern architecture into London.

As to distinguished foreign architects active in the UK, and teaching through their example, there were hardly any. One exception, however, was the Paris-trained Ernö Goldfinger, who had come to Britain in the 1930s and had built a block of three pilotified modern houses, one of them for his family, at 1–3 Willow Road, NW3, in 1940.[22] His muscular style made him as many critics as admirers. The Willow Road plans were blocked at first by the local authority, which was over-ridden by the LCC.[23] He found it hard to secure contracts from cautious clients but as a Marxist he was happy to join in the Modernist reconstruction of the *Daily Worker* offices on Farringdon Road in 1946.[24] His dominating Alexander Fleming House (1960–67) at the Elephant and Castle echoed early Soviet Constructivism. He built two tall flat projects for the Greater London Council, Balfron Tower on the Rowlett Street estate (1966) in Poplar and Trellick Tower (1968–73) at Edenham Street, Paddington. Both were towering slabs emphasising their powerful concrete frames. They had a separate service tower and connecting decks, one between every three floors. Trellick Tower was the tallest block of flats in England when built. The design was much admired though it was overshadowed by the partial collapse of Ronan Point, a greatly inferior systems-built block, in 1968. Goldfinger lived in a top-floor flat at Balfron Tower for two weeks to 'test' it, securing much favourable comment in the media.[25]

The shortage of foreigners left room for English leaders of the Modern Movement. The most influential were a young married London couple and architectural partnership, Alison and Peter Smithson. They published their first statement, 'New Brutalism', in *Architectural Design* in 1955.[26] As prominent CIAM members and admirers of Le Corbusier they called for a reassertion of the principles of the Modern Movement to replace what they called the 'modern' or 'contemporary' architecture which had emerged since the war – or the Modern Free Style as it is termed in this chapter. This meant praising the pre-war Modern Movement and its post-war leaders such as Le Corbusier and Mies van der Rohe. They shared in the interest in East End community life which had become fashionable by the mid-1950s. The Smithsons built little, mainly because their radical work discouraged clients, but they lectured, published and entered competitions. They became known for their advocacy of 'brutalism', the word used by Le Corbusier to describe materials left in their natural state after inclusion in a building. The Smithsons developed this concept so that it applied particularly to reinforced concrete. They also moved beyond Le Corbusier to develop, between about 1952 and 1954, the idea of a 'new brutalism', which applied to the design of the building as a whole. This ended with their 'Brutalist Manifesto' in 1955, which also called for architect involvement in local communities. In the 1960s intellectual and artistic inter-

299 No. 2 Willow Road, Hampstead, by Ernö Goldfinger.

est in the working class helped the Smithsons to gain support for their demotic approach.[27] While providing a suave, 'contextual' home for *The Economist* (1960–64) in St James's Street, to the admiration of nearly all the architectural profession, they built two large deck-access blocks, facing each other across a large open space, in the East India Dock Road in 1964–70. This was their biggest deck-access achievement, after an advocacy of deck access, slab blocks and linking walkways going back to their Golden Lane Housing Competition entry of 1951–2. Known grotesquely as Robin Hood Gardens, this estate of two kinked slabs was short on gardens and robbed the poor of the low-rise environment with private gardens which the large, sloping site could have allowed.[28] At the same time, it did not appear to promote 'association' or 'community' and had no 'contextual' qualities at all. By 1970 the Smithsons had lost their leading role in the profession.

The influence of the Smithsons affected many architects building high-rise public housing, which expanded from the mid-1950s. One of these was Denys Lasdun. Lasdun's reputation soared in the late 1950s thanks to his housing work and his theorising, which stressed the importance of context and continuity. Much of his work recalled Parisian Modernism of the 1920s and 1930s, which had first impressed Lasdun in his student days, and the horizontality of Frank Lloyd Wright. Dark interiors lowered behind horizontal bands, with height often disguised, allowing congruity with smaller, older buildings or the natural landscape.[29] He had a large and competent office and he secured much praise for his spartan

Peter Robinson department store at 65 the Strand (1958), which respected the traditional heights of neighbouring buildings while, one suspects, honouring Joseph Emberton's Simpson's department store (1935) in Piccadilly. He built a sensitive block of flats at 26 St James's Place (1958–60), overlooking Green Park. His building for the Royal College of Physicians, Outer Circle, Regent's Park (1960–64), on the Crown Estate, was a triumph, deliberately merging the new, the old and nature in a multi-purpose building. His daring megastructure for the Institute of Education and Law, London University, designed in 1965 but not built until the 1970s, retained the striking linearity and the transversal wings of Holden's huge university project of 1933, and confirmed Lasdun as the great London public architect of the Post-Classical age.

Lasdun's star commission was the National Theatre on the South Bank (1969–76), part of the delayed completion of the South Bank arts complex. Lasdun, who always sought to set his buildings in context, insisted that he had not clashed with the Festival Hall but the public, which by now used the term Brutalism freely, applied it to the design even though the architect himself did not make that claim. The interior spaces worked well but reinforced concrete was everywhere. The exterior design directly reflected the interior, with a pyramidal arrangement of concrete decks topped by lift towers and ventilation shafts, related persuasively to the Thames vista, to the other South Bank buildings and to the deck concept which united the whole area. Lasdun sometimes referred to it, pretentiously, as an 'urban landscape'.

Lasdun's unrivalled way with words, while convincing the architectural community, could not protect this highly visible London building from the barbs and darts of an aggressive media.[30] The public never liked it. Nor did Prince Charles, who compared it to an old Olivetti typewriter (this was not one of his best). The National Theatre was a major stimulus to the reaction against modern architecture which began in the late 1970s, though it was a palace in comparison with the adjacent Queen Elizabeth Hall, Purcell Room, Hayward Gallery and National Film Theatre complex designed by various architects under the general control of the GLC Architects' Department and opened in the late 1960s. *Private Eye* called this concrete bunker the 'National Car Park' (this was spot on). By this time, the 'New Brutalism' had degenerated into 'aesthetic formalism', as even a sympathetic observer like Robert Maxwell called it.[31] It still worked well on university campuses but by the early 1970s it was in danger of undermining the whole reputation of modern architecture in London.

★   ★   ★

THE CITY

Rebuilding the City was the main focus of a lively wartime debate. The main emphasis was on planning, beginning with the MARS Plan of 1942, the Royal Academy plan also of 1942 which grew out of the 1938 Bressey Report on roads, the incomplete RIBA report (1943), the London County Council Plan (1943) and the City Corporation plan (1944–51).

The MARS Plan dealt mainly with spatial structure and communications. Lord Esher, of the Royal Academy, attacked its failure to deal with aesthetics and buildings which could add to the character of London.[32] The Royal Academy report, product of a committee chaired by Lutyens which was intended to redress the balance, concentrated on Bressey's big, planned intersections, stressing piazzas and associated buildings in the Classical style.[33] Lutyens had prepared detailed treatments for a number of these intersections. Most were of the 'gateway' or 'forum' type and all were Classical in design. Scale, skyline and vista were carefully considered, on lines apparently inspired by Beaux-Arts principles.[34] The RIBA (London Regional Reconstruction Committee) Plan was an advisory city plan much more than a contribution to architecture. It dealt mainly with communications, looking to the Bressey Report as its main starting-point.

There was no sign of a London architectural revolution and even the planning results were disappointing. The City of London was in the doldrums. In 1944 the City's Improvements and Town Planning Committee reported that it had 'pursued a level course in the best interests of the whole City of London'.[35] It rejected the idea of comprehensive replanning, boldly asserting that 1666 had not been a missed opportunity. The artist's impression of the post-war City, opposite the first page of its report, shows building up to the Victorian ceiling height, the blocks fully occupied by building and some streets widened. It expected an increase of fifty per cent in floorspace and seemed indifferent to the creation of landmarks or vistas, except at Charles Holden's piazza round St Paul's.[36] The committee anticipated that the height of London buildings would still be governed mainly by the 1894 Building Act, which fixed the maximum cornice height at 24.3 metres, with two further storeys in the roof or in setbacks, making a maximum height of 30.5 metres. This concept was uncannily like post-Fire London.

The City's 1944 plan was severely criticised and in 1945 the Minister of Town and Country Planning, W. S. Morrison, told the City to appoint new planning consultants. Charles Holden and (Lord) William Holford were selected.[37] Holden's experience with large office structures and groups of monumental buildings was by now unrivalled and he reassured what was still a notably cautious City. Holford, a younger man of South African birth whose experience in town planning and architecture had won him a senior position in the Ministry of Town and Country Planning in 1943, offered a prospect of modernity and originality. He also had an expert knowledge of the new planning methods being developed by the Ministry for urban reconstruction.[38]

Holden and Holford presented their final report to the Common Council of the City in 1947.[39] Their crucial recommendation was that the area of floorspace in the City should be restored to its 1939 level, with a daytime population of about half a million. With no serious decentralisation proposed, they tackled the problem of congestion in the City by measures to reduce site coverage and allow greater heights. They also proposed the creation of views and vistas across the City and towards the Thames. This was a conservative proposal, designed to maintain the City's pre-war role as a world business centre and to reassure City interests, including landowners and developers. It predicted a development boom if City prosperity increased after the war, and it pointed the way to greater heights, up to 36.5 metres in some cases in the east of the City, well away from St Paul's.[40] The Common Council, predictably, welcomed the report.

The report's most original proposals were for plot ratios and daylighting controls for the entire City, designed to open up more offices to direct daylight. This was the first practical demonstration of plot ratios in Britain, after the concept had been developed by Holford and his colleagues between 1944 and 1947.[41] The maximum plot ratio for the whole of the City was 5:1, except around the Bank of England, where it was 5.5:1. The pre-war maximum ceiling heights were retained. The practical application of these plot ratios was delayed, as little building was going on in the City, but the Holden and Holford plan was incorporated into the City Development Plan of 1951, by which time the LCC had become the planning authority.[42]

The quality of office building in London after 1945 was poor for some years. Lord Esher later described some of it as being of 'quite incredible ugliness'.[43] Much was carried out by 'commercial firms' (builder-developers), employing their own architects, which could build quickly and efficiently but for whom design quality and originality were not a priority.[44] From 1948 the City was empowered to create large sites by compulsory purchase and to cede them to builders on long leases. This 'lessor scheme', which allowed developers to build offices and then lease them to government departments, produced some conventional architecture such as the Neo-Georgian New Change House, Cheapside (1952–8), by Victor Heal and Smith.[45] Their design sought to defer to the cathedral after an earlier proposal by Sir John Burnet, Tait and Partners had been rejected by the City. Its long, curved frontage and colonnade were the product of Holden's piazza concept.

The relaxation of building controls in 1954 led to developers building speculative schemes, all over the City, which sought little more than maximum, cheap floorspace while satisfying local authority requirements.[46] American practice was highly influential.[47] Where corporate clients commissioned work, they often sought an outdated grandeur and had limited concepts of design, favouring Neo-Georgian or Stripped Classical.[48] Bracken House, Cannon Street (1955–9), a twin block in brick built for *The Financial Times* by (Sir) Albert Richardson, was considered to be one of the better new buildings in the City at this time but it was essentially Neo- or Stripped Classical.[49]

Criticism was mounting by the mid-1950s. Much of it was related to the undistinguished townscape that was beginning to emerge and which contrasted with the LCC's attractive Barbican comprehensive planning scheme by Chamberlin, Powell and Bon, adopted in 1956, which the public admired. The lack of buildings which could be regarded as modern disturbed the professionals, the architectural journals and the public at large.

The first block to secure praise for its modernity was Bucklersbury House, Queen Victoria Street (1953–8), by Owen Campbell Jones. The product of lengthy discussions among the developer, the architect, the Royal Fine Arts Commission and the LCC planners, it took advantage of the plot ratio to combine a fourteen-storey slab with lower buildings on the street frontages.[50] The daylighting which Holden and Holford had wanted was secured but the building was heavy with towering frontages and wings. It was noted less for its design than for the discovery of a huge Roman mosaic and a Mithraic temple as construction proceeded.

By the mid-1950s a number of such buildings were securing planning permission. Fountain House, Fenchurch Street (1954–8), by W. H. Rogers and Sir Howard Robertson, was the first to use the slab and podium formula and a glazed curtain wall, both already established in New York at Lever House by Skidmore Owings and Merrill. London Wall (Route 11), a length of new road planned by the LCC and the City Corporation and begun in 1955, included several such towers, with a pedestrian deck taking the place of individual podiums.

300, 301 and 302 Barbican views in 2004. This mixed-development-with-decks scheme looks good but the pedestrian often treks long distances and climbs plenty of steps without encountering much social interest apart from the occasional convenience store or Starbuck's.

It was nearly complete by 1965. The Institute of Chartered Accountants building, Copthall Avenue, by William Whitfield, 1964–70, had striking massing and glazing.

By the 1960s the public could see a new, modern City emerging but the architecture was mainly Modern Free Style, a collection of up-ended cornflake boxes with glass and ceramic curtain walling. Double-height entrance areas began to appear in the 1950s but they were complicated by the LCC 'pedway' system (walkways at first-floor level) which affected most new buildings in the City from 1963. At the time, however, the new City looked impressively modern.

The move towards very tall buildings in the City culminated in Richard Seifert's tower for the National Westminster Bank (later, Tower 42; 1970–81) on Old Broad Street. This was a dull and gloomy affair, 183 metres high, which won little affection. However, by the mid-1970s towers were on the wane and the NatWest Tower was given a surprisingly easy ride by press and public who saw it as a unique statement, even though it was the biggest insult yet to Wren's city of domes and spires.

303 Barbican (Wood Street) Police Station, 1962–6. This is a late example of the Lutyens Monumental style, by McMorran and Whitby. McMorran had worked with one of Lutyens's assistants. It is unique for its date.

304 A scarcely used pedway bridge over Bishopsgate, in 2004.

COMMERCIAL ARCHITECTURE OUTSIDE THE CITY

With business maintaining its wartime movement into the West End, much office building took advantage of the new heights, using the plot ratios. Thorn House (1957–9), Upper St Martin's Lane, by Sir Basil Spence and Partners, and Castrol House (1960), Marylebone Road, by Gollins, Melvin, Ward and Partners, were London's first modern towers. Both used the podium and slab formula with geometrical glazing and transoms on New York lines. They were welcomed as a clean, rational alternative to the pre-war styles and as a stimulating backdrop to older buildings. For instance, the Sunday newspaper colour supplements, which were just starting, dwelt on the contrast between old and new and on the new aesthetics created by contrasting dimensions, perspectives and colours.

New Zealand House (Robert Matthew, Johnson-Marshall and Partners; 1960–63) at Haymarket and Pall Mall was another tower above a podium but its position just off Trafalgar Square made it potentially a big visual challenge. Jones and Woodward are critical of it on visual environment and skyline grounds but in its day it was seen as breaking up the townscape and creating a useful vertical feature.[51] The high quality of its finish and the ground-level spaces were intended to justify its position in an elegant area.

305 Looking west from St Paul's in 1973. Most of this view is in the West End and few tall buildings are visible.

306 Looking east from St Paul's in 1973. Low buildings are visible in the foreground in the St Paul's Churchyard area and the first towers now stand up in the east of the City.

307 New Zealand House soaring above St James.

The thirty-two storey Vickers Building (1960–63) on Millbank, by Ronald Ward and Partners, offered a different vision as a great monolith rising from the Thames and silhouetted again the changing sky. Many architects found it trite but it did more to convince Londoners of the modern tower as a quality contribution to the townscape than any other building of its day. The London Hilton, Park Lane (1963), by Lewis Solomon Kaye, did the opposite but this was mainly a standard 'visual intrusion on Hyde Park' issue, with most Londoners tolerant of the Miami design. Another big Hyde Park debate centred on the brick-built Knightsbridge Cavalry Barracks (1967–9) by Sir Basil Spence (and Partners), whose London buildings in the 1960s combined modernity and tradition to the general dissatisfaction of the Smithsons and their friends. As a man who would probably have been happier reconstructing the Basilica of Maxentius, he was accused of building large, insensitive structures of which the Hyde Park barracks was the most notorious. Curiously, another intrusion on the park, the Royal College of Art on Kensington Gore (1962–73) by H. T. Cadbury-Brown and Sir Hugh Casson, was given a much easier ride by the critics.

Closer to the historic centre was the Shell Centre Building (1953–63) on the South Bank, by Sir Howard Robertson and R. Maynard Smith, the product of LCC planning for the South Bank.[52] A bulky 103-metre monolith with a smaller, adjacent structure, both clad in Portland stone, it was an awful building in itself but in addition it belittled the Palace of Westminster and the Festival Hall. Some of the best architect-decorators of

the day were brought in to add lustre to the interior but this application of London's 'better inside than outside' principle did not help the average Londoner, who could only view this lumpy mass from across the Thames. Public concern built up during construction and for a while undermined the case for more office towers in London.

By the 1960s commercial firms were becoming the leading forces in development schemes in the West End, as in the City. Richard Seifert and Partners were among the most prominent. In 1963–7 they built the 121-metre Centre Point at a big West End crossroads (101 Oxford Street). This reflected a fashion in the early 1960s for placing major buildings at big traffic intersections, which was encouraged by LCC planners.[53] It was visible from ground level over a wide area and was sufficiently close to the Post Office Tower (1960–64), the tallest building in London when built, to transform the Oxford Street and the Tottenham Court Road area by striking vertical 'statements'. The value of all this as architecture was less clear. The Post Office Tower had been designed by Sir Eric Bedford, Chief Architect of the Ministry of Works, apparently to serve a range of purposes, none of which required a location at that point. Centre Point was a guaranteed moneymaker from the start. Seifert, as London's businessman architect *par excellence*, worked hand in hand with the developer and the LCC planners. The building remained deliberately unlet for years and caused a furore among the London intelligentsia but its 'layered' facade with deep reveals created by hundreds of muscular pre-cast concrete units produced ever-changing lighting and shadow effects which made it a key West End landmark. The Post Office Tower never acquired much of a following after its brief heyday in the Carnaby Street era but the public gradually warmed to Centre Point, leading to its Grade II listing (that is, a minor historic monument) in 2003.

THE DEVELOPER AS THE MASTER DESIGNER

By 1975 most architects found themselves more constrained than in the past. Big schemes were often initiated by the developers in connection with road and renewal schemes. They generally had preconceptions about the architecture. Design practices were larger and some employed a number of specialists including, at one time, sociologists. The young architect was often given defined jobs at a low level but clung on, hoping for promotion.

L. S. Marler, O.B.E., T.D., chairman of Capital and Counties Property Company Ltd, gave the game away.

In 1963 he was asked to lecture on 'private urban renewal' at 'People and Cities', a conference organised by the British Road Federation and the Royal Town Planning Institute in the aftermath of the official 'Buchanan report', *Traffic in Towns*. Following the trend, Marler called for extensive precinct development with high-rise buildings and claimed that ideal sites for private urban renewal would be of forty to fifty acres. He referred to his own current scheme, Knightsbridge Green, which on the evidence of the illustrations and models shown, did not need an architect.[54]

Meanwhile, where they could get large sites, developers replaced Victorian structures along main streets and roads, especially in the outer districts. For instance, early in the 1960s the busiest part of the traffic-packed, admittedly nondescript, Ilford High Road was transformed by two huge department stores in the Modern Free Style. The local authority planners tolerated the reinforcement of a corridor shopping street and there was no talk of precincts. They probably went beyond their remit and influenced the architecture in their talks with the developers, partly bypassing the architects. Meanwhile, the local press was ecstatic about the rejuvenation of Ilford High Road, especially as both buildings had rooftop restaurants and one had a night club. The locals were impressed. And so was the author of this book, who was taken to lunch in the cheaper of the restaurants. Wasn't very good though – the steak was thin and dry.

THE OIL CRISIS AND LONDON ARCHITECTURE

In 1973 the world entered an era of uncertainty. Some economists claim that the world economy had been approaching serious difficulties much earlier but London building speculation had not noticed them. The sharp fall in oil production undermined the British economy and building in London was held back until well into the 1980s. One of the earliest responses was the refurbishment and re-use of older buildings.

Conservation and restoration began to expand from the 1970s.[55] Interiors especially attracted attention.[56] The reconstruction of the Royal Opera House to designs by Dixon Jones and the Building Design Partnership, using the adjacent Floral Hall for front-of-house space (1984–2000), was acclaimed. This was not, however, purely a conservation project and the result was, in effect, a redesign. The refurbishment of Liverpool Street Station in the 1980s by Architecture and Design Group was accompanied by the modernisation of Charles Barry Jr's Great Eastern Hotel (1884). A number of older office blocks were refurbished and modernised in the City into the 1990s.[57]

Public houses, most of which had been built between 1830 and 1910, and which were regularly refurbished every twenty years, started to acquire enhanced Victorian interiors from the 1970s. Even more recent pubs acquired these Victorian interiors and production of ironwork for tables and chairs expanded, together with decorated mirrors and street lanterns. With the value of older properties increasing, pubs were among the many types of commercial building to benefit from jet cleaning, which was began to be applied extensively to brickwork for the first time.

308   The refaced 'Cittie of York', High Holborn, 1923, near Staple Inn. The reputation of Charles Dickens was at its height and the interior is an idealised version of a lawyer's tavern, complete with carrels. Go early as the carrels fill up very quickly, some of them with real lawyers.

309 Old Greenwich from the Thames in 2005. Gentrification and conservation turned many of London's village nodes into tourist attractions from around 1970.

The word 'refurbishment' (or 'refurb' in the pub) now came into wide use for the upgrading of both interiors and exteriors. The effect was to take much of what was left of the public London of the late Victorian era, when design had been at its most varied, and make it look new or even better than it had been. Much housing in inner London received similar treatments, with degraded areas such as Islington and Greenwich improved through what became known as 'gentrification'. By 2000, very little of London had not been 'refurbed' to some degree.

All this meant that much of an ageing nineteenth-century London greatly increased its rental value. It not only generated its own capital for improvements but it drew in new funds which were used to upgrade ordinary districts which a few years earlier would not have attracted the 'gentrifiers'. Living in the suburbs, with its attendant commuting, became less attractive. Small and single-person households, now growing rapidly in numbers, were attracted to small dwellings and house-shares in inner London. These residential choices changed the character and status of whole districts. They also affected attitudes to modern architecture.

★   ★   ★

THE REACTION AGAINST THE MODERN

By the 1970s the London intelligentsia was beginning to agree that architecture had sold out to the money men. From the late 1940s to the 1970s, the Modern Free Style had dominated London architecture. Some voices were raised in criticism. An outspoken architectural journalist, Ian Nairn, launched an attack on 'Subtopia' – the ugly and tasteless development of town and country – in 1955.[58] The loss of older buildings such as the Doric arch at Euston and the Coal Exchange, both in 1962, hit the headlines in the Sunday papers. These and a host of redevelopment episodes undermined confidence in the new Britain of the Modern Free Style but fundamental doubts about the quality of London's architecture began to surface after 1972, when the Stock Exchange (Llewelyn-Davies, Weeks, Forestier-Walker and Bor) was completed.[59] Pevsner's terse description of it as 'a massive irregular heptagon', 97.5 metres high, seems about right.

In 1975 Colin Amery and Dan Cruickshank published *The Rape of Britain*. 'Rape' was a popular journalistic expression at the time, implying the brutal destruction of traditional townscapes and their replacement by inferior design. Charles Jencks has drawn attention to the twenty or so large hotels, built with government subsidies to encourage tourism, which were opened in 'Hotellandia' on the route to Heathrow Airport between 1969 and 1973. These were the equivalent of the stan-

310 No. I Poultry and Tower 42 in 2004. Stylistic variety and the struggle to create office space and electronic networks maintained the City's tradition of architectural individualism.

dard City office block, and Jencks knocks them all down like skittles with his 'On the outside they are uptight International Style; on the inside Lapidus Ersatz.'[60] In the 1980s a reaction against almost all modern architecture occurred, with Prince Charles's campaign for a more humane architecture launched in 1984.

Prince Charles showed, in his sensitive and stimulating *A Vision of Britain* (1989), that he knew a great deal about design and its context. He also had a commitment to the British environment as a whole which few architects could match or even understand. It was, however, his comments on individual modern buildings, enhanced by the media, which caught the eye. For instance, he became involved with the redevelopment of an office site by Peter Palumbo, a City developer and art lover. Palumbo wanted to use a classic Mies van der Rohe design, commissioned by his father and dating from 1962–8, but there was much opposition from conservationists seeking to preserve listed Victorian buildings on the site.[61] After a long debate the design was rejected in 1985 on planning grounds. James Stirling then designed a Post-Modern structure in 1986–8, known as No. I Poultry (1994–7), which looked like a joke, the

equivalent of Wren's Warrant Design. However, after further conservationist manoeuvres, the new building secured planning permission in 1988. It was completed in 1997, after Stirling's death in 1992, the delay being mainly due to the collapse of the property market in the early 1990s. The Stirling building had the distinction of being the second design for the same site to be lambasted by Prince Charles (the 'old 1930s wireless'), now that he had shifted his attack from the Modernists to the Post-Modernists.

PRINCE CHARLES AND THE CHALLENGE TO THE MODERN

In 1982 the RIBA opened its 'Great Debate' on architecture.[62] They secured more interest than they expected when Prince Charles commented unfavourably on the design for the National Gallery extension which at that point seemed likely to be built. This scheme was the product of a competition in 1982 and the designs presented by Ahrends, Burton and Koralek (ABK) in 1984 were a revision of their winning proposals. They included a tower with aerials. The uproar which followed Prince Charles's comments on the 'carbuncle' (which, they say, may have been aimed at Richard Rogers's entry) led to the client's rejection of the ABK

311 Trafalgar Square in 1986.

proposals. Venturi Scott Brown were commissioned to design what became known as the Sainsbury Wing and it was completed in 1991. Robert Venturi had a reputation in the US as an architectural theorist and it was assumed that he would please Prince Charles and his growing group of followers. So he did – on the inside. The exterior, which had to meet some extremely awkward requirements, was completely beyond him. This mess started the decline in Prince Charles's design campaign, which had faded away by 1995.

Meanwhile, however, the RIBA had invited Charles to give an address at a meeting at Hampton Court to celebrate their 150th anniversary. The date was 30 May 1984. This turned out to be a 'much-loved London' address with Charles referring, among other things, to desecration of the view of St Paul's. References to Wren were of course in order given the location of the occasion and Prince Charles made the most of these. The Englishman's birthright, a humane environment and open decision-making all figured in his persuasive address.[63] This was one of his best speeches and the effect was overwhelming. He went on to make a series of speeches, widening his aim, between 1984 and 1988.[64] Then he set up his own Institute and alternative School of Architecture and launched a luxurious architectural journal, *Perspectives* (later, *Perspectives on Architecture*) in 1994.

Speeches, interventions and publications led to Prince Charles's direct involvement in a number of design schemes. Paternoster Square was much the biggest and involved him with some very big developers, owners and architects as well as the LCC. The name applied to a large area to the north-west of St Paul's which had been burned down in 1940. It had been rebuilt by Trehearne and Norman Preston and Partners on lines laid down by Holford as chief planner in 1956. Much praised on completion in 1967 by the supporters of modern architecture, its gaunt concrete slabs rising above plazas and decks in the East Berlin style were causing adverse comment before Prince Charles's 1984 speech. In 1987 the new owner, (Sir then Lord) Stuart Lipton of Mountleigh Estates, responded to the new emphasis on quality created by Prince Charles by inviting seven architectural firms to take part in a limited competition to replace the offices, which no longer met modern business requirements. They included Richard Rogers, James Stirling, Norman Foster and Arata Isozaki.[65] Mindful of the Prince's influence, the developers showed him the results. Rumour had it that Rogers was the 'front-runner' with his high-coverage scheme of low buildings.[66] Prince Charles did not like the Rogers scheme, even though it was thoughtful and technically advanced,

312   The Grand Staircase of the Sainsbury Wing, National Gallery.

especially in relation to underground access to the cathedral area. Instead, Philip Dowson and Arup Associates were declared the winners of the competition with a Post-Modern scheme on classical lines which at first sight looked capable of satisfying all interests, including Prince Charles's.[67]

The prince then put forward his own concept of the rebuilt area. In a speech at the Mansion House in December 1987 he presented his ideal which was essentially a pastiche of the area as it might have been rebuilt after the Fire. He had already seen a scheme prepared in 1985 by John Simpson, a historicist architect with whom he was now in touch and who had been advised by the Prince's favoured architect-planner, Léon Krier. This further encouragement from the prince and the favourable reaction to his speech persuaded Simpson

313 Office buildings on the edge of the Paternoster Square area and facing the west front of St Paul's. Completed in 2004, they revive the Modern Neo-Classical tradition which flourished in London in the 1930s. *Private Eye*'s 'Piloti' sees a whiff of Italian Fascist design here.

to prepare a detailed scheme which extended beyond Paternoster Square to other areas near the cathedral where Holford's planning had arguably detracted from the surroundings of Wren's masterpiece. The Simpson buildings were of traditional construction and materials. Simpson worked on Paternoster Square from 1987 to 1992. Public support and the deference of the owner, by then Arup Associates, suggested for a while that Simpson might be allowed to guide the whole scheme.[68]

Simpson's proposals were ably presented at an exhibition held in the crypt of St Paul's in 1988. The other seven entries invited by Lipton were also displayed. The exhibition had been requested by Prince Charles as part of his effort to open up architecture and planning to public gaze and participation. Simpson's project secured massive public support and London's only evening newspaper, the *Evening Standard*, offered to seek outline plan-

ning permission, a move which would have taken the initiative away from the developers. Arup Associates, who had become the owners, now sold the site and, after some complex commercial moves, an astoundingly international pro-Simpson consortium of developers and architects, Paternoster Associates, produced a revised project which was exhibited in 1991. Despite the participation of (Sir) Terry Farrell and Quinlan Terry, the scheme conceded a great deal to commercial considerations and Prince Charles, though careful this time not to pass comments on architecture which might deprive its authors of future work, did not seem entirely happy with it. However, a revised scheme secured planning permission in 1992 with some returns to the Simpson concept, mainly in the form of lower buildings and a central square with market hall.[69]

The collapse of the property market now prevented work on the scheme, which did not start until 1999, under Mitsubishi Estates, who were by then the sole owner of most of the area. By this time the public had largely reverted to favouring modern architecture, while architects had never been won over by the Simpson scheme. Prince Charles, meanwhile, had decided to give

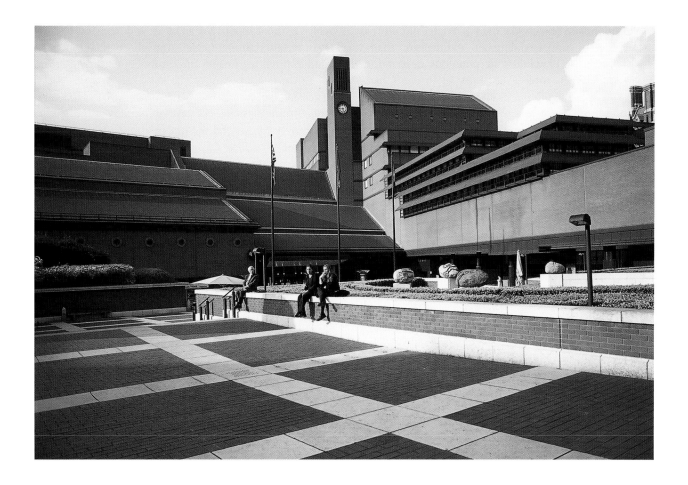

314 The forecourt of the British Library. Scandinavian brick and swooping roofs, and bright colours, work well here.

up his advocacy of specific styles of architecture and his support for individual schemes. In terms of plan and height, much of Simpson's scheme survived but the idea of a pastiche office district on expensive land in the City had proved too ambitious. Paternoster Square was completed in 2003 to a master plan by Sir William Whitfield. Apart from a column in the middle of the square, and Temple Bar's return to London, explicit Classicism had been banished but scale and layout were a tribute to Prince Charles's initial intervention.[70]

One of the biggest of Prince Charles's targets was the new National Library, begun in 1974 and finished in 1998, by Sir Colin St John Wilson with the Property Services Agency. In one of his most telling comparisons, Prince Charles said that anyone would think that Scott's St Pancras Hotel was the national library and that the British Library was a new railway station.[71] This tale of alteration and retrenchment was like Scott's Government Buildings but far worse – the 'Thirty Years War', as Wilson

called it.[72] At least Scott's site did not end up half-empty. Wilson's frustrating struggle with his masters ended with a Scandinavian solution drawing on Alvar Aalto, with a hint of the Post-Modern in the exterior colour scheme. The great expanses of red brick were said to defer to Scott's hotel but they, the swooping roofs and the long green balconies/sunbreakers, all looked cheap. However, the library revives the Palladian tradition of 'better inside than out' and the subtle atrium over the entrance area and the planning and lighting of some welcoming interior spaces are a great success.

Prince Charles's interventions as an architectural commentator and educated client gave amateurism a good name, at least for a while. The counter-attack by the modern architects in 1987 questioned the Prince's competence but he had much public support by this time.[73] He generated more thinking about architecture than any of his predecessors since the Prince Regent. He returned architecture to the people and reminded them that it was a source of pleasure. Not since the 1940s had the public responded so well to the presentations of designs which were easy to understand and which went directly to the heart as well as the mind. His habit of comparing buildings to mundane objects like the typewriter did more to encourage an understanding of architecture than a hundred sets of drawings and pompous descriptions. Modern architects took a dim view of Prince Charles ('he understands nothing about architecture!') but the Neo-Modern architecture of the 1990s would not have emerged in the same way without him. Developers recognised the public pressure for better buildings and worked more closely with leading architects, using competitions and exhibitions to draw on a wider range of design ideas.

POST-MODERNISM

The reaction against the Modern contributed to the rise of what became known as Post-Modernism (though the term New Classicism was often used). This was a completely undisciplined approach based on random forms, colours and allusions, born along American freeway strips and at Las Vegas. It emerged in the 1970s and reached London in the 1980s.[74] Post-Modernism was a deliberate reaction against the ascetic and didactic char-

acter of the Modern Movement and was inspired by pleasure, entertainment, relaxation and crude symbolism. It sought striking images and symbols, often drawn from the urban environment of the past. The most advanced structural techniques were used but in appearance it ranged from pastiche to comic-book illustration.

Many architects and the media were fascinated by the Post-Modern and it throve, though more in print than on the ground, from about 1985 to 1995.[75] Garish or jokey Post-Modernism of the American type was rare in London. Charles Jencks, the fashionable architectural critic from Los Angeles, with (Sir) Terry Farrell, remodelled his family house in Bayswater in 1979–81 on 'dream houses of LA' lines but this was more an assertion than a model.[76] However, some of the more daring London architects, while denying their allegiance to Post-Modernism, moved into expressionism, symbolism and historicism. Farrell was the best-known of these. He had been partly trained in the USA and admired the creative urban theories of Venturi, Rowe, Koetter and others. Freed of his partnership with (Sir) Nicholas Grimshaw in 1980, he launched into experiments with urban forms. In 1981–3 he converted a large garage at Hawley Crescent, NW1, into an expressionist television studio. His Embankment Place (1990), a huge commercial structure over Charing Cross Station, commissioned by the developer Geoffrey Wilson, offered a symbolic

315 The Guildhall Art Gallery, 1999, London's outstanding example of Post-Modern design and a threat as much as a promise.

profile over the Thames, its vaults reminding the observer of the tracks underneath. The public was impressed. He followed it with Vauxhall Cross, Albert Embankment (1993), headquarters of the secret services (MI6), where he developed some of his ideas from Charing Cross. His Alban Gate (1988–92), an office development in the City, was a further exercise in vaults and was much admired.

For a while, Farrell made it seem that there was a future for commercial Post-Modernism but this was not to be. However, there was often a dash of Post-Modernism in Neo-Modern offices built in the 1990s and after 2000. For instance, the Neo-Gothic Minster Court, Mincing Lane (1987–91) by GMW Partnership, was an effective, tall building with steep roofs contrasted with strip windows. Plantation Wharf, Battersea, by Moxley and Frankl, was a picturesque combination of tall and low buildings, using gables. Images drawn from the past, fairly common in these buildings, suited London and their quality materials and finish were welcome. The bright colours, rare in London over the centuries, made a big impact. When London revived from the recession in the mid-1990s, the Classical Revival of the Prince of Wales was finished. So was the Post-Modern. Prince Charles had never supported the Post-Modern as such but it suffered from the change in climate. Post-Modernism of the Stirling type, always unconvincing, quickly faded away after Stirling's death. Although the Post-Modern was dead by 2000, with Farrell renouncing it as early as 1990, it contributed much to Modern architecture when the Modern came back to favour. It was relaxed and did not take itself as seriously as the Modern Movement had done. It had shown how colour could live in the 'Smoke' and it had opened architecture out to the street. Above all, it had destroyed the old view that a building had to obey the rules. Post-Modern's contribution to broader developments in modern architecture can be detected in Jencks's perceptive *Post-Modern Triumphs in London* (1991), published when London's Post-Modern was already in decline. Post-Modern was soon replaced after its brief run by a very different Modern, referred to in this book as Neo-Modern. Yet the spirit of Jencks's Post-Modern never died.[77]

Meanwhile, ecological design came more into favour. The most spectacular example was Ralph Erskine's London Ark (1990–91) at Hammersmith. This was London's biggest ecological building, with a shape to indicate its novelty. It applied Erskine's Scandinavian-influenced architecture to a large office building. However, this ecological branch never rose beyond the experimental level in London, except in minor adjustments to ventilation and lighting.

PASTICHE

From the 1980s interest grew in two types of pastiche. The first was the creation of new buildings on old lines. The other was the rebuilding of structures that had disappeared or had never been built at all. The pastiche made a fragmentary impact on London building but it impressed the public.

London had boasted one serious pastiche building since the 1920s. This was Liberty's department store, a huge half-timbered structure standing back from Regent Street on Great Marlborough Street. It was built in 1924 by E. T. and E. S. Hall when Liberty's Regent Street frontage was reconstructed by the same architects in a Neo-Classical style. Though admired for its honesty and high standards, it had not been emulated and modern architects distrusted this type of work. In the 1980s and 1990s the return to the pastiche was led by Quinlan Terry's six beautiful pastiche villas in Regent's

316 The Globe Theatre, in 2004.

199

Park (1988–2003), for the Crown Estate. The commission came indirectly from Prince Charles, who wanted to show the best that could be done in a variety of old styles, while continuing the picturesque tradition of John Nash round the park. They were in a wide variety of historic styles, including Gothick and Italianate.[78] Impressive of its kind was Terry's river ensemble at Richmond riverside (1986–8), a mixture of existing and pastiche buildings, though it had something of a film set and the effect gradually palled.[79] The Globe Theatre, rebuilt in the 1990s, though a persuasive reconstruction, was even more like a film set, as was much of the restored and rebuilt South Bank. Pastiche dockside inns were built on the South Bank and near Tower Bridge as central features of a modernised Dickensian London. The alluring Vinopolis under Doresque railway arches near Southwark cathedral could have been the setting for a Dickens novel on the evils of drink.

More scholarly was the rebuilding of the gateways flanking Inigo Jones's Covent Garden church, which had been removed in 1877. This work was carried out from 1991 by Donald W. Insall and Associates. Crosby Hall (c. 1466–75), which had been moved from the City to Chelsea by the architect Walter Godfrey in 1908, was improved and extended from 1988 by Christopher Moran, a property developer.[80] He built a small palace in fifteenth-century style round the hammerbeam hall, estimating that about one-third was renovation and two-thirds rebuilding. Much of it was ready by 2003, with completion expected in 2010.[81]

The New Queen's Gallery at Buckingham Palace, by John Simpson and Partners (1997–2002) is an eclectic Classical building with hints of Schinkel, Robert Adam and no doubt others which are invisible to this author.[82] For Kenneth Powell it calls up some of the design climate of the Regency.[83] The workmanship is first class, suggesting that for once a palace architect could draw on all the money he needed.[84] It was bigger, more ambitious and more lavish than the original Queen's Gallery, built in 1962.

One of the most interesting types of pastiche was the pastiche Modern. Coutts Crescent (1986–9), St Alban's Road, NW5, by Chassay Wright Architects, is a crescent of tall houses, partly drawing on the Dutch example of the 1920s. In 1991 the Renton Howard Wood Levin partnership completed One America Square, near the Tower. The entrance block seemed to be inspired by the Streamline Moderne, including Odeon cinemas.[85] Riverside Apartments at Rotherhithe, by Troughton McAslan, was a pastiche Streamline Moderne, complete with white rendering, strip windows and curved bays recalling Ibex House. Demetri Porphyrios Associates'

Regency house in Kensington looked like a carefully refurbished Modern original.[86]

THE NEO-MODERN: LONDON GETS IT RIGHT

The last twenty years of the twentieth century were unique in London's architectural history. Impetus for change came mainly from the commercial sector. The 'Big Bang', an expansion and deregulation of business services in 1986, was a stimulus to office building. American fast construction methods, in many cases introduced by American firms, affected design, with an emphasis on metal and structural elements. Complex wiring systems were inserted between the floors and buildings could go out of date quickly on grounds of wiring alone. Meanwhile, the City tried to replace some of the early post-war office buildings.[87]

Symbolic of the change was Lloyd's of London, Leadenhall Street (1978–86), by the Richard Rogers Partnership with engineering support from Ove Arup and Partners. The big, internal spaces here were inspired by Louis Kahn, the American architect who built some classic factories between the wars, and the external arrangement of the services echoed the Pompidou Centre. The tall atrium out-atriumed the other atria built in the City since the idea had been imported from America in the late 1970s. Atria became popular in the 1980s with big trading floors and office employment stabilised.[88] Europe House, St Katharine Docks, was built by the Richard Rogers Partnership from 1987, drawing on the lessons of Lloyd's. (Lord) Rogers went on to build 88 Wood Street (1991–9). It emerged from a limited competition held in 1990 by the Japanese banker Daiwa. This was another Lloyd's-like building.[89]

These achievements allowed the charismatic figure of Rogers to take Lasdun's place as London's leading architect. In 1992, with Prince Charles and the Post-Modern out of the way, Rogers and other Modernist architects took the initiative. They wanted to show that architects had the vision needed to create a new London, stretching far beyond the individual building. With the General Election approaching, Rogers published *A New London*, an outline proposal for a new, modern but ecological London. This was at a time when London seemed to many to be tired, dirty and in decline. In the summer of 1992, Rogers put on an exhibition at the Royal Exchange to publicise the recent achievements of the City.[90] By the mid-1990s Rogers had become an authority on London improvements who recalled Wren. Consulted at every turn and a 'darling of the media', he became almost a household name in London. His

317　The sunlit Vauxhall Cross. and nearby Neo-Modern developments, in 2004.

peerage in 1996 and his growing role in strategic decisions allowed him to influence planning as well as architecture. He had an especially close understanding with Sir Stuart Lipton. Happily, he also built up a good understanding with Prince Charles, who became an admirer of Neo-Modern buildings. Readers will note that a princely, lordly and knightly circle of architects and patrons was an active force in London architecture, as in the 1660s and the 1720s.

DOCKLANDS

By the year 2000 the City of London had been expanding into a new area to the east. This was the London Docklands, a unique environment for Neo-Modern architecture. The London docks had fallen into decline from the 1950s, beginning with the Pool of London, west of Tower Bridge, and continuing from Tower Bridge eastwards to Woolwich. The main cause of the decline was containerisation, which required more extensive facilities and deep-water berths which were provided at Tilbury. The redevelopment of the London Docklands, beginning in the 1970s and at first much derided, led to the creation of a completely new cityscape within London.

Closures and industrial decline began in the docks area in the late 1960s. The resulting 22 square kilometres of redundant space were soon heralded, with striking originality, as 'London's biggest redevelopment opportunity since the Fire of London'. The London Docklands Development Corporation (LDDC) was set up in 1981, following the example of the New Towns Development Corporations. It gave a low priority to design, seeking above all to generate development. In 1982 it issued the Isle of Dogs Design Guide, following the example of the Essex Design Guide, but this was not very precise. Andrew Derbyshire, once a board member of the LDDC, said: 'we had to nod through some awful schemes'.[91]

The core of Docklands was a plan for a huge office city on the West India Docks, at the top of the Isle of Dogs. This plan was commissioned from New York's most active commercial architects, Skidmore, Owings and Merrill, by an American developer, G. Ware Travelstead. The plan was completed in 1985. From 1987 Travelstead's successor, Olympia and York, put the plan into effect, in association with the LDDC.[92] The architecture was mainly by American firms, though Foster and Partners designed one of the towers. By 1999 the development housed 25,000 workers. It was best known for its central core, Canary Wharf, which was developed from 1985 on a master plan designed in America. Its central tower, Cabot House (1991), was designed by the Argentinian-born architect Cesar Pelli. I. M. Pei, of the Crystal Cathedral in California and the Louvre, was one of several distinguished consultant architects. With a height of 244 metres and a bold silhouette, Cabot Tower received a good press. Canary Wharf as a whole was hard hit by the depression of the 1990s but by 2000 the

318   Approaching Canary Wharf from the west in 2004.

319   Canary Wharf, in 2004.

320   Canary Wharf from the Docklands Light Railway (DLR) in 2004.

321 and 322 Canary Wharf DLR station in 2004.

scheme was a commercial success and the focus of a dozen sandwich-and-juice outlets.

Canary Wharf was lambasted by the press at first. Their objections were trivial and ignorant and do not merit review here. By the end of the century, with surrounding buildings in place and the dreamy Docklands Light Railway (DLR) in full operation, the allusive, Neo-Modern design of the whole area made it the symbol of

both a traditional and a new London. Cabot Tower could be seen from the City and parts of the West End, often unexpectedly, a reminder that the City now had a rival in a new urban landscape which the past could not drag down. The swarms of garish Thames passenger boats were speeded up. Used by tourists more than Docklands workers, they pointed the way to a futuristic transport system with computerised air buses and air taxis flying from Tower Bridge to Tilbury via the City Airport. The Docklands gave a new expression to modernity. None of the City's crowding occurred here but the landscape was strongly urban. The public appreciated it or so at least did the passengers vying for the best seats at the front of the driverless DLR trains. The sharp curves and vaulted stations in the Canary Wharf area produced constant changes of view. Catch a DLR train in the twilight and you will see.

Canary Wharf was the first of many big Docklands schemes. In 1984 the Richard Rogers Partnership was commissioned to prepare a master plan for the Royal Docks, which stretched eastward from the Isle of Dogs. This was the biggest redevelopment scheme in Docklands and Rogers's practice went on to design several important buildings and layouts there. The Reuters Data Centre, for instance, was built from 1987 to 1992, drawing on the solutions developed at Rogers's Lloyd's.[93] Some other schemes in Docklands were, however, less impressive. Odyssey, a complex by Alan Selby and Partners for Redrow, completed in 2002, was an awkward design.[94]

THE CITY IN THE DOCKLANDS ERA

In the 1980s and 1990s the creation of some huge office plazas with attendant shopping, recreational and cultural space took place. They helped cater for the new City workers' one-hour-and-no-more sandwich lunch which replaced the leisurely and alcoholic style of the 1960s and 1970s. Most brought their own food in plastic boxes but sandwich-making became a major industry and included deliveries to offices. Cold-drinks cabinets loomed everywhere. Pubs played little part in these new schemes, while developers provided open space and seating for use when the weather was fine. The most impressive, Broadgate/Bishopsgate (1985–91), provided 330,000 square metres of office space in and around Liverpool Street station. It was built by Rosehaugh Stanhope jointly with British Rail. Most of the new space was provided over tracks running into Liverpool Street station and on the site of Broad Street station. Arup Associates and Skidmore, Owens and Merrill were the architects.

323　The City skyline from the OXO building in 2004.

This was widely recognised as a quality scheme with an artistic element and it influenced other, smaller schemes. Ludgate (1989–92), another scheme over railway tracks (76,000 square metres), was the work of the same developers. Journalists liked to write loosely about 'air rights', as in the original development north of Grand Central Terminal in the 1920s. The term did, however, reflect the massive American involvement in London development which had built up by the 1990s. These new firms used new construction methods, including prefabrication, and accelerated project management on lines already normal in America.[95]

At the turn of the century there was a return to the concept of the very tall building, in abeyance since Seifert's Tower 42. This was partly the product of changes in the use of the plot ratios in 1993 which tolerated applications for tall buildings where space was reduced lower down. The Norman Foster partnership's Swiss Re Tower (1997–2004), forty storeys high and thicker in the middle than at the bottom, was only the start. Swiss Re, together with the Mayor of London's offices near Tower

324　Neo-Modern scene in the City at Fenchurch Street, London Street, and Mark Lane (including the Swiss Re), 2004.

325 The City from South Bank in 2004.

Bridge, another bulging building, were both designed by Ken Shuttleworth. Shuttleworth's astounding formalism, verging on expressionism, waved the last goodbye to Wren's world of dome and spires but it was often argued that this had been destroyed long before. At the Swiss Re, as often now, the Post-Modern paved the way for the Neo-Modern. Yet it reminds one that Buckminster Fuller, the geodesic dome specialist, has been a major influence on Foster's career. Its media nicknames, most of them variants on gherkin, are much too trite but 'Hindenburg resurgens' – this author's bid for immortality – may be too scholarly to catch on. As these pages were being written, news came of a 217-metre tower to be built at Aldgate by a development company, Minerva, and known reassuringly as the Minerva Building. The architect is Sir Nicholas Grimshaw. The artist's impression makes it look like a 'shard of steel' (or razor), now all the rage in the City.[96]

HOUSING

Since the 1890s the creation of public housing had played an important part in the developing architecture of London. The main agents had been the London County Council and the London boroughs. After the Second World War the role of the LCC and the boroughs had been enhanced by the clearance and redevelopment operations, particularly in the East End. The Greater London Council carried on when it replaced the LCC in 1965. This housing was variable in quality, especially when the boroughs were doing the work.

326 Docklands housing in 2004.

From the 1970s this public housing role was diminished and eventually snuffed out. In the early 1980s the GLC housing stock was transferred to the London boroughs and in 1986 the GLC was abolished. Peter Jones, Director of Architecture at the outgoing GLC, detected a change in housing and school architecture between 1976 and 1986.[97] The change was linked to a reduction in the volume of new building, especially in education. In housing, design was on a smaller scale and the authority made more effort to consult the users. There was a shift from new building to renovation.

Where new housing was built in the late 1970s and the early 1980s, it was mainly in what became known as the Neo-Vernacular manner. This usually meant two-storey houses with pitched roofs at high density, much of it on infill sites, with public greenery and small gardens. Steep roofs, elevations with a horizontal emphasis and colour contrasts were strongly emphasised. Brick was used for the most part. There were some low blocks of flats, with pitched roofs. Jeremy and Fenella Dixon used this formula in Lanark Road, w9, to echo the two-storey terraces disguised as villas so common in the first London suburbs in the early nineteenth century. At Petticoat Lane, a block of nineteenth-century model dwellings was refurbished and complemented by low blocks of flats in a conforming style.[98]

Neo-Modern swept into private housing in the 1990s, especially in prestigious locations with views. Centurion, a shimmering, balconied block at Chelsea Bridge Wharf, Queenstown Road, by Berkeley Homes, was completed in 2002.[99] Private flats were built in Docklands in some numbers, especially facing south along the Thames or forming courts round the docks. London had become so rich that the quality of new private housing was usually outstanding, especially in west London.

TRANSPORT

The extension of the Jubilee Line produced a number of striking stations, the subject of a special design programme. The architect-in-chief of the Jubilee line extension, Roland Paoletti, decided to secure design continuity over eleven new or rebuilt stations, in the manner of Charles Holden. He did not impose a single, 'High-Tech' aesthetic but the acres of stainless steel cladding suggest that all the architects had the same

dream about a Delorean production line. The biggest and most impressive was the Canary Wharf junction station (1990–2000), designed by Foster and Partners. The concrete vaults and stainless steel facings were used to produce an ultra-modern building which from certain angles looked like a film set. Construction methods recalled some of the stations on the Paris Metro around 1900, in that a huge concrete box was sunk into a large dock and the station was built up inside it. The most dramatic station was Michael Hopkins and Partners' Westminster (1991–2000), which created a dire sense of impending doom in this author on his first visit. They should play Holst's 'Mars' through the loudspeakers.

Completion of the Channel Tunnel prompted a number of railway station improvements. The Waterloo International Terminal by Sir Nicholas Grimshaw and Partners, completed in 1993, was an extension of the existing station to accommodate Eurostar trains from Paris and Brussels. Work on a Eurostar terminal at St Pancras began in 2000, involving the refurbishment of the Victorian St Pancras station and the redevelopment of a large area to the north. The canopy, opened in 2004, must be the largest temporary structure built in London since the Festival of Britain.

CONCLUSION

By 2000 London architecture had achieved an unprecedented brilliance and variety, sharing in a world movement of Neo-Modern architecture. Britain was now the richest country in the European Union and London retained or even enhanced its world role. Drawing heavily on American contributions and on British architects with a worldwide activity, London's architecture was well up with the other top world cities. However, Kenneth Powell, the chronicler of British Neo-Modern, has gone further than this, asserting that since 1990 London had been 'arguably the most significant centre of architectural creativity anywhere.'[100] Many of the most successful London practices, Powell points out, have more prestigious projects abroad than at home.[101] Architects were honoured in a spectacular fashion. Rogers and Foster were members of the House of Lords and Foster was awarded an O.M., while Grimshaw, Farrell and Hopkins were all knights. Was this a new Augustan Age?

327   Percy Circus in 2004.

7 Conclusion: Has There Ever Been an Architecture of London?

In Chapter 1 I asked whether London had an architectural tradition. An architectural history of Bath could present a Bath Classical tradition over three hundred years, but other examples of such longevity are rare. We certainly cannot discern a London architecture over two thousand years. London's longest tradition, the Palladian style, lasted only about two hundred years without serious challenge. However, certain elements have been present throughout and others have been extremely long-lived. Most have already been mentioned, but we can now see clearly how they shaped London.

THE BOX HOUSE

The box house emerged from the obscurity of the early Middle Ages and is still with us. By the time of the Great Fire of 1666 most houses in the City and its suburbs had a rectangular plan with one or two rooms on the ground floor and between one and four floors above. There was little space behind the house, so it tended to retain a clear, box-like form (though low kitchens and workshops often stood behind the houses). Many post-Fire sites were probably smaller than their predecessors and there was a tendency to greater height but the box format survived. Most were built in rows of adjoining houses, with strong party walls. By the eighteenth century the houses of richer people were becoming deeper as well as higher, producing gloom in the middle of the house, but retaining the box form in its vertical variant.

In the suburbs of the nineteenth century sites became longer. Although the houses did not cover all their sites, the depth of terraced houses was usually much greater than their breadth. In the twentieth century there was a move towards a square plan. Many suburban houses were still built in rows but the detached and semi-detached house multiplied in outer areas. Even detached houses were normally of the box type but there was a move towards better natural lighting which enhanced the suburban lifestyle.

The box house influenced layout and design. When built in rows, it encouraged architects and even the most illiterate of builders to value conforming facades which were related, often only remotely, to Classical principles. It had a conservative influence on London architecture, creating a reassuring environment for those who were used to it. Some foreign observers, and especially the French, found it stultifying but most Londoners have lived in streets lined by nearly identical box houses from the Fire to the present day.

THE PARTY WALL

All but the houses of the rich shared a side wall, or walls, with a neighbouring structure or structures. These party walls were more important than their invisibility might suggest, with the authorities striving from the Middle Ages to make them strong and fireproof. Later, efforts were made to make them soundproof as well. Although cheaper materials could be used than on the facade, party walls were usually strong and a good support for the floor joists and roof timbers. They often survived fires and could be re-used.

THE TOWER OR SPIRE

Towers or spires adorned most London churches from the Fire onwards. Churches in the City were generally much smaller than those on the Continent because the parishes were small. Many pre-Fire churches were so tiny that they had only a bell turret, but when the number of parishes was halved after 1666, nearly all the survivors insisted on a tower or spire, a wish that Wren encouraged in pursuit of his great concept of a dome surrounded by a forest of spires.

When church building moved outside the City and the inner suburbs early in the eighteenth century, it responded to the large parishes there with correspondingly large new churches. Hawksmoor's East End churches were among the biggest of the day. Towers and spires became higher, with many exceeding sixty metres into the nineteenth century. They extended Wren's forest to the edge of the built-up area. The demand for a vertical feature is reflected in St Pancras New Church (1822–4) where a temple-like building in the most careful Greek Revival style was equipped with a Wren-like bell tower (though inspired by the Tower of the Winds in Athens).

The emancipation of the Roman Catholics and other religious minorities in the nineteenth century added to the number of churchbuilders and even some of the synagogues had their towers. From the 1970s large mosques added to the throng. The Hindus, Sikhs and Buddhists generally did not require large premises and often used their homes for worship but they were the exception in London's religious history, at any rate since the eighteenth century. This is not the place to start a religious census, but no other large western city appears to have as great a density of places of worship as London. These places give London its architectural character as much as any other building type.

PORTICOES, COLUMNS AND PILASTERS

Londoners are so used to porticoes that they rarely notice how many there are. The first portico was added to the west end of St Paul's cathedral by Inigo Jones in about 1630. In 1631–8 Jones built a smaller portico for his church of St Paul, Covent Garden. Attached porticoes using pilasters multiplied after 1660. Wren built a number, some of them decorative rather than actual entrances. The Palladian revival early in the eighteenth century produced a feast of porticoes, leading to the Neo-Classical and Greek Revival styles which were marked by further porticoes. A new surge of porticoes occurred from the 1880s to the 1930s during the great revival of the Classical styles. George Bernard Shaw's 'Pygmalion' starts under a portico.

After 1630 no other European city had as many porticoes. The portico flourished in America and in the British Empire but attached and decorative porticoes were always mainly a London feature. Painters often used porticoes as backgrounds and foreign artists were especially aware of them. The perceptive Jacques Tissot, who exhibited in both London and Paris, included three porticoes in his *London Visitors* (c. 1874) (two on the

328 and 329   Tissot's *London Visitors* (c. 1874) and (*below*) a contemporary photographic version of his subject.

National Gallery and one on the church of St Martin-in-the-Fields). The photographer Cyril Arapoff chose the same subject in about 1935.

Porticoes were expensive but impressive and they simplified the design of large buildings. At the same time, they spared the architect the task of developing alternative treatments and they usually influenced or determined the design of the other main elevations. The resulting Palladian conformity helped generate a conventional architecture which culminated in the weighty commercial buildings of the West End between 1890 and 1930, typified by the reconstruction of Regent Street. Fortunately, Modern architecture began to change all that but London's Roman inheritance lives on in the West End and in much of the City, often without much obvious distinction.

STONE, BRICK AND STUCCO

Materials constraints were a major factor until the nineteenth century. London's lack of local or regional building stone capable of forming ashlar was an obstacle to polite architecture. It could of course be obtained from a distance but it was never cheap enough to be used in the houses of most Londoners or in the general run of commercial buildings until the nineteenth century. Instead, London became a city of brick from the fifteenth century.

Brick

Brick could be made in London using clay dug from the foundations of new buildings or from nearby vacant land. Most London gardeners will tell you that there is no shortage of clay in London. Brick could also be imported from brickfields just outside London. It was a cheap and durable material. In 2000 it was still in much use, partly for aesthetic and traditional reasons but mainly because it was easy to lay and still the best material for exterior cladding in the London climate.[1] As the Romans also had used brick, it could be regarded as a timeless element of London architecture, though the only brick used between the departure of the Romans and the late Middle Ages was rescued from Roman ruins.

330   Brick frontages, Grays Inn Road, opposite the Water Rats headquarters (slightly disturbing pub and music hall linked to theatrical charities) on 24 May 2004. The houses appear to date from about 1840 except the one on the right (Ashlee House) where the frontage appears to have been rebuilt after war damage.

331   'A hundred years of brick'. The main structure here is the extravagant headquarters of the Theosophical Society, built by Lutyens in 1938 with funds provided by his wife and rich believers, and now part of the buildings of the British Medical Association. The brick terraces further down the street date from the first half of the nineteenth century.

211

London has become the world's largest brick city. However, brick cannot build more than simple walls and arches. Stone ornaments can be built into it, it can be 'rubbed' as it often was in the Tudor era and it can be carved (though with difficulty). Variants such as terracotta and faience are easy to mould but they are more expensive. Moulded bricks, known as 'specials', can be produced but London tradesmen rarely reached the Dutch level of skill in this area.[2] The combination of differing sizes and colours of brick on Dutch lines has almost never been attempted.

Brick weathers well, though all but glazed brick is liable to discolouring by smoke and until the recent development of pressure hosing it was difficult to clean. 'White brick', as sometimes used in the eighteenth century, could look a little like ashlar when well laid, as at Brooks's Club. Victorian architects generally believed that yellow London stock brick, being less pervious, resisted the London atmosphere better than red brick and it was widely used in the East End and in the eastern suburbs where, however, it quickly became horribly black. All brick nevertheless provides a solid base for coatings such as stucco, plastic coatings or stone paint which can be easily cleaned or repainted. Brick tends to generate rectangular window spaces and right-angled corners, sometimes modified by shallow, segmental arches, so it is often linked to simple structures of which the London box house is the main example. When concrete frames became common after 1945, stock brick was widely used as a filler on external walls. Brick has served London well, in its modest way.

★　★　★

332　Nash's garden front of Buckingham Palace, in 2004.

Stone

Only one stone could resist the London climate while being workable without too much trouble. This was Portland stone. Its strength, however, was also its weakness. Its self-cleaning qualities responded well to London's wind and rain but sheltered areas, quickly blackened, could make an embarrassing contrast. It was shaped in the Dorset quarries mainly in the form of solid ashlar blocks or in the thin, rectangular slabs which were used for cladding when the metal frame arrived after 1900. Portland stone statuary and carving, on the rare occasions when they were commissioned, often looked crude and over-assertive. For all this, Portland stone carried on as a prestigious building material from 1550 to 2000, surviving the Industrial Revolution and the rise of Modern architecture in the twentieth century.

A variety of limestones, sandstones and ironstones were quarried from a broad belt running from Bristol to York. Sandstone was almost never used in London; it deteriorated quickly even in country districts and it was far too soft and porous to resist the London climate. Ironstone was difficult to work and its russet colour could startle. The limestones had the most potential in London but by the nineteenth century the increasingly smoky and acidic air was causing difficulties. The most valued limestone of all, Bath stone, which resembles the limestone used in Paris, was first used in London on a large scale in the construction of St Bartholomew's Hospital (1730–68), where Ralph Allen of Bath hoped to publicise his quarries.[3] However, it was vulnerable to the atmosphere and, though used from time to time, especially on the houses of the rich, it often needed replacing or patching. The garden front of Nash's Buckingham Palace, for instance, shows much patching with new blocks of Bath stone. St Bartholomew's Hospital had to be recased by Philip Hardwick in 1836.[4]

Other types of stone were tried. Caen stone, a pure limestone from Normandy, was imported for some of the early Norman cathedrals and castles. It continued to be used on some major buildings until it fell out of use in the sixteenth century after coal smoke began to damage it. Edward Blore used it on Buckingham Palace after its use for church restorations in France had improved its reputation but his unusual choice deteriorated rapidly. Marble was imported from many sources, mainly in Italy, and was used in interiors, but to apply it to exteriors was a waste of good marble. John Nash hoped for the best with his Marble Arch but its brilliant surfaces quickly dulled. Granite, which came mostly from Dartmoor, the Lake District, Scotland or Scandinavia, was used from the nineteenth century onwards for bridge piers, dock walls, cladding, podiums, bases or the lower floors of large buildings. Even more resistant than Portland stone, it required too much work to produce a smooth, ashlar surface or small blocks. Polished granite could look like marble but it was normally used in huge, Cyclopean blocks with a rough or convex surface. Tower Bridge, New Scotland Yard and the Ritz Hotel used much granite but most London buildings, however large, did not. Perhaps the decisive factor was that granite for government buildings could be supplied free from the quarries at Dartmoor Prison.[5] One startling exception is Lasdun's flats at 26 St James's Place, where it was used with other highly resistant materials, including bronze for the window frames.[6] Knott's London County Hall was built of granite and Portland stone and is as solid as a rock.

A final type of 'stone' deserves mention. This was Coade Stone, an artificial stone whose origins dated back to 1722. Coade Stone could be shaped in moulds to produce durable, waterproof reproductions of carvings which looked like Portland stone. It was made on the South Bank (where County Hall now stands) and production expanded under the direction of Mrs Eleanor Coade from about 1769. It was used for a wide range, from quoins and trimmings to monumental statues and bas-reliefs.[7] In an age of brick, Coade Stone features could add cheap, Classical distinction to the most spartan of buildings. Its pretensions knew no limits. As seen, Coade Stone dressings were used on Blore's frontage at Buckingham Palace, where they lasted longer than his Caen stone. Coade Stone products were normally stamped visibly with the name of the company, which became widely known in consequence. The Coade Lion, a thirteen-ton mould made in 1837, stood over the entrance of the Lion Brewery and later over the entrance to Waterloo Station. It now stands on Westminster Bridge. However, Coade Stone had its competitors and the company was wound up in 1840.[8] Various other makes of artificial stone were used on London buildings, especially for ornaments, into the twentieth century.

Stucco

London's pollution led to stucco. This was a mixture of water, plaster, sand, lime, cement and other materials favoured by the maker. Perfected in the late eighteenth century by Robert Adam and others, it provided a cheap answer to problems of colour, carving and damp penetration. Applied to a base of common brick, it produced a smooth, paintable surface. Vertical surfaces of stucco were not greatly prone to weathering and even fine

333   Coade Stone caryatids at St Pancras Church.

details such as cornices and architraves survived without harm, especially when painted. Much early stucco was lined in paint to look like masonry blocks, and Nash ironically used a 'frescoing' technique to simulate weathering, but by the nineteenth century the favoured colours were unmarked white or cream. Pastel shades did not become popular until about 1960 when they were used in restorations. Stucco remained in wide use until about 1870 when brick became fashionable, largely under the influence of Philip Webb and Richard Norman Shaw.

BUILDING FOR THE SHORT TERM

Most building materials are judged on their solidity and durability. In London this is not necessarily so. As we have seen, London has a long tradition of building for a short life, perhaps more than any large western city except New York. The length of this life settled in the eighteenth century at about a hundred years and this target still inspires most London building.

It is usual to link the short life to the leasehold system but the explanation is much broader. In the Middle Ages the constant fires did not encourage owners to build to last. There was no alternative to timber, except for the very wealthy. Fire insurance did not become effective

334　Repairs at Bedford Place in 2003.

2000, though the usual period of lease tended to lengthen to 200 or even 999 years.

The conservation movement and the reduced rate of slum clearance slowed down the demolition of buildings in London from the 1970s. The successful conservation and re-use of Covent Garden market after 1974 followed a long campaign which aroused great public interest. More money was then put into the maintenance and refurbishment of buildings which were lasting well beyond their expected life. The exemption from Value Added Tax of work on listed buildings was not only a major encouragement but a symbol of change in official attitudes. The Burton terraces on the Bedford Estate secured a surge of investment by the end of the century as profitable hotel and business uses were found for what had often become listed buildings in conservation areas. London squares, in particular, proved flexible and ideal for a number of uses including offices.

until after the Fire. The average London house would have lasted forty years. Building regulations may have increased the sense of security as London moved towards the Great Fire, but greater densities and heights had an opposite effect.

Post-Fire building controls and insurance generated greater confidence but building leases then spread through the West End as aristocratic owners developed their estates. With buildings and improvements reverting to the lessor at the end of the lease, the lessee (developer or builder) had no interest in building to last. For instance, the land for the Adam brothers' Adelphi scheme was secured in 1768 on a ninety-nine year lease. Building started in 1772. The Adelphi looked built to last, with its frontage of noble, four-storey houses standing on giant brick vaults in a towering composition unrivalled in Europe. However, the elevations were radically remodelled according to Victorian taste in 1872 and most of the Adelphi was demolished for redevelopment in 1936. So it lasted more than ninety-nine years but not much more.

In the nineteenth century the standard period of lease settled at ninety-nine years and much building responded. Many of the rows built by James Burton on the Bedford estate in Bloomsbury after 1800 looked cheap from the start. Much housing in inner London deteriorated in the later years of the lease as maintenance was skimped and the district went downhill socially. In the twentieth century speculation in building land produced rapid rises in values which discouraged the outright sale of the freehold and the leasehold system flourished until

FIRES

London's fires were a constant problem until the mid-nineteenth century. They were not just due to cheap construction and high densities. London had a tradition of heating and cooking by open fires, fed by the universal taste for roast meat. The great houses of the rich often caught fire when unreliable servants failed to tend the ranges, usually after falling asleep. Inattentive servants were, however, a problem anywhere in the house and the bigger the house, the worse the problem. A subsidiary danger was lighting by unprotected candles, which lasted well into the nineteenth century.

Some buildings were more at risk than others. Public buildings let out in private offices were always in danger, among them the post-Fire Royal Exchange, which burned down in 1838, and Wren's Custom House of 1669, which lasted only until a fire in 1718. As Saunders has pointed out, the Custom House, first opened in 1382, was burnt down four times thereafter.[9] Theatres burnt down frequently until the end of the nineteenth century, when fireproof design and electric light came in. Until then, twenty years was a normal life for a theatre. Industrial fires were recurrent. So were warehouse fires until fireproof building became universal and obligatory in the mid-nineteenth century. Only church fires were rare, owing to the lack of flammable contents. Those burnt included St Martin Outwich, Threadneedle Street (1765), and St Paul, Covent Garden (1795).

Major conflagrations were less frequent after 1666 but they persisted in the East End and south of the Thames until the mid-nineteenth century.[10] E. L. Jones and his

335 High Holborn in the late nineteenth century, looking east with Staple Inn on the right. This is a sunny summer's day but coal pollution nevertheless mars the view.

336 Holborn Circus, looking up Holborn Viaduct, c. 1890. This is a clearer day but there is enough pollution to blur the distant buildings.

colleagues have detected fifty-seven 'multiple house fires' (more than ten buildings) in London between 1666 and 1839.[11] Large groups of buildings remained vulnerable, like the Palace of Whitehall which burned down in 1698, only Jones's Banqueting Hall surviving, and the adjacent Palace of Westminster which went up in flames in 1512 and 1834. After about 1850 conflagrations were less common owing to stronger building regulations and the spread of the suburbs at lower densities.

CLIMATE AND POLLUTION

London architecture has always struggled against the weather. The struggle was at its height between about 1750 and 1950, when the density of coal smoke reached a high plateau.[12] Between 1950 and 2000 the smoke was reduced, thanks mainly to the Clean Air Act of 1956, but motor and heating fumes arising from the use of oil replaced it. These fumes did not combine with damp weather as disastrously as coal smoke, which produced sulphuric acid and the black droplets of the London fog, and although they often blurred distant views they did not obscure or distort nearby buildings.[13] With sunny days apparently more common in London towards the end of the twentieth century, architects could venture more freely into colour and subtlety.

Even without pollution, however, the London climate challenged the architect. Flat roofs were always likely to leak sooner or later and architects clung to pitched roofs from Roman times until large housing and commercial blocks with roofs supported by powerful beams and girders came on the scene from about 1850, following advances in warehouse construction. This meant that many roofs on buildings of Classical inspiration had to be hidden by balustrades or parapets, or artistically emphasised as at County Hall or Lutyens's banks. Voids and balconies were likely to accumulate damp and their floors deteriorated fast. Even Inigo Jones's loggia at the Queen's House has needed frequent repair.[14] As a result, architects and builders avoided insets on their facades and tried to protect windowsills from drips. Balconies were rare until added to local authority flats as drying and storage space after 1918.

LIGHT

Even at its sunny best, London light was far different from Italy's. It was weaker and more sharply angled. Moisture in the air was thicker than in Italy and images were often slightly blurred. Light and colour contrasts were sharper in Italy. In the winter with its mists, fogs and rain, the outlines and details of London buildings were often difficult to see clearly. Paris had much better light. Architects often created bold, strong outlines, as in Wren's great spires, or in the Streamline Moderne cinemas of the 1930s. Detail, especially higher up a building, was often strengthened even though it often became cruder as a result. On features like cornices, however, detail was simplified or abandoned. Turrets, spires and cupolas were used to direct attention to the top of a building and to prevent the eye being disappointed when it reached it.

Colour responses varied. Stucco could be painted but repainting was ideally carried out every three to five years. With houses in the stucco areas rising up to five or six storeys, repainting was often neglected and a dull

337 The Quadrant, Piccadilly, as rebuilt, mainly by Sir Reginald Blomfield but on lines sketched by Shaw and Webb, in the 1920s. The simple elevations, Tyrolean roofs and multiple dormers enhance a unified concept of great power. This is the epitome of Britain's crescent tradition, following Nash and his successors. There is nothing like it anywhere in the world.

brown or yellow was often the result.[15] Not until faience, a glazed form of terracotta tile, became available from about 1900 was it possible to use materials which would produce a white, or light-coloured, building without further treatment. It was used sparingly because of its cost and because owners of neighbouring buildings might resent a glaring contrast. The Regent Palace Hotel (1910) was entirely clad in faience tiles and so were Summit House, Red Lion Square (1925) and the White House, Albany Street, off Regent's Park (1936). In these cases the colour chosen was similar to Bath stone. The tiles weathered well though where exposed on the upper levels they became much whiter. Bright colours were not normally used because architects knew that they appeared tawdry under the London light.[16] The other response was to design a dark building with strong features, as Richard Norman Shaw often did, for instance with his towering chimneys (though these may have been a practical contribution to clearing the smoke). Such features could produce a mysterious, threatening city. Observers were especially aware of these effects in the winter but the advantage of the 'dark city' solution was that it justified the use of brick.

ARCHITECTURAL STYLES

Complete continuity of architectural style cannot be expected over two thousand years but one style, or group of styles, certainly did its best. This was the Classical mode, within which the Palladian was dominant. Classical architecture provided the main face of authority, title, wealth, status, fashion and taste in London from early in the seventeenth century to the early part of the twentieth. As this design tradition was largely inspired by Ancient Rome, one can add the years 43 to 410 as an early effort to build a Classical London (though even the largest buildings in Roman London bore little resemblance to the mighty structures of Rome itself). This

338 The Quadrant in 2004.

means that London has passed through some seven hundred years of Classical architecture. Only in the years after about 1830, when the Gothic and other styles produced a revolutionary eclecticism, was Classical architecture challenged but it was not completely surpassed until the 1950s when Modern architecture began to dominate. Even then, the brief revival of the Classical in the 1980s and 1990s was still to come.

The Palladian was London's main Classical style until about 1770 when its derivative, the Neo-Classical, began to become popular. The main effect of London's Neo-Classical was, however, on interiors as in the work of the Adam brothers. Neo-Classical exteriors, in houses, churches and public buildings, did not diverge greatly from the Palladian tradition. The Greek Revival of the early 1800s was something new but it failed to establish itself. Wren's English Baroque was often influential but Continental Baroque had only a brief success in the early eighteenth century and Rococo was only used for interiors.

Other London styles included the Romanesque (1040–1200), the Gothic (1150–1500) and the Tudor (1500–1600). Castles and other defences were the products of military engineering. What is now called Mannerist design, derived from distant gleams of the Italian Renaissance via Holland and France, emerged from about 1520 and lasted until about 1700. The Classical and its derivatives swept all this away after 1600. Non-Classical alternatives throve under Victoria. Modern architecture, which has much in common with the Classical, began to transform London from about 1930 and will probably last well beyond the seventy-five years which it has endured so far. However, the rise of preservation, conservation and environmental concern since about 1970 means that most of Classical London has many years of healthy life ahead of it. With the Modern free to flourish in the Docklands and the City, the post-war battle between heritage and redevelopment came to an end in about 1980. Classical London was safer in 2000 than at any time since Victoria's day.

The question remains: why was the Classical so influential in London, and for so long? Yet why did it dominate Paris for even longer, and without a period of

217

339 The (?)last gasp of the Palladian: an office block facing the Thames, north of Charing Cross. This one makes every mistake in the book.

disruption in the nineteenth century? Part of the answer lies in the fact that the Parisian Classical was different from London's. To begin with, much of it retained medieval elements, including tall roofs, dormer windows and conical turrets. The seventeenth century saw the addition of purely practical features such as the mansard roof, which emphasised the upper level of the building, the ground-floor arcade, the entresol and the metal window-guard. Perrault's eastern and southern fronts of the Louvre, built between 1667 and 1680, laid the foundation of a French royal style on impressive, but relaxed, Classical lines. Many of the mansions built in the eighteenth century were in an eclectic Baroque or Rococo. Round-headed arches were frequent. In the nineteenth century statuary was often placed above the cornice line. Continuous metal balconies and external shutters were often features of apartment blocks and small cupolas became quite frequent. The result was ordered, impressive and easy on the eye, a combination of the rational and the picturesque.

London's Classical followed a different course. The pursuit of Palladian perfection, beginning with Inigo Jones, produced a more austere aesthetic. The Baroque's association with Toryism, France and the Roman Catholic Church held it back in the eighteenth century. The Palladian then became associated with economical building and repetition. It became thoroughly predictable in the eighteenth century and though leavened by the Neo-Classical its limitations helped stimulate the Gothic-Eclectic alternative. The Italianate, not the Palladian, became the equivalent of the Parisian Classical in the nineteenth century. However, it was rarely

carried out with the same skill as in Paris. London Classical revived at the end of the nineteenth century and the Palladian flourished in public buildings until the 1930s.

In Paris the Classical was a more attractive style than in London and many streets and squares were ideal Classical architecture. Nineteenth-century Parisian architects valued the Romantic and the Picturesque as much as the Londoners but they never allowed them to disrupt the aesthetic of their city. So the Classical, broadly defined, lived on until the 1950s.

TRAINING

The lack of a national school of architecture, similar to the French Ecole des Beaux-Arts and its predecessors, was probably less of a handicap in London than it might appear. From about 1750 most young architects were articled in the offices of senior men and Summerson sees this as equivalent to a programme of training.[17] It has been suggested that employment in the Office of Works also provided something approaching a systematic architectural training.[18] However, Paris offered a demanding, formal programme of instruction and practice which produced a high standard of competence especially in Classical design and in its aesthetic and philosophical background. It tended to encourage conservatism but the Paris-trained architect usually achieved the highest quality in all his buildings. A series of prestigious prizes encouraged study abroad. The Parisian architect was confident and proud of the tradition in which he worked, which dated back to Henry IV and Louis XIV.

By the late eighteenth century the young English architect could choose between a number of lecture programmes in London and prizes were on offer. However, Britain lacked the great synthetic treatises or textbooks like those of Perrault, Blondel and Durand. Most of these huge French works were the product of lectures given in Paris and were used by students and young architects all over France. The lack of formal, examined training programmes in London until late in the nineteenth century meant that such comprehensive works were not needed in England. Indeed, some English students used the French texts. The best-known early British treatise was Sir William Chambers's *Treatise on Civil Architecture*, which appeared in 1759 and was republished in 1768 and 1791.[19] Chambers was a French laureate and more closely in touch with French architecture than any Englishman but he eschewed the lengthy theorising which was normal in the French texts and limited himself mainly to the decorative aspects.[20] Of course, students used Palladio and the other Italian masters, all of which were available in translation.

Education in architecture was available at the Royal Academy Schools from 1768. John Soane and Richard Norman Shaw, among many others, studied there. Training took the form of series of lectures, often given by famous architects. In 1870 the Schools were reorganised under the influence of the Architectural Association's training programme, founded in 1847.[21] Shaw, for instance, was a Visitor in the Architectural School there in 1881 and G. E. Street gave a course of lectures there in the same year.[22] Most of the students worked for their practices during the day, attending the Royal Academy Schools in the evening. The young Shaw, for instance, attended the Class of Design on some evenings each week, where he was taught by C. R. Cockerell.[23] Students could enter for the Royal Academy Gold Medal and winners often went to study in Italy, sometimes with the support of the highly competitive Travelling Studentship. The Gold Medal was a less formal, and less well endowed, equivalent of the French Prix de Rome but it offered considerable prestige.

In the eighteenth and early nineteenth centuries young architects often went to study in Rome with the support of aristocratic patrons and some met potential clients there. One of the earliest was James Gibbs, Burlington's reject. Few took advantage of French training at this time, no doubt seeing that the great Italians were better mentors. However, from about 1850 a growing number of English architects went to study, formally and informally, at the Ecole des Beaux-Arts and they mingled with the many Americans who studied there towards the end of the century.

Beginning with Henry Holland's work at Carlton House and Nash's at Buckingham Palace, and going on to the development of the Aldwych in the 1920s, a persuasive French influence was visible in central London. The Prince Regent, later George IV, was a strong supporter. By the end of the nineteenth century architects were familiar with the elegant Beaux-Arts styles of the day and a new, elegant London was emerging.

The (Royal) Institute of British Architects, founded in 1834, also built up a programme of lectures and moved towards a formal course and qualification. Voluntary examinations began there in 1863 and they became a requirement for associate membership in 1882. The Architectural Association was set up in 1847 by more than a hundred young architects who wanted to be free of the articled pupil system and to set up an educational system 'for architects by architects'. A design class was held every two weeks, with additional courses, given on a voluntary basis, in later years. Its training had become

extensive and respected by the end of the century and in 1901 it set up a day school. In the twentieth century a full system of training was in place, leading to the RIBA Associateship. Ralph Knott, the young architect of London County Hall, was among many who attended classes there. However, articled pupils were still abundant at the turn of the century and most paid for the privilege, with a top architect like Aston Webb able to charge up to £500.[24] In 1892 Banister Fletcher set up a full-time course in architecture at King's College, London. The Bartlett School of Architecture and the Polytechnic School of Architecture, Regent Street, followed. Evening courses were offered in a number of places and the Royal Academy School of Architecture remained active. Provincial schools were founded, notably at Liverpool in 1904. The RIBA and other bodies set up a Rome Prize in 1912, with winners studying in the Faculty of Architecture at the British School in Rome, which had been founded in 1901. The Rome Prize crowned a hierarchy of prizes which was by now comparable to those on offer to young French and American architects but there was some suggestion at the time that it encouraged deferential conservatism rather than innovation.[25]

By the 1920s most architects entering independent practice had qualified on a three- or four-year course or its equivalent in evening study. They took a broader view of architecture than most of their articled predecessors and they were tolerant of, or even enthusiastic about, the Modern. Ironically, their French equivalents did not break away from their Beaux-Arts mentality to the same extent. London had accepted the need for training at last and its architects went into the Modern era on a much firmer footing than those of Paris.[26]

COMPETITIONS

Competitions became quite common from the 1820s, with the competition for the Travellers' Club in 1828 setting a trend.[27] Many, however, were closed competitions intended to attract well-known architects and to encourage them to put in some serious work. Young architects were often attracted to the small number of open competitions but these were mainly provincial affairs. Even there, they knew that they had little chance of winning and they frequently submitted little more than draft plans and elevations.[28] The open competitions were often determined by an elite of invited competitors, some of whom were transformed into assessors in the final stages. In theory, promising young entrants could be selected as winners on the assumption that their designs could be developed later on but this rarely happened. Their best chance was in the 'battle of the styles' period between about 1830 and 1880 when the great Gothic challenge to the Palladian had 'broken the mould' and the choice of prize-winning designs was unusually unpredictable. The influence of Arts and Crafts, Free Style and Art Nouveau from the 1870s probably favoured younger architects. When the handling of the Law Courts competition in 1866 was widely criticised, competitions became less popular, partly on the grounds that they favoured senior architects who often produced mediocre designs.[29] An important exception was the London County Hall competition in 1907, won by a very young architect.

There was still a future for the closed competition, or consultation. This technique was revived by London developers in the 1980s and it generated a clear focus on the design and planning issues. By 2000 these competitions were in decline but they had helped create a positive climate for Neo-Modern architecture.

FOREIGN ARCHITECTS

Until the 1920s London was built almost entirely by British architects. This changed between the wars when Americans arrived to build some large, steel-framed structures. The Americans returned from the 1970s. Some of the best British architects, like Richard Rogers who had trained at Yale, became international in their activities and outlook. Rogers and Renzo Piano built the astounding Pompidou Centre in Paris in the 1970s, transforming Rogers's career and allowing him to return to London as one of the greatest architects of his day. This degree of innovation was new for London and it contributed to the creation of Lloyd's and other revolutionary buildings in the City. It also contributed to the astounding environment of Docklands where Rogers further enhanced his reputation.

Until the Americans arrived, foreign architects had built little in London, with the exception of the eleventh and early twelfth centuries when Norman masons were active. During the Renaissance the English Crown did little to attract foreign architects, in contrast to the French royalty and aristocracy which valued the presence of Italian architects in particular. Italian and French decorators were common enough in London but not architects. John Harvey detects an influential contribution from Antonio Toto dell' Nunziata of Florence and John of Padua, employed by the Crown in the 1540s and 1550s, and by implication blames them for the growth of Mannerism.[30] However, English Mannerism could

emerge readily enough from Serlio and other books and a few more Italians might well have restrained its excesses. It may be surmised that these two Italians worked at Henry VIII's Nonsuch Palace (demolished) but this had little influence. Antonio and John appear to have been exceptional and they did not lead to much recruitment of Italians in the mid-sixteenth century, partly no doubt because Elizabeth would not have wanted to pay them. Isaac de Caus, a Frenchman who worked for members of the Court from the 1630s, was mainly a designer of gardens and grottoes, though he worked with Inigo Jones on the Banqueting House and perhaps at Covent Garden.[31] The Italian James Leoni, whose English edition of Palladio was published in 1715, built three houses in London and several country houses.[32] His work was impeccable and he had a considerable reputation until his death in 1746, though Richard Hewlings maintains somewhat controversially that Leoni adopted English Palladianism rather than introduced the Venetian variety.[33] During the eighteenth century a number of French craftsmen worked on the interiors of London houses but few designed the exteriors.[34] Robert Adam employed a number of Italian, and one Belgian, draughtsmen.[35] An unknown French architect worked for a while on the clubhouse of the Society of Dilettanti but Sir Francis Dashwood reported in 1753 that 'my rascally french architect is ran off and has left nothing but his debts', leading to the abandonment of the scheme.[36]

Not all the American architects and engineers who worked on London buildings were based in England. Daniel Burnham was the main creator of Selfridge's but his contribution was made from Chicago. Raymond Hood, winner of the *Chicago Tribune* competition, co-designed Palladium House in 1928 but worked from New York. Bush House was built by an American firm, Corbett and Hemle, which kept a London office. Americans were involved in many lesser department stores and big hotels. They played a large part in London's Streamline Moderne in the 1930s. From the late 1970s they returned to London to work for big international developers and they had a huge impact in the towering City and Docklands. London was by then the international world city to which all could contribute, as long as they could function in English.

The Continental architects who came to Britain in the 1930s made a big impact in London, especially by reinforcing the Modern Movement. Even though some, like Gropius, soon left, they inspired the MARS Group. With public taste already moving towards the Modern, the work of Eric Mendelsohn and other leading foreigners showed what could be done. Most worked and lived in London where they mingled with the native intelligentsia and rich. The parties held at Ernö Goldfinger's house in Hampstead drew artists, writers and clients, many of whom seem to have lived in the Hampstead area. Most Modern Movement building was done outside London, but Highpoint 1 and 2 by Berthold Lubetkin and Tecton owed part of its influence to its London location.

BUILDING REGULATIONS

Efforts to control London building began in the Middle Ages. The regulations were directed mainly at houses but in the nineteenth century warehouses, factories and commercial buildings came under control. Churches and other public buildings were subject only to basic requirements relating to building and fire safety. In the twentieth century new building materials and techniques, and the drive to greater heights, led to new controls or exceptions. Town planning norms and decisions increasingly merged with the building regulations to allow new urban forms. Overall, the regulations were cumulative, which meant that their general effect was conservative.

Did London's building regulations help shape its architecture? Or did they merely reflect tendencies in building techniques, design and demand? London's medieval controls sought mainly to secure fireproof building, and fire and structural safety for adjoining houses, by stressing the party walls. What made them necessary, however, was the London pattern of adjoining, timber houses of up to five storeys. The regulations appear to have reinforced a type of building which would have grown up in any case.

The emphasis on fire continued after 1600 but with greater attention to the outer walls. In 1605 brick or stone was required for all new buildings except window and door frames and shop fronts, while aesthetic issues came into play, with efforts made to secure uniform frontages. Minimum ceiling heights date from 1619, when jettying was banned. The post-Fire Building Act of 1667 required 'uniform' roofs and the maximum number of storeys was related to street widths for all but mansions standing within their own sites. The maximum height for buildings on high and principal streets was five storeys, while houses fronting onto the lowest class of street, by-streets and lanes, could not exceed three storeys. Window dimensions were restricted to prevent the spread of fire along the outer walls and the result was that all but the smallest houses generally had a row of two or more identical windows on each floor. To secure more light through these windows, a progression occurred from mainly square windows after the Fire to tall, rectangular sash windows. Where houses were built adjoining in rows, long lines of identical windows built up, producing crude perspective effects. These were reinforced by the ban on gables in 1707 which tended to produce a continuous horizontal line at the level of the eaves, cornice or parapet.

By the early eighteenth century much of the City and the West End displayed a conformity without parallel in Europe. This conformity was largely a result of the building regulations and especially of London's radical post-Fire measures. The Act of 1774 then followed the naval example by allocating each building to a 'rate' with defined characteristics and appropriate regulations. It extended regulation to churches, factories and com-

340 and 341 Flexibility in London terraced housing on the Hornsey estate of the Artisans', Labourer' and General Dwellings Company, c. 1870.

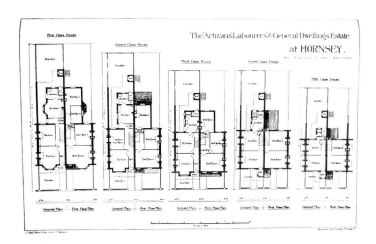

221

mercial buildings but removed the street-related height limits of 1667, allowing tall buildings to be erected on narrow streets and alleys, foreshadowing the congested commercial City of the nineteenth century. The design of terraced houses, which fell into three of the rates, became even more standardised after 1774 than it had been before.

The first Building Act to take public health and traffic into account was passed in 1844. Repealing the Act of 1774, it fixed minimum widths for new streets and established that building heights on these streets should not exceed their width. It did not restrict the height of buildings on existing streets but it paved the way towards a new, suburban architecture. As smaller and lower houses multiplied in the suburbs from about 1850, they were less constrained by the Building Acts and architects such as Shaw and Voysey were able to design more freely. In 1894 a rare concession to the architect occurred when projecting gables or eaves were allowed in detached or semi-detached houses to allow the overhanging roofs pioneered by Voysey and others outside London.

In central London, meanwhile, taller buildings were a growing problem, especially when combined with high ground coverage. The Act of 1894 fixed the maximum height at 24.4 metres plus two storeys in the roof, a total of 30.5 metres. The turn of the century saw Acts dealing with steel-frame, and later concrete-frame, construction. A formal height limit of 30.5 metres was set by the London Building Acts (Amendment) Act of 1939.

After 1945 the emphasis switched towards exceptions to the Building Acts in response to developments in modern architecture and commercial requirements and to town planning concepts. Creative architecture was clearly in command and London changed rapidly from its traditional, conformist appearance to an unconstrained one, at least in the City, the West End, the East End and Docklands. Elsewhere, however, conservation and community ideals reinforced the traditional townscape.

The connection between architecture and building relations requires much more consideration than can be undertaken here, and the following conclusions are speculative. First, as we have seen, from the Middle Ages to the eighteenth century the London regulations were intended mainly to prevent fire in residential buildings. The form of those buildings was mainly determined by the land market and the builders. Buildings of the rich, churches and public buildings were not greatly affected by regulation. Inigo Jones and Christopher Wren clearly wanted to use the regulations to create a Renaissance city of beauty and order but little was done to that effect. Traffic and health concerns, and increasing heights,

played little part until the 1844 Act and its successors. By this time, regulation was purely practical and the aesthetic result was left to the market and to the architects who served it. Suburban building was not greatly affected by building regulations and architecture was at its freest here.

By 1914 the corpus of London building regulations was thorough and extensive, though still lacking in aesthetic requirements like those of Paris. Already under pressure from the 1920s, it was challenged in the 1960s and architects became free to draw on the potential of Modern architecture.

CONCLUSION

So has there ever been an architecture of London? Yes, there has. London has always had an architecture that can keep out rain and damp. Since the seventeenth century it has largely been an architecture of brick, though concrete has played a big part in the twentieth century. Pitched roofs have been present since Roman times. Balconies and loggias have been rare. Interiors have been very comfortable as Londoners spend most of their free time inside. Flimsy building lasted until the twentieth century. Fires discouraged expensive building until the middle of the nineteenth century. The leasehold system had a similar effect from the beginning of the seventeenth. Longer leases and the spread of freehold in the twentieth century encouraged greater solidity though much municipal housing and the cheaper private estates conformed to the older London tradition.

From the seventeenth century London architecture gave a big place to greenery, except in the City. With the leasehold system keeping land values low, and residential development for the rich requiring the provision of open space, London created more open space than any other European capital, mostly in the form of squares and crescents and private gardens lying mainly at the back of the house. With many of the richest houses facing the squares, architects began to design facades which looked good when fronted by large trees and viewed down planned paths. The City, which became increasingly congested, could not join in this aesthetic, but much of the rest of London shared in it. Streets had little greenery, it is true, but when low-density expansion developed from the mid-nineteenth century, many acquired trees and other greenery grew up in the front gardens. Architects responded by designing stronger frontage features which were visible through the branches and cottage-style houses which looked good in a green environment. From the 1950s opponents of tall buildings objected to those which could be seen from inside public parks and some architects modified their dimensions and treatments to make them less 'intrusive'. The City and the Docklands never had an architecture of greenery but elsewhere it was an essential part of London in 2000.

The royal parks were the foundation of green London but London lacked impressive royal palaces. This feature dates back to the Middle Ages when Whitehall Palace and Westminster Palace grew up into a ragged collection of mainly modest buildings. St James's Palace, though built by a spendthrift Henry VIII, was small and conservative in its design. Kensington Palace was small and built on the cheap and Buckingham Palace grew out of a modest country house, with limited funds provided by Parliament. Some monarchs retired to Windsor Castle whenever possible. London never had a giant palace like the Louvre on which the finest architects worked with no expense spared. Of course, that was the price of democratic monarchy.

That young architects learned their trade mainly on the job until the twentieth century is a fundamental feature of the architecture of London. It helped create architectural 'dynasties' within which design traditions were passed on, like the Wyatt dynasty and the Scott–Street–Shaw–Lethaby tradition which covered much of the nineteenth century. It could also produce limited, conventional architects who emerged from nondescript practices. The overall effect is hard to assess but it looks as though the trainees ended up as good, or as bad, as their masters. This book is full of young English architects who went to study in Italy or France but not many foreigners ever wanted to train in England, at least until after 1945.

Most European cities have wide areas of common building heights and London has been no exception. Pre-Fire London was largely three storeys high and this was a common height after 1667. When taller houses were built, as had become common by the early nineteenth century, their design formula was little different, with extra floors and rows of windows simply added on. Simple facade designs were a feature of London houses between the Fire and the late nineteenth century. Most other west European capitals had more decorative and varied domestic facades than did London. The London three-storey brick row of box houses which lasted from 1666 to about 1900 was astoundingly ordinary and only the simple street perspective could rescue it.

Much of this ceased to be true in the twentieth century. London's enthusiastic adoption of Modern architecture has allowed it to join a world movement. Young architects from abroad now come to study at the Architectural Association and other schools and many go on to work in London. Some of the best London architects now work abroad as much or more as they do in Britain. Technical prowess, helped by the Americans, ranks London with Chicago, Hong Kong and Tokyo. Conservation architecture in London is an example to the rest of the world. It is too soon to say whether a new architecture of London has come on the scene but a trip on the Docklands Light Railway will suggest that London has created an entirely new cityscape.

342   Docklands in 2004. The new urban landscape.

Notes

Preface

1   A. Sutcliffe, *Paris: An Architectural History*, New Haven and London: Yale University Press, 1993.
2   D. Watkin, *The Rise of Architectural History*, London: Architectural Press, 1980, pp. vii–viii.
3   D. Gentleman, *London*, London: Weidenfeld and Nicolson, 1985.

Chapter 1

1   Beer stone was brought to London in 1347 for use on the Palace of Westminster; J. Harvey, *English Mediaeval Architects: A Biographical Dictionary down to 1550* (2nd edn), Gloucester: Alan Sutton, 1984, p. 1.
2   Christopher Wren quoted in A. Clifton-Taylor and A. Ireson, *English Stone Building*, London: Victor Gollancz, 1983, p. 16.
3   For Roger Pratt's notes on the costs of using Portland stone, which suggest that it was twice as expensive to carve as softer stones, see R. Gunther, *The Architecture of Sir Roger Pratt*, Oxford University Press, 1928, p. 221.
4   W. Te Brake, 'Air Pollution and Fuel Crises in Pre-industrial London, 1250–1650', *Technology and Culture*, XVI (2), 1975, p. 339; see also P. Brimblecombe, *The Big Smoke: A History of Air Pollution in London since Medieval Times*, London: Routledge, 1987, pp. 5–9.
5   Te Brake, 'Air Pollution', p. 340.
6   Brimblecombe, *The Big Smoke*, pp. 29–30.
7   *Ibid.*, p. 34.
8   *Ibid.*, p. 38. Some blackened and damaged limestone from the old cathedral is on view in the triforium of Wren's St Paul's.
9   Brimblecombe, *The Big Smoke*, pp. 54–65.
10 Jones and Woodward, pp. 422–3.
11 Bradley and Pevsner, 1, p. 341.
12 C. Barron, 'London, 1300–1540', in D. Palliser (ed.), *The Cambridge Urban History of Britain*, Cambridge University Press, 2000, 1: 600–1540, p. 397. See map in Jones and Woodward, p. 426.

Chapter 2

1   For John Schofield's informed dicussion of timber building, see his *Medieval London Houses*, New Haven and London: Yale University Press, 1995, pp. 140–50.
2   For an up-to-date and clear survey of building in Roman London, see G. Milne, *Roman London: Urban Archaeology in the Nation's Capital*, London: Batsford, 1995.
3   *Ibid.*, p. 45.
4   W. F. Grimes, *The Excavation of Roman and Medieval London*, London: Routledge, 1968, p. 11.
5   See reconstruction of the Cheapside bath house in J. Morris, *Londinium: London in the Roman Empire*, London: Weidenfeld and Nicolson, 1982, pl. 13.
6   Milne, *Roman London*, p. 73; Bradley and Pevsner, 1, p. 40.
7   Bradley and Pevsner, 1, pp. 39–40.
8   E. Howe, *Roman Defences and Medieval Industry: Excavations at Baltic House, City of London*, Museum of London Archaeology Service, 2002, pp. 1–25.
9   Contribution by Martin Millett to B. Watson (ed.), *Roman London: Recent Archaeological Work*, Portsmouth, R.I: *Journal of Roman Archaeology*, 1998, p. 7, n. 1.
10 Milne, *Roman London*, p. 53.
11 P. Marsden, *The Roman Forum Site in London: Discoveries Before 1985*, London: HMSO, 1987.
12 *Ibid.*, pp. 38–64.
13 *Ibid.*, p. 67.
14 To compare like with like between London and Rome, see e.g. S. B. Platner, *A Topographical Dictionary of Ancient Rome*, Oxford University Press, 1926. See esp. the contemporary Basilica Ulpia in Trajan's Forum, only slightly longer than the London basilica but boasting marble columns and bronze quadrigae. Its walls were faced with marble and its timber roof was covered with bronze. Its floor was paved with white marble (pp. 241–2).
15 See Grimes, *Excavation*, pp. 92–117; for a full report see J. Shepherd, *The Temple of Mithras, London*, London: English Heritage, 2002.
16 See photographs in R. Merrifield, *The Roman City of London*, London: Ernest Benn, 1965, pls 72–83.
17 Marsden, *Roman Forum Site*, p. 32.
18 See Grimes, *Excavation*, pp. 15–39.

19 Gravel was used in the construction of roads in the Southwark area. It came from large gravel pits there: P. Hinton (ed.), *Excavations in Southwark 1973–76: Lambeth 1973–79*, Museum of London, 1988, pp. 19–30.

20 Grimes, *Excavation*, pp. 47–78; Bradley and Pevsner, I, pp. 37–40.

21 Tim Eaton's *Plundering the Past: Roman Stonework in Medieval Britain*, Stroud: Tempus, 2000, a national review of the re-use of Roman materials, makes no reference to spoliation in London.

22 The text and plates in Merrifield, *Roman City of London*, provide an extensive picture of Roman London's buildings and artefacts.

23 See A. Vince, *Saxon London: An Archaeological Investigation*, London: Seaby, 1990, pp. 26–37.

24 Schofield, *Medieval London Houses*, p. 27. Schofield (pp. 28–9) provides examples of house plans of the eleventh, twelfth and thirteenth centuries which, even in the absence of plot boundaries, suggest that each house had little land behind or at the side and certainly nothing similar to a burgage plot.

25 D. Palliser (ed.), *The Cambridge Urban History of Britain*, I: *600–1540*, Cambridge University Press, 2000, p. 170.

26 J. Campbell, *Brick: A World History*, London: Thames & Hudson, 2003, p. 78.

27 See R. Harris, *Discovering Timber-framed Buildings* (3rd edn), Princes Risborough: Shire Publications, 1993, p. 50.

28 See E. Gee, *A Glossary of Building Terms used in England from the Conquest to c. 1550*, Frome Historical Research Group, 1984, p. 78.

29 M. Reed, 'The Urban Landscape, 1540–1700', in P. Clark (ed.), *The Cambridge Urban History of Britain*, II: *1540–1840*, Cambridge University Press, 2000, p. 293. Houses with a one-room plan are discussed by Schofield, *Medieval London Houses*, p. 53.

30 Summerson coined the term 'unit-house' for this type: Summerson, I, p. 50. For the conflation of rural building plans in towns, which produced this concentrated plan, see Harris, *Timber-framed Buildings*, p. 53.

31 See plans in F. Brown, 'Continuity and Change in the Urban House: Developments in Domestic Space Organisation in Seventeenth-century London', *Comparative Studies in Society and History*, XXVIII, 1986, pp. 558–90.

32 *Ibid.*, pp. 561–6.

33 Harris, *Timber-framed Buildings*, p. 53.

34 See Schofield, *Medieval London Houses*, p. 173.

35 Drawing reprinted in F. Parker and P. Jackson, *The History of London in Maps*, London: Barrie and Jenkins, 1990, p. 19.

36 J. Harvey, *English Mediaeval Architects: A Biographical Dictionary down to 1550* (2nd edn), Gloucester: Alan Sutton, 1984, p. 24.

37 P. Hammond, *The Tower of London*, London: Department of the Environment, 1987, pp. 4–5.

38 J. Campbell, 'Power and Authority, 600–1300', in Palliser, *Cambridge Urban History*, I, p. 60.

39 D. Watkin, *A History of Western Architecture* (3rd edn), London: Laurence King, 2000, pp. 128–9; R. Gem, 'The Romanesque Architecture of Old St Paul's Cathedral and its Late Eleventh-century Context', in L. Grant (ed.), *Medieval Art, Architecture and Archaeology in London*, London: British Archaeological Association, 1990, p. 47.

40 Harvey, *English Mediaeval Architects*, p. 125.

41 J. Schofield, 'Medieval and Tudor Buildings in the City of London', in Grant, *Medieval Art*, p. 20.

42 C. Barron, *London in the Later Middle Ages: Government and People, 1200–1500*, Oxford University Press, 2004, p. 248.

43 Summerson, I, p. 50.

44 Schofield, *Medieval London Houses*, pp. 171, 173.

45 *Ibid.*, pp. 41–4.

46 Bradley and Pevsner, I, pp. 155–8; Gem, 'Romanesque Architecture' p. 58.

47 X. Baron (ed.), *London 1066–1914: Literary Sources and Documents*, 3 vols, Robertsbridge: Helm Information, 1997, I, p. 118.

48 R. Morris. 'The New Work at Old St Paul's Cathedral and its Place in English Thirteenth-century Architecture', in Grant, *Medieval Art*, p. 75.

49 Harvey, *English Mediaeval Architects*, p. 244.

50 Cherry and Pevsner, 2, pp. 564–72.

51 Harvey, *English Mediaeval Architects*, p. 252. For Robert Branner's detection of important Parisian influences, including the Sainte-Chapelle, see his 'Westminster Abbey and the French Court Style', *Journal of the Society of Architectural Historians*, XXIII (1), 1964, pp. 3–18.

52 John Harvey wrote what amounts to a biography of Yevele in his *Henry Yevele, c. 1320 to 1400*, London: Batsford, 1944.

53 For a full discussion of the principles on which the design of Westminster Abbey was based, see F. Bond, *Westminster Abbey*, London: Henry Frowde and Oxford University Press, 1909, pp. 77–110.

54 Bradley and Pevsner, I, p. 51.

55 J. Schofield and G. Stell, 'The Built Environment, 1300–1500', in Palliser, *Cambridge Urban History*, I, p. 380.

56 Bradley and Pevsner, I, p. 50.

57 See D. M. Palliser, *et al.*, 'The Topography of Towns, 600–1300', in Palliser, *Cambridge Urban History*, I, p. 180.

58 For the large number of religious houses and hospitals, see W. Page (ed.), *The Victoria History of London*, I, London: Constable, 1909, pp. 407–588.

59 G. Cobb, *The Old Churches of London*, London: Batsford, 1942, p. 1.

60 Harvey, *English Mediaeval Architects*, p. 195.

61 Cobb, *Old Churches*, p. 2.

62 John Schofield provides an excellent discussion of the use of stone for houses in early medieval London in *Medieval London Houses*, pp. 31–2.

63 John Stow, *Survey of London*, London: Dent, 1956, p. 11.

64 Harvey, *English Medieval Architects*, p. 161.

65 Bradley and Pevsner, I, p. 316; P. Murray and M. Stevens (eds), *Living Bridges*, London: Royal Academy of Arts, 1996, p. 46.

66 Stow, *Survey of London*, p. 29.

67 Palliser, *Cambridge Urban History*, I, p. 184; Harris, *Timber-*

framed Buildings, p. 53. It is sometimes suggested that builders may have followed the example of Hanseatic merchants whose London houses perhaps used jettying as in their home ports.

68 D. Keene, 'Growth, Modernisation and Control: The Transformation of London's Landscape, c. 1500–c. 1750', in P. Clark and R. Gillespie (eds), *Two Capitals: London and Dublin, 1500–1840*, Oxford University Press, 2001, p. 21.

69 D. Yarwood, *The Architecture of England from Prehistoric Times to the Present Day*, London: Batsford, 1963, p. 167.

70 For John Schofield's suggestion that the original structure was composed of small panels, see his *Medieval London Houses*, pp. 1, 189–90. See p. 145 for two photographs showing two stages in the history of this frontage.

71 Harris, *Timber-framed Buildings*, p. 61.

72 Schofield, *Medieval London Houses*, p. 146.

73 Schofield and Stell, 'The Built Environment', p. 371.

74 See Barker and Jackson, *London*, p. 91.

75 Schofield, 'Medieval and Tudor Buildings', p. 17; Schofield, *Medieval London Houses*, pp. 150–52.

76 Harris, *Discovering Timber-framed Buildings*, p. 21.

77 Schofield, 'Medieval and Tudor Buildings', p. 25.

78 *Ibid*.

79 Summerson, 1, p. 92.

80 Harris, *Discovering Timber-framed Buildings*, p. 15.

81 N. Lloyd, *A History of the English House*, London: Architectural Press, 1975, pp. 71, 80.

82 See H. Colvin (ed.), *The History of the King's Works*, 7 vols, London: HMSO, 1963–82, 1, pp. 527–33; J. Cherry and N. Stratford, *Westminster Kings and the Medieval Palace of Westminster*, London: British Museum Press, 1995, pp. 50–106.

83 Harvey, *English Mediaeval Architects*, p. 139.

84 Harris, *Discovering Timber-framed Buildings*, p. 15; Harvey, *English Mediaeval Architects*, p. 139.

85 Royal Commission on Historical Monuments (England), *An Inventory of the Historical Monuments in London*, II: *West London*, London: HMSO, 1925, p. 121.

86 See C. Barron, *The Medieval Guildhall of London*, Corporation of London, 1974; Schofield, *Medieval London Houses*, pp. 114–19.

87 Bradley and Pevsner, 1, p. 54.

88 Harvey, *English Mediaeval Architects*, pp. 26, 76.

89 *Ibid.*, p. 26.

90 *Ibid.*, p. 123.

91 A. Saunders, *The Art and Architecture of London*, Oxford: Phaidon, 1984, p. 31.

92 Barron, 'London, 1300–1540', pp. 430–31.

93 Schofield, *Medieval London Houses*, p. 41.

94 Schofield, 'Medieval and Tudor Buildings', p. 22.

95 Bradley and Pevsner, 1, p. 55.

96 For the scholarly recreation of Crosby Hall by an enthusiast, Christopher Moran, c. 2000, see Chapter 6, p. 200, below.

97 Cherry and Stratford, *Westminster Kings*, pp. 11–49.

98 J. Harris and G. Higgott, *Inigo Jones: Complete Architectural Drawings*, New York: Drawing Center, 1989, p. 108.

99 J. Mackie, *The Earlier Tudors, 1485–1558*, Oxford: Clarendon Press, 1952; J. Gloag, *The English Tradition in Architecture*, London: A. and C. Black, 1975, p. 131.

100 Summerson, 1, p. 16; J. Musgrove (ed.), *Sir Banister Fletcher's A History of Architecture* (19th edn), London: Butterworth, 1987, p. 1014.

101 M. Girouard (ed.), 'The Smythson Collection of the Royal Institute of British Architects', *Architectural History*, V, 1962, p. 75.

102 This frontage is illustrated and discussed in R. Simon (ed.), *Somerset House: The Building and the Collections*, London: British Art Journal, 2001, pp. 6–8.

103 Summerson, 1, p. 50.

104 John Smythson's sketch of the front elevations of this house makes it look nothing like the work of Inigo Jones.

105 Bradley and Pevsner, 1, p. 295. For the successive Custom House buildings, including illustrations, see London County Council, *Survey of London*, XV. London County Council, 1934, pp. 31–43.

106 Bradley and Pevsner, 1, p. 328.

107 D. Keene, 'Growth, Modernisation and Control', p. 10.

108 Schofield, *Medieval London Houses*, p. 25.

109 For a surviving, but more recent (1676), example of the galleried inn, see the George Inn, 1 Borough High St in Jones and Woodward, p. 275.

110 J. Bowsher, *The Rose Theatre: An Archaeological Discovery*, Museum of London, 1998, pp. 11–13.

111 *Ibid.*, pp. 11–12.

112 R. Leacroft, *The Development of the English Playhouse*, London: Methuen, 1988, pp. 39–50.

Chapter 3

1 For a full introduction to Palladianism, see R. Tavernor, *Palladio and Palladianism*, London: Thames and Hudson, 1991; see also H. M. Colvin, p. xxiii, in T. Barnard and J. Clark (eds), *Lord Burlington: Architecture, Art and Life*, London: Hambledon Press, 1995.

2 D. Watkin, *A History of Western Architecture* (3rd edn), London: Laurence King, 2000, p. 273.

3 W. Kuyper, *Dutch Classicist Architecture*, Delft University Press, 1980, p. 1.

4 J. Harris and G. Higgott, *Inigo Jones: Complete Architectural Drawings*, New York: Drawing Center, 1989, p. 14.

5 Summerson, 1, p. 62.

6 See J. Bold, *John Webb: Architectural Theory and Practice in the Seventeenth Century*, Oxford: Clarendon Press, 1989.

7 See Jones's meticulous notes on Palladio's *Four Books of Architecture* in the library of Worcester College, Oxford. A more convenient source is *Inigo Jones on Palladio*, 2 vols, Newcastle: Oriel Press, 1970.

8 J. Lang, *Rebuilding St Paul's after the Great Fire of London*, London: Oxford University Press, 1956, pp. 2–4.

9 G. Worsley, *Classical Architecture in Britain: The Heroic Age*, New Haven and London: Yale University Press, 1995, pp. 10–11, 46.

10 See Serlio's house with a steep roof and dormers, designed especially for French conditions, in *Tutte l'opere d'architettura, et prospetiva, di Sebastiano Serlio Bolognese . . .*, Venice: Giacomo de' Franceschi, 1619, Book 7, Chapter 71; *Sebastiano Serlio on Architecture*, trans. V. Hart and P. Hicks, New Haven and London: Yale University Press, 2005, I.

11 Nicholas Stone quoted in J. Newman, 'Nicholas Stone's Goldsmiths' Hall: Design and Practice', *Architectural History*, XIV, 1971, pp. 36–7.

12 Bradley and Pevsner, I, p. 63.

13 For the spread of pilasters, see *ibid.*, p. 66.

14 C. Wren, *Parentalia*, London: C. Wren, 1701, pp. 220–21.

15 Watkin, *History of Western Architecture*, p. 335.

16 A. Sutcliffe, *Paris: An Architectural History*, New Haven and London: Yale University Press, 1993, pp. 24–5.

17 K. Downes, *Christopher Wren*, London: Allen Lane, Penguin Press, 1971, p. 55.

18 Among the exceptions were the big fire of the 120s, which burned down most of the west of London, and those of 1077, 1087, 1133, 1136 and 1212. See G. Milne, *Roman London: Urban Archaeology in the Nation's Capital*, London: Batsford, 1995, p. 73; R. Gem, 'The Romanesque Architecture of Old St Paul's Cathedral and its Late Eleventh-century Context', in L. Grant (ed.), *Medieval Art, Architecture and Archaeology of London*, London: British Archaeological Association, 1990, p. 59; T. Baker, *London: Rebuilding the City after the Great Fire*, Chichester: Phillimore, 2000, p. 2; P. Ackroyd, *London: The Biography*, London: Chatto and Windus, 2000, p. 59.

19 For the form the rebuilding took, see the outstanding collection of illustrations, including many instructive drawings, in Baker, *London: Rebuilding the City*.

20 See engraving in G. Beard, *The Work of Christopher Wren*, Edinburgh: John Bartholomew, 1982, pl. 44.

21 Lang, *Rebuilding St Paul's*, pp. 8–10.

22 *Ibid.*, p. 35.

23 Bradley and Pevsner, I, p. 82.

24 Lang, *Rebuilding St Paul's*, pp. 48–59.

25 V. Hart, *St Paul's Cathedral*, London: Phaidon, 1995, p. 6.

26 Beard, *Work of Christopher Wren*, p. 21.

27 See the beautifully illustrated D. Kendall, *The City of London Churches: A Pictorial Rediscovery*, London: Collins and Brown, 1998.

28 Bradley and Pevsner, I, p. 76.

29 Kuyper, *Dutch Classicist Architecture*, pp. 34–56.

30 Baker, *London: Rebuilding the City*, p. 7.

31 See views in C. Amery, *Wren's London*, Luton: Lennard Publishing, 1988.

32 Summerson, I, pp. 119–28.

33 Beard, *Work of Christopher Wren*, p. 21.

34 P. Booth, *Planning by Consent: The Origins and Nature of British Development Control*, London: Routledge, 2003, p. 34.

35 C. Knowles and P. Pitt, *The History of Building Regulation in London, 1189–1972*, London: Architectural Press, 1972, pp. 19–22.

36 Harris and Higgott, *Inigo Jones*, p. 88.

37 See Kuyper, *Dutch Classicist Architecture*; Summerson, *Architecture in Britain*, p. 91.

38 Harris and Higgott, *Inigo Jones*, p. 88.

39 *Ibid.*, p. 298.

40 *Ibid.*

41 The frontage of this house has been rebuilt in the bookshop of the Victoria and Albert Museum.

42 Knowles and Pitt, *History of Building Regulation*, p. 41.

43 W. Godfrey, *A History of Architecture in London*, London: Batsford, n.d. [1912], p. 195; N. Lloyd, *A History of the English House*, London: Architectural Press, 1975, pp. 117–18.

44 The origins and development of the sash window are discussed in H. J. Louw, 'The Origin of the Sash Window', *Architectural History*, XXVI, 1983, pp. 49–72; H. Louw and R. Crayford, 'A Constructional History of the Sash-Window, c. 1670–c. 1725', Part 1, *Architectural History*, XLI, 1988, pp. 82–130; Part 2, XLII, 1989, pp. 172–239.

45 Knowles and Pitt, *History of Building Regulation*, p. 41.

46 D. Cruickshank and P. Wyld, *London: The Art of Georgian Building*, London: Architectural Press, 1975, pp. 40–64, provide a number of photographs and measured drawings of small London houses, 1670–1750, stressing variety and creative design. However, many of these are on the fringes of London, outside the authority of the Building Acts.

47 See A. Kelsall, 'The London House Plan in the Later 17th Century', *Post-Medieval Archaeology*, VIII, 1974, pp. 80–91. This summary does not do justice to Kelsall's article, which focuses on the staircase.

48 Summerson, *Architecture in Britain*, p. 227.

49 See elevation and plan in P. Thorold, *The London Rich: The Creation of a Great City from 1666 to the Present*, London: Viking, 1999, p. 54.

50 Bradley and Pevsner, I, p. 68.

51 Map reprinted in P. Glanville, *London in Maps*, London: The Connoisseur, 1972, pp. 98–101.

52 P. Guillery, *The Small House in Eighteenth-Century London*, New Haven and London: Yale University Press, 2004, p. 43.

53 Summerson, 2, p. 58.

54 Baker, *London: Rebuilding the City*, p. 12.

55 E. McKellar, *The Birth of Modern London: The Development and Design of the City, 1660–1720*, Manchester University Press, 1999, pp. 178–80.

56 Summerson, I, p. 227.

57 Bradley and Pevsner, I, p. 597.

58 G. Milne, *The Great Fire of London*, New Barnet: Historical Publications, 1986, p. 20.

59 B. Cherry, 'John Pollexten's House in Walbrook', in J. Bold and E. Chaney (eds), *English Architecture, Public and Private*, London: Hambledon Press, 1993, p. 90.

60 J. Boulton, 'London, 1540–1700', in P. Clark (ed.), *The Cambridge Urban History of Britain*, II: *1540–1840*, Cambridge University Press, 2000, pp. 325, 346.

61 Summerson, I, pp. 85–8; P. Thorold, *The London Rich: The Creation of a Great City from 1666 to the Present*, London: Viking, 1999, p. 40.

62 N. Silcox-Crowe, 'Sir Roger Pratt, 1620–1685: The

Ingenious Gentleman Architect', in R. Brown (ed.), *The Architectural Outsiders*, London: Waterstone, 1985, p. 15.

63 J. Harris, *William Talman: Maverick Architect*, London: Allen and Unwin, 1982, p. 18.

64 J. M. Crook, *The British Museum*. London: Allen Lane, Penguin Press, 1972, pp. 54–8.

65 K. Downes, *English Baroque Architecture*, London: Zwemmer, 1966, p. 5.

66 Summerson, 2, p. 24.

67 See Baker, *London: Rebuilding the City*, p. 34.

68 Guillery's *Small House in Eighteenth-Century London* gives a clear impression of the largely ramshackle, disordered east London which emerged in the eighteenth century.

69 Downes, *English Baroque Architecture*, pp. 3–4.

70 See *ibid.*, pp. 49–54.

71 See J. Bold, *Greenwich: An Architectural History of the Royal Hospital for Seamen and the Queen's House*, New Haven and London: Yale University Press, 2000.

72 J. Summerson, *Heavenly Mansions*, London: Cresset Press, 1949, pp. 65, 81–2; Summerson, 1, p. 138.

73 J. Harris, *The Palladian Revival: Lord Burlington, his Villa and Garden at Chiswick*, London: Yale University Press and Royal Academy of Arts, 1994, p. 1.

74 K. Downes, *Hawksmoor*, London: Thames and Hudson, 1970, pp. 10–11.

75 *Ibid.*, p. 12; J. Summerson, *Architecture in England since Wren* (rev. edn), London: British Council, 1948, p. 9.

76 Worsley, *Classical Architecture in Britain*, pp. 54–63.

77 Colvin, p. 402.

78 Hawksmoor's churches are seen at their dramatic best in V. Hart, *Nicholas Hawksmoor*, New Haven and London: Yale University Press, 2002.

79 Summerson, 1, p. 169.

80 C. Campbell, *Vitruvius Britannicus, 1715*, Introduction, p. 8.

81 Worsley, *Classical Architecture in Britain*, p. 103.

82 Harris, *Palladian Revival*, p. 1.

83 Summerson, 1, p. 214.

84 McKellar, *Birth of Modern London*, p. 138.

85 See *The Modern Builder's Assistant*, London: Robert Sayer *et al.*, 1742, and W. Pain, *The Builders' Companion*, London: Robert Sayer, 1762.

86 Summerson, 2, pp. 72–6.

87 J. Bryant, 'Villa Views and the Uninvited Audience', in D. Arnold (ed.), *The Georgian Villa*, Stroud: Alan Sutton, 1996, p. 23.

88 Pevsner, 1, p. 623.

89 L. Stone, 'The Residential Development of the West End of London in the Seventeenth Century', in B. Malament (ed.), *After the Reformation: Essays in Honour of J. H. Hexter*, Manchester University Press, 1980, pp. 173–7, notes and explains this demise of the London palace.

90 Summerson, 1, p. 196.

91 Jones and Woodward, p. 171.

92 H. Stutchbury, *The Architecture of Colen Campbell*, Manchester University Press, 1967, p. 38.

93 Cruickshank and Wyld, *London: Art of Georgian Building*.

94 J. Fowler and J. Cornforth, *English Decoration in the Eighteenth Century*, London: Barrie and Jenkins, 1974, pp. 45, 49.

95 Worsley, *Classical Architecture in Britain*, p. 127.

96 *Ibid.*, p. 235.

97 A. Bolton, *The Architecture of Robert and James Adam*, 2 vols, London: Country Life, 1922, I, pp. 99–100.

98 The wings were built by Soane (1827) and Sir Charles Barry (1844).

99 R. White, 'John Vardy, 1718–65: Palladian into Rococo', in Brown, *Architectural Outsiders*, pp. 65–6.

100 M. Jourdain, *The Work of William Kent*, London: Country Life, 1948, pp. 56–7.

101 Summerson, 1, p. 217.

102 Worsley, *Classical Architecture in Britain*, p. 261.

103 Colvin suggests that Edwin may have had a second commission in the mid-1770s. This was the Hanover Square Concert Rooms.

104 See J. Friedman, 'The Town Houses', in J. Harris and M. Snodin (eds), *Sir William Chambers, Architect to George III*, New Haven and London: Yale University Press, 1996, p. 89.

105 *Ibid.*, pp. 90–91.

106 *Ibid.*, pp. 90–94, 105.

107 Harris, *Palladian Revival*, pl. 99.

108 These comparisons are facilitated by Leonora Ison's perceptive drawings in her *English Architecture through the Ages*, London: Arthur Barker, 1966, p. 34.

109 Cruickshank and Wyld, *London: Art of Georgian Building*, pp. 192–3.

110 Summerson, 2, p. 130.

111 *Ibid.*, p. 69.

112 Summerson, 1, p. 218.

113 See D. Stillman, *English Neo-Classical Architecture*, I, London: Zwemmer, 1988, pp. 27–48.

114 For the complete work of Robert and James Adam, only a small part of which was in London, see D. King, *The Complete Works of Robert and James Adam*, Oxford: Architectural Press, 1991.

115 See quotation in Colvin, p. 47.

116 King, *Complete Works of Robert and James Adam*, p. 8.

117 A. Saunders, *The Art and Architecture of London* (2nd edn), Oxford: Phaidon, 1988, p. 158. Much light is shed on the building of the house by Bolton, *Architecture of Robert and James Adam*, II, pp. 1–17.

118 Summerson, 1, p. 265.

119 Summerson, 2, p. 137.

120 Bolton, *Architecture of Robert and James Adam*, I, p. 100.

121 See J. Barrier, 'Chambers in France and Italy', in J. Harris and M. Snodin (eds), *Sir William Chambers, Architect to George III*, New Haven and London: Yale University Press, 1996, pp. 19–34.

122 J. Harris, *Sir William Chambers: Knight of the Polar Star*, London: Zwemmer, 1970, pp. 10–11, 108.

123 For an account of Chambers's work at Somerset House, see R. Simon (ed.), *Somerset House: The Building and the Collections*, London: British Art Journal, 2001, pp. 6–13.

124 J. Newman, 'Somerset House and other Public Buildings', in Harris and Snodin, *Sir William Chambers*, p. 112; J. Harris, 'Sir William Chambers and his Parisian Album', *Architectural History*, VI, 1963, p. 5.

125 Summerson, 1, pp. 256–8.

126 H. Colvin, *Royal Buildings*, London: RIBA, 1968, pp. 40–45.

127 Summerson, 1, p. 218.

128 See plates in Harris, 'Sir William Chambers', pp. 54–90.

129 Summerson, 1, p. 269.

130 *Ibid.*, p. 273; D. Stroud, *George Dance, Architect, 1741–1825*, London: Faber and Faber, 1971, p. 97.

131 H. Kalman, 'Newgate Prison', *Architectural History*, XII, 1969, p. 54.

132 Summerson, 1, p. 272.

133 *Ibid.*, p. 275.

134 *Ibid.* For the important French contribution to the furnishings, see D. Stroud, *Henry Holland: His Life and Architecture*, London: Country Life, 1966, pp. 77–85.

135 A. Dale, *James Wyatt*, Oxford: Basil Blackwell, 1956, pp. 6–14; J. Robinson, *The Wyatts: An Architectural Dynasty*, Oxford University Press, 1979, p. 1, pl. 1.

136 R. Carter, 'The Drury Lane Theatres of Henry Holland and Benjamin Dean Wyatt', *Journal of the Society of Architectural Historians*, XXVI (3), 1967, pp. 200–16.

137 Robinson, *The Wyatts*, p. 98, pl. 58.

138 *Ibid.*, p. 40, pl. 28.

139 See H. Steele and F. Yerbury, *The Old Bank of England, London*, London: Ernest Benn, 1930, pp. 11–26.

140 The origins of the usage are explained by J. M. Crook, *The Greek Revival: Neo-Classical Attitudes in British Architecture, 1760–1870*, London: John Murray, 1972, p. 63.

141 Summerson, 1, p. 304; Colvin, p. 741.

142 G. Tyack, '"A gallery worthy of the British people": James Pennethorne's Designs for the National Gallery, 1845–1867', *Architectural History*, XXXIII, 1990, pp. 120–34.

143 Pugin quoted in A. Service, *Architects of London and their Buildings from 1066 to the Present Day*, London: Architectural Press, 1979, p. 95.

144 Summerson, 1, p. 307.

145 H. Hobhouse, *Lost London*, London: Macmillan, 1971, p. 83. For a map of all the squares in London, see Jones and Woodward, pp. 422–3.

146 See the map of London's 'great estates' in Jones and Woodward, pp. 420–21.

147 F. Sheppard, *London: A History*, London: Oxford University Press, 1998, p. 176.

148 See Cruickshank and Wyld, *London: Art of Georgian Building*, pp. 2–3.

149 Booth, *Planning by Consent*, p. 21.

150 N. Brett-James, *The Growth of Stuart London*, London: Allen and Unwin, 1935, p. 67.

151 J. Lubbock, *The Tyranny of Taste: The Politics of Architecture and Design in Britain, 1550–1960*, New Haven and London: Yale University Press, 1995, pp. 30–33.

152 See Summerson, 2, pp. 29–31; Summerson, 1, pp. 76–9.

153 Summerson, 1, pp. 77–8.

154 Summerson, 2, p. 33.

155 Used with care, T. Mowl and B. Earnshaw, *Architecture without Kings: The Rise of Puritan Classicism under Cromwell*, Manchester University Press, 1995, pp. 135–6, can shed some light on the move towards harmonious frontages. The care is needed because of their over-concentration on pilasters.

156 Saunders, *Art and Architecture of London*, p. 141.

157 Summerson, 2, p. 40.

158 Summerson, 1, p. 230.

159 Summerson, 2, p. 104.

160 *Ibid.*, pp. 21–2.

161 D. Olsen, *Town Planning in London: The Eighteenth and Nineteenth Centuries*, New Haven and London: Yale University Press, 1982, pp. 90–93.

162 H. Hobhouse, *A History of Regent Street*, London: Macdonald and Jane's, 1975, p. 10.

163 Summerson, 2, pp. 177–90.

164 *Ibid.*, pp. 198–201.

165 T. Davis, *The Architecture of John Nash*, London: Studio, 1960, p. 7.

166 *Ibid.*, p. 9.

167 Summerson, 2, p. 23.

168 *Ibid.*, pp. 24–5.

Chapter 4

1 See A. Service, *Edwardian Architecture: A Handbook to Building Design in Britain, 1890–1914*, London: Thames and Hudson, 1977, pp. 6–7.

2 *Ibid.*, p. 303.

3 A. Service, *Architects of London and their Buildings from 1066 to the Present Day*, London: Architectural Press, 1979, p. 155; Service, *Edwardian Architecture*, p. 311.

4 B. Little, *Catholic Churches since 1623*, London: Robert Hale, 1966, pp. 142–3.

5 Service, *Architects*, p. 64; *Edwardian Architecture*, p. 303.

6 Service, *Edwardian Architecture*, pp. 303, 320–23. For Holden see Chapter 5, pp. 164–8 below.

7 For a full design history and assessment, see Royal Commission on the Historical Monuments of England, *Survey of London*, XVII, London: Athlone Press, 1991.

8 Bradley and Pevsner, 1, p. 390.

9 Jones and Woodward, p. 188.

10 Bradley and Pevsner, 1, p. 106.

11 Service, *Edwardian Architecture*, p. 81.

12 I used to attend this church as a teenager and wondered why it looked unusual. The Diocletian windows were especially puzzling. Only my later visits to Rome allowed me to see it in its true historical context of the third century, rather than of the late 1950s to which I had assumed it belonged.

13 Summerson, 1, p. 313.

14 C. and J. Riding (eds), *The Houses of Parliament: History, Art, Architecture*, London: Merrell, 2000, is a mine of information on the destruction and reconstruction of the Palace of Westminster and a full guide to the literature.

15 S. Sawyer, 'Sir John Soane and the Late Georgian Origins of the Royal Entrance', in *ibid.*, pp. 137–48; S. Sawyer, 'Sir John Soane's Symbolic Westminster: The Apotheosis of George IV', *Architectural History*, XXXIX, 1996, pp. 54–76; D. Stillman, *English Neo-Classical Architecture*, II, London: Zwemmer, 1988, pp. 370–71.

16 See Barry entry in Colvin.

17 I. Toplis, *The Foreign Office: An Architectural History*, London: Mansell, 1987.

18 J. Robinson, *The Wyatts: An Architectural Dynasty*, Oxford University Press, 1979, pp. 210–13, pl. 124.

19 Pevsner, 1, p. 480.

20 G. Stamp (ed.), *Personal and Professional Recollections by the Late Sir George Gilbert Scott*, Stamford: Paul Watkins, 1995, p. 273 (hereafter, *Scott*).

21 See S. Bayley, *The Albert Memorial: The Monument in its Social and Architectural Context*, London: Scolar Press, 1981.

22 Stamp, *Scott*, p. 271.

23 Picturegoers were allowed a peep into the hotel when it was the setting for the royal court in 'Richard III' (1996).

24 See M. H. Port, 'The New Law Courts Competition, 1866–67', *Architectural History*, XI, 1968, pp. 75–93.

25 Stamp, *Scott*, pp. 273–6.

26 See B. Clarke, *Parish Churches of London*, London: Batsford, 1966, pp. 1–11 for a concise account of the national, diocesan and local church building schemes affecting London from 1711 to 1954.

27 D. Cole, *The Work of Sir Gilbert Scott*, London: Architectural Press, 1980, pp. 34–7.

28 For a sympathetic review of Teulon's career, see M. Saunders, 'Samuel Sanders Teulon, 1812–1873: A Pragmatic Rogue', in R. Brown (ed.), *The Architectural Outsiders*, London: Waterstone, 1985, pp. 132–52.

29 Cherry and Pevsner, 3, pp. 673–4.

30 M. Girouard, *Sweetness and Light: The 'Queen Anne' Movement 1860–1900*, Oxford: Clarendon Press, 1977, p. 1.

31 E. Hollamby, *Red House*, London: Architecture Design and Technology Press, 1991, n.p.

32 See *ibid.*

33 Girouard, *Sweetness and Light*, pp. 19–25.

34 See J. Crook, *The Dilemma of Style: Architectural Ideas from the Picturesque to the Post-Modern*, London: John Murray, 1987, p. 171.

35 Service, *Architects*, p. 133.

36 A. Saint, *Richard Norman Shaw*, New Haven and London: Yale University Press, 1976, p. 153.

37 *Ibid.*, pp. 194–5.

38 *Ibid.*, pp. 142–3.

39 See illustration in R. Macleod, *Style and Society: Architectural Ideology in Britain, 1835–1914*, London: RIBA Publications, 1971, fig. 2.4.

40 See Jones and Woodward, p. 324.

41 G. Stamp and A. Goulancourt, *The English House, 1860–1914: The Flowering of English Domestic Architecture*, London: Faber and Faber, 1986, pp. 176–7.

42 Girouard, *Sweetness and Light*, pp. 64–70.

43 A. Crawford, *C. R. Ashbee*, New Haven and London: Yale University Press, 1985, pp. 237–59.

44 The frontage was replaced between the wars but the treatment still survives on a side wall.

45 G. Alex Bremner has pointed out the connection between imperial Eclectic and the work of British architects building in India: '"Some Imperial Institute": Architecture, Symbolism and the Ideal of Empire in Late Victorian Britain, 1887–93', *Journal of the Society of Architectural Historians*, LXII (1), 2003, pp. 50–74.

46 Alastair Service has done more than anyone to identify the Free Style as a distinct movement in architecture before 1914: see *Edwardian Architecture, passim.*

47 *Ibid.*, pp. 3–8.

48 *Ibid.*, pp. 41ff.

49 *Ibid.*, p. 10.

50 Several of the LCC fire stations are pictured in *Historic Buildings of London*, London: Academy Editions, 1975.

51 Service, *Edwardian Architects*, pp. 71–2.

52 *Ibid.*, p. 51.

53 S. Muthesius, *The English Terraced House*, New Haven and London: Yale University Press, 1982, p. 183.

54 S. Durant, *The Decorative Designs of C. F. A. Voysey*, Cambridge: Lutterworth Press, 1990, p. 6.

55 This dating is drawn from S. Muthesius, *The High Victorian Movement in Architecture, 1850–1970*, London: Routledge and Kegan Paul, 1972, p. 196.

56 I worked as a BBC messenger at The Langham in 1960 and often tried to beat my record for running down all eight floors, swinging round on the banisters at each level. My best performance in this Newtonian exercise was 50 seconds. I also ran up the eight floors but less often. My best time, as I recall, was 2½ minutes.

57 A. Sutcliffe, *Paris: An Architectural History*, New Haven and London: Yale University Press, 1993, p. 128.

58 See Service, *Edwardian Architecture*, pp. 432–42.

59 *Ibid.*, p. 113.

60 J. Friedman, *Inside London: Discovering London's Period Interiors*, New York: Prentice Hall, 1988, p. 28.

61 For the Committee's design, see P. Beaver, *The Crystal Palace, 1851–1936: A Portrait of Victorian Enterprise*, London: Hugh Evelyn, 1970, p. 18.

62 G. Chadwick, *The Works of Sir Joseph Paxton*, London: Architectural Press, 1961, pp. 247–8.

63 Jones and Woodward, p. 180.

64 See J. S. Curl, *Victorian Architecture: Its Practical Aspects*, Newton Abbot: David and Charles, 1973, pls 49–52.

65 Bradley and Pevsner, 1, p. 106.

66 *Ibid.*

67 See D. Watkin, *The Life and Work of C. R. Cockerell*, London: Zwemmer, 1974, pp. 207–13.

68 Pevsner, 1, pl. 145.

69 See illustration in Macleod, *Style and Society*, fig. 5.3.

70 H.-R. Hitchcock, *Early Victorian Architecture in Britain*, II, London: Architectural Press, 1954, p. 29.

71 H. Hobhouse, *Lost London*, London: Macmillan, 1971, p. 103.

72 *Ibid.*, p. 123.

73 See Clarke, *Parish Churches*, p. 89, pl. 65.

74 Let it be said that a positive assessment of this church appears in *Betjeman's London,* a videotape published by Green Umbrella (n.d.).

75 See Crook, *Dilemma of Style*, p. 146.

76 D. Gentleman, *London*, London: Weidenfeld and Nicolson, 1985, p. 8.

77 Jones and Woodward, p. 291.

78 See illustration in Hobhouse, *Lost London*, p. 101.

79 See Crook, *Dilemma of Style*, 1987, p. 84. Crook provides a fuller account in his *William Burges and the High Victorian Dream*, London: John Murray, 1981, pp. 238–9.

80 See J. Robinson, *Buckingham Palace: A Short History*, London: Michael Joseph, 1995, pp. 56–7.

81 For a detailed account of Blore's work on the east front, see H. Hobhouse, *Thomas Cubitt, Master Builder*, London: Macmillan, 1971, pp. 394–426.

82 *Ibid.*, p. 399.

83 Robinson, *Buckingham Palace*, pp. 59–108.

84 A full account of the Buckingham Palace works under Nash, Blore and Pennethorne, stressing the many difficulties faced by the architects, appears in H. Colvin (ed.), *The History of the King's Works*, London: HMSO, 1963–82, VI, pp. 263–99.

85 Robinson, *Buckingham Palace*, p. 129. The courtyard range of Blore's east wing is still in painted Caen stone while the Bath stone of Nash's garden frontage still survives, though with much patching.

86 *Ibid.*, p. 125.

87 D. Schubert and A. Sutcliffe, 'The "Haussmannization" of London?: The Planning and Construction of Kingsway-Aldwych, 1889–1935', *Planning Perspectives*, XI (2), 1996, pp. 134–7.

88 For Croston Street see *Historic Buildings of London*, p. 49.

89 Summerson, 2, p. 81.

90 A. Saint, *The Image of the Architect*, New Haven and London: Yale University Press, 1983, p. 60. For Cubitt, see the authoritative biography by Hobhouse, *Cubitt*.

91 *Country Life*, 7 November 2002.

92 Robinson, *The Wyatts*, p. 199.

93 See the comprehensive, informative, painstaking and detailed map in Jones and Woodward, pp. 422–3.

94 R. Dixon and S. Muthesius, *Victorian Architecture* (2nd edn), London: Thames and Hudson, 1985, pp. 59–61.

95 See the excellent photograph of houses in Amtill Road, E3, built about 1860–1870, in Muthesius, *English Terraced House*, 1982, p. 91.

96 W. Besant, *East London*, London, Chatto and Windus, 1912, p. 16.

97 J. Tarn, 'French Flats for the English in Nineteenth-century London', in A. Sutcliffe (ed.), *Multi-Storey Living: The British Working-Class Experience*, London: Croom Helm, 1974, p. 24.

98 *Ibid.*, p. 25.

99 See J. Tarn, *Five Per Cent Philanthropy: An Account of Housing in Urban Areas Between 1840 and 1914*, Cambridge University Press, 1973.

100 See S. Beattie, *A Revolution in London Housing: LCC Housing Architects and Their Work, 1893–1914*, London: Greater London Council and Architectural Press, 1980.

101 See Service, *Edwardian Architecture*, pp. 406–11.

102 A. A. Jackson, *Semi-Detached London*, London: Allen and Unwin, 1973, p. 21.

103 H. J. Dyos, *Victorian Suburb: A Study of the Growth of Camberwell*, Leicester University Press, 1961, p. 19.

104 Jackson, *Semi-Detached London*, pp. 44–5.

105 Susie Barson, 'Infinite Variety in Brick and Stucco:

1840–1914', in English Heritage, *London Suburbs*, London: Merrell Holberton, 1999, pp. 70–71.

106 See Girouard, *Sweetness and Light*, pp. 160–76; M. J. Bolsterli, *The Early Community at Bedford Park*, London: Routledge, 1977.

107 Robinson, *The Wyatts*, pp. 111, 115, pls 63, 64; Pevsner, 1, pp. 511–12.

108 Pevsner, 1, p. 504.

109 J. Crook, *The Rise of the Nouveaux Riches: Style and Status in Victorian Architecture*, London: John Murray, 1999, pp. 153–4.

110 *Ibid.*, p. 74.

111 *Ibid.*, p. 160.

112 P. Thorold, *The London Rich: The Creation of a Great City from 1666 to the Present*, London: Viking, 1999, p. 298.

113 Robinson, *The Wyatts*, pl. 128.

114 Hobhouse, *Lost London*, p. 39.

115 Crook, *Rise of the Nouveaux Riches*, pl. 104.

116 See plate in Hobhouse, *Lost London*, p. 37.

117 See M. Ignatieff, *A Just Measure of Pain: The Penitentiary in the Industrial Prison, 1750–1850*, Harmondsworth: Penguin, 1978, pp. 3–11.

118 T. Bruning, *Historic Pubs of London*, London: Prion Books, 1998, p. 13.

119 B. Spiller, *Victorian Public Houses*, Newton Abbot: David and Charles, 1972, p. 60.

120 See Curl, *Victorian Architecture*, pp. 71–6.

121 Crook, *Dilemma of Style*, p. 205.

122 T. Bruning, *Historic Pubs of London*, London: Prion Books, 2000, p. 143.

123 O. Lancaster, *A Cartoon History of Architecture* (2nd edn), London: John Murray, p. 90.

124 Spiller, *Victorian Public Houses*, p. 7.

125 Bruning, *Historic Pubs*, 1998, p. 16.

126 V. Glasstone, *Victorian and Edwardian Theatres*, London: Thames and Hudson, 1975, pp. 13–14.

127 G. Spain and N. Dromgoole, 'Theatre Architects in the British Isles', *Architectural History*, XIII, 1970, pp. 79–90.

128 Glasstone, *Victorian and Edwardian Theatres*, p. 7.

129 For a more positive assessment of this theatre, see *ibid.*, pp. 84–5.

Chapter 5

1 See esp. P. Oliver, I. Davis and I. Bentley, *Dunroamin: The Suburban Semi and its Enemies*, London: Pimlico, 1981.

2 See D. Cottam, *Sir Owen Williams, 1890–1969*, London: Architectural Association, 1986.

3 See D. Ryan, *The Ideal Home through the Twentieth Century*, London: Hazar, 1997.

4 D. Schubert and A. Sutcliffe, 'The "Haussmannization" of London?: The Planning and Construction of Kingsway-Aldwych, 1889–1935', *Planning Perspectives*, XI (2), 1996, pp. 134–7.

5 H. Clunn, *The Face of London* (6th edn), London: Simpkin Marshall, 1935, p. 126.

6 See A. Forsyth, *Buildings for the Age: New Building Types, 1900–1939*, London: HMSO, 1982.

7   For the Roman reference, see Jones and Woodward, p. 296.

8   A. Service, *Architects of London and their Buildings from 1066 to the Present Day*, London: Thames and Hudson, 1979, pp. 185–7.

9   C. Hussey, *The Life of Sir Edwin Lutyens*, London: Country Life, 1953, p. 462.

10 R. Gradidge, *Edwin Lutyens: Architect Laureate*, London: Allen and Unwin, 1981, pp. 73–5.

11 Hussey, *Life of Sir Edwin Lutyens*, p. 461.

12 See C. Percy and J. Ridley, *The Letters of Edwin Lutyens to his Wife Emily*, London: Collins, 1985.

13 Bradley and Pevsner, I, p. 493.

14 J. Gloag, *The English Tradition in Architecture*, London: A. and C. Black, 1963, p. 205.

15 J. Friedman, *Inside London: Discovering London's Period Interiors*, New York: Prentice Hall, 1988, p. 36.

16 *Daily Telegraph, Property*, 7 June 2003.

17 A. Eyles and K. Skone, *London's West End Suburbs*, Sutton: Keytone Publications, 1991, pp. 57–8.

18 Some superb photographs appear in C. Hines, *Art Deco London*, Twickenham: Park House Press, 2003.

19 P. Bayer, *Art Deco Architecture*, London: Thames and Hudson, 1992, pp. 14–15, 88.

20 *Ibid.*, p. 116.

21 *Ibid.*, p. 123.

22 M. Hebbert, *London: More by Fortune than Design*, Chichester: John Wiley, 1998, p. 54.

23 D. Watkin, *A History of Western Architecture* (3rd edn), London: Laurence King, 2000, p. 641.

24 The importance of Burnet was first given due prominence by A. Service in his *Architects of London and their Buildings from 1066 to the Present Day*, pp. 179–81.

25 D. Walker, 'Sir John James Burnet', in A. Service (ed.), *Edwardian Architecture and its Origins*, London: Architectural Press, 1975, p. 205.

26 Bradley and Pevsner, I, pl. 127.

27 Pevsner identifies Francis Lorne, a member of the partnership, as the author of this design: *ibid.*, p. 610.

28 Jones and Woodward, p. 190.

29 Bayer, *Art Deco Architecture*, p. 177.

30 *Ibid.*, p. 167.

31 R. Simpson, 'Classicism and Modernity: The University of London's Senate House', *Bulletin of the Institute of Classical Studies*, XLIII, 1999, p. 45.

32 For German interest in tall city towers in the 1920s, see e.g. D. Neumann (ed.), *Film Architecture: Set Designs from Metropolis to Blade Runner*, Munich: Prestel, 1999, pp. 94–103.

33 A painting of Holden's total concept in 1933 appears in F. Borsi, *The Monumental Era: European Architecture and Design, 1929–1939*, London: Lund Humphries, 1987, pp. 102–3.

34 Simpson, 'Classicism and Modernity', pp. 71–2.

35 *Ibid.*, p. 63.

36 *Ibid.*, pp. 64–5.

37 Bayer, *Art Deco Architecture*, p. 115, sees it as an Art Deco building, but its style is as much determined by its Portland stone cladding and its Expressionist southern aspect.

38 Jones and Woodward, p. 249.

39 Cottam, *Sir Owen Williams*, pp. 52–9.

40 Now a luxurious and welcoming hotel, it is called the Meliá White House at Regent's Park.

41 Hebbert, *London*, p. 55.

42 See Cottam, *Sir Owen Williams*, pp. 35–9.

43 See N. Bullock, *Building the Post-War World: Modern Architecture and Reconstruction in Britain*, London: Routledge, 2002.

44 For views of the stadium, including the interior, see the 1939 feature film, *The Arsenal Stadium Mystery*.

45 As in Bayer, *Art Deco Architecture*, p. 17.

46 P. M. Shand, *Modern Theatres and Cinemas*, London: Batsford, 1930.

47 See photograph in Bayer, *Art Deco Architecture*, p. 158.

48 D. Atwell, *Cathedrals of the Movies*, London: Architectural Press, 1980, p. 97.

49 Bayer, *Art Deco Architecture*, p. 145.

50 *Ibid.*, p. 152.

51 Atwell, *Cathedrals of the Movies*, p. 88.

52 This assessment is drawn from Bullock, *Building the Post-War World*, p. XI.

53 See C.-P. Warncke, *De Stijl, 1917–1931*, Cologne: Taschen, 1998, pp. 90–197. But 1–10 Wells Rise, NW8, heavily rectangular terraced houses built by Francis Lorne and Tait, c. 1933, are loosely De Stijl in appearance.

54 See J. Gold, '"Commoditie, firmenes and Delight": Modernism, the MARS Group's "New Architecture" Exhibition (1938) and Imagery of the Urban Future', *Planning Perspectives*, VIII (4), 1993, pp. 357–76.

55 Information from Professor Peter Fawcett.

56 I am indebted to Professor Peter Fawcett for this derivation.

57 I am grateful to Professor Peter Fawcett for directing me to this quotation.

Chapter 6

1   N. Bullock, *Building the Post-War World: Modern Architecture and Reconstruction in Britain*, London: Routledge, 2002, p. 247.

2   *Ibid.*

3   *Ibid.*, p. 41.

4   See *ibid.*, pp. xi–xii, 25–60.

5   *Ibid.*, p. 62.

6   *Ibid.*, p. 64.

7   See J. McKean, *The Royal Festival Hall*, London: Phaidon, 1992.

8   Charles Jencks refers to this type of architecture as 'modern vernacular' but the vernacular does not normally involve architects; C. Jencks, *Modern Movements in Architecture* (2nd edn), London: Penguin, 1985, pp. 248–9.

9   E. Mills, *1946–1953: The New Architecture in Great Britain*, London: Standard Catalogue Company, 1953, pp. 27–38.

10 *Ibid.*, pp. 63–74.

11 *Ibid.*, pp. 189–208.

12 Matthew Sturgis, *Daily Telegraph, Property*, 18 October 2003.

13 Bullock, *Building the Post-War World*, pp. 89–90.

14 Jones and Woodward, p. 71.

15 Bullock, *Building the Post-War World*, p. 91.

16 R. Banham, *The New Brutalism*, London: Architectural Press, 1966, pp. 108–9. Matthew Sturgis wrote a good article on these houses, *Daily Telegraph*, *Property*, 10 January 2004.

17 Service, *Architects*, p. 194.

18 Banham, *New Brutalism*, pp. 102–6. To follow Le Corbusier's internal treatments for houses of this type would have pushed the price or rent well above the means of the expected clientele.

19 Jones and Woodward, p. 130.

20 Bullock, *Building the Post-War World*, pp. 39–40.

21 *Ibid.*, p. 42. For a report, see *Journal of the Royal Institute of British Architects*, 3rd series, LV(3), 1948, p. 107.

22 See N. Warburton, *Ernö Goldfinger: The Life of an Architect*, London: Routledge, 2004.

23 Jones and Woodward, p. 47.

24 Warburton, *Goldfinger*, pp. 127–9.

25 *Ibid.*, pp. 157–8.

26 Bullock, *Building the Post-War World*, p. 95.

27 See Banham, *New Brutalism*.

28 H. Webster (ed.), *Modernism without Rhetoric: Essays on the Work of Alison and Peter Smithson*, London: Academy Editions, 1997, pp. 8, 20, 24, 32, 46, 53, 73–7, 89.

29 Lasdun's buildings are fully discussed in W. Curtis, *Denys Lasdun: Architecture, City, Landscape*, London: Phaidon, 1994, p. 6.

30 *Ibid.*, p. 10.

31 R. Maxwell, *New British Architecture*, London: Thames and Hudson, 1972, p. 30.

32 Lord Esher, cited in M. Marmaras and A. Sutcliffe, 'Planning for Post-war London: The Three Independent Plans, 1942–3', *Planning Perspectives*, IX(4), 1994, p. 438.

33 *Ibid.*, p. 440.

34 *Ibid.*, pp. 440–43.

35 *Reconstruction in the City of London*, London: Corporation of London and Batsford, 1944, p. 'a'.

36 G. Cherry and L. Penny, *Holford: A Study in Architecture, Planning and Civic Design*, London: Mansell, 1986, pp. 136.

37 *Ibid.*, pp. 138–9.

38 Bullock, *Building the Post-War World*, p. 252.

39 Cherry and Penny, *Holford*, pp. 136–8.

40 C. Holden and W. Holford, *The City of London: A Record of Destruction and Survival*, London: Architectural Press, 1951, p. 46.

41 Bullock, *Building the Post-War World*, p. 253.

42 Cherry and Penny, *Holford*, pp. 138–9.

43 L. Esher, *A Broken Wave: The Rebuilding of England, 1940–1980*, Harmondsworth: Penguin, 1983, p. 111.

44 See Bullock, *Building the Post-War World*, p. 251.

45 See *ibid.*, pp. 254–5.

46 W. Holford, 'The Changing Face of London', in Centre for Urban Studies (ed.), *London: Aspects of Change*, London: MacGibbon and Kee, 1964, pp. 148–50.

47 Bradley and Pevsner, I, p. 127.

48 This assessment is based on Bullock, *Building the Post-War World*, pp. 255–7.

49 *Ibid.*, pp. 255–6.

50 *Ibid.*, pp. 256–7.

51 Jones and Woodward, p. 256.

52 *Designing the Future of the South Bank*, London: Academy Editions, 1994, p. 7.

53 Jones and Woodward, p. 257.

54 *People and Cities*, London: British Road Federation, n.d. [1964], pp. 97–104.

55 See J. Harvey, *Conservation of Buildings*, London: John Baker, 1972.

56 J. Friedman, *Inside London: Discovering London's Period Interiors*, New York: Prentice Hall, 1988, p. 13.

57 See R. Burdett (ed.), *City Changes: Architecture in the City of London, 1985–1995*, London: Architecture Foun-dation, 1994.

58 I. Nairn, *Outrage*, London: Architectural Press, 1955; I. Nairn, *Counter-Attack*, London: Architectural Press, n.d.

59 C. Jencks, *The Language of Post-Modern Architecture* (6th edn), London: Academy Editions, 1991, p. 9.

60 *Ibid.*, pp. 24–5. Colin Amery and Dan Cruikshank, *The Rape of Britain*, London: Paul Elek, 1975.

61 See illustrations of buildings on the site in R. Rowsome, *Heart of the City: Roman, Medieval and Modern London Revealed by Archaeology at 1 Poultry*, Museum of London, 2000, pp. 72–8; HRH Prince Charles, *A Vision of Britain*, London: Doubleday, 1989.

62 C. Jencks, *The Prince, the Architects and New Wave Monarchy*, London: Academy Editions, 1988, p. 7.

63 E. Morris, *British Town Planning and Urban Design: Principles and Policies*, London: Longman, n.d., p. 209.

64 The speeches were reprinted by Jencks in *The Prince*, pp. 43–50.

65 K. Powell, *Richard Rogers, Complete Works*, 2 vols, London: Phaidon, 2001, II, p. 84.

66 *Ibid.*, pp. 84–90.

67 Jencks, *Language of Post-Modern Architecture*, p. 17.

68 See R. John and D. Watkin, *John Simpson: The Queen's Gallery, Buckingham Palace, and Other Works*, London: Andreas Papadakis, 2002, pp. 90–98.

69 For the market hall, a small, Doric design, see *Contemporary British Architects*, Munich: Prestel, 1994, pp. 148–9.

70 *Daily Telegraph*, 5 November 2003; 'Piloti', *Private Eye*, 9–22 January 2004, p. 15.

71 Prince Charles, *A Vision of Britain*, p. 65.

72 Colin St John Wilson, cited in R. Stonehouse and G. Stromberg, *The Architecture of the British Library at St Pancras*, London: Spon Press, 2004, p. xv.

73 Jencks, *The Prince*, p. 21.

74 The growing influence of the Post-Modern is exemplified among the award winners and competitors in *British Architecture*, London: Academy Editions, 1982.

75 See N. Ellin, *Postmodern Urbanism*, Oxford: Blackwell, 1996.

76 N. Moffett, *The Best of British Architecture, 1980–2000*, London: Spon, 1993, p. 44.

77 For a division of Modern into some of the more varied categories in use in the 1990s, see Moffett, *Best of British Architecture*, Contents; C. Jencks, *Post-Modern Triumphs in London*, London: Academy Editions, 1991.

78 K. Powell, *New Architecture in Britain*, London: Merrell, 2003, p. 155.

79 Moffett, *Best of British*, p. 57.

80 Harvey, *Conservation of Buildings*, p. 191.

81 *Daily Telegraph*, 7 October 2003.

82 For a far different interpretation, stressing coherence, appropriateness, deference to history and innovation, see John and Watkin, *John Simpson*, pp. 16–59.

83 Powell, *New Architecture in Britain*, p. 76.

84 See John and Watkin, *John Simpson*, pp. 16–59.

85 P. Bayer, *Art Deco Architecture*, London: Thames and Hudson, 1992, pp. 208–9.

86 These houses appear in K. Powell, *World Cities: London*, London: Academy Editions, 1993, pp. 221, 232, 245.

87 K. Powell, *New London Architecture*, London: Merrell, 2001, p. 8.

88 P. Hall, *London 2001*, London: Unwin Hyman, 1989, pp. 12–14.

89 Powell, *Richard Rogers*, pp. 196–209.

90 Powell, *New London Architecture*, p. 7.

91 S. Brownill, *Developing London's Docklands: Another Great Planning Disaster?*, London: Paul Chapman, 1990, p. 146.

92 Powell, *New London Architecture*, p. 8.

93 Powell, *Richard Rogers*, p. 54.

94 Advertised in *Country Life*, 2 November 2002.

95 Powell, *New London Architecture*, p. 8.

96 *Daily Telegraph*, 14 January 2004.

97 B. Klatt (ed.), *GLC/ILEA Architecture, 1976–1986*, London: Architectural Press, 1986, p. 7.

98 *Ibid.*, p. 7.

99 Advertised in *Country Life*, 7 November 2002.

100 Powell, *New London Architecture*, p. 30.

101 Powell, *New Architecture in Britain*, p. 7.

Chapter 7

1 Maxwell Fry, the Modern Movement pioneer, developed a lifelong preference for brick as a London material, beginning in 1938; see A. Service, *Architects of London and their Buildings from 1066 to the Present Day*, London: Architectural Press, 1979, p. 192.

2 But see N. Lloyd, *A History of English Brickwork* (repr.), New York: Blom, 1972, for a review of shaped bricks, 1000–1800.

3 G. Worsley, *Classical Architecture in Britain: The Heroic Age*, New Haven and London: Yale University Press, 1995, p. 223.

4 Burlington had used Bath stone to clad his Westminster School dormitory in 1722.

5 A. Saint, *Richard Norman Shaw*, New Haven and London: Yale University Press, 1976, p. 269.

6 Jones and Woodward, p. 256.

7 Summerson, 2, pp. 130–32.

8 J. Ruch, 'Regency Coade: A Study of the Coade Record Books, 1813–21', *Architectural History*, XI, 1968, p. 34; A. Kelly, 'Coade Stone in Georgian Architecture', *Architectural History*, XXVIII, 1985, pp. 71–95.

9 A. Saunders, *The Art and Architecture of London* (2nd edn), Oxford: Phaidon, 1988, p. 90.

10 See L. Frost and E. Jones, 'The Fire Gap and the Greater Durability of Nineteenth-century Cities', *Planning Perspectives*, IV(3), 1989, pp. 333–47.

11 E. Jones, S. Porter and M. Turner, *A Gazetteer of English Urban Fire Disasters, 1500–1900*, Norwich, Geo Books, 1984, pp. 4, 46.

12 See M. Warner (ed.), *The Image of London: Views by Travellers and Emigres, 1550–1920*, London: Trefoil, 1987, pp. 7–28.

13 The thickest London fogs were known as 'blacks' because of their heavy coal content. Normal fogs were known as 'London particulars'.

14 J. Bold, *Greenwich: An Architectural History of the Royal Hospital for Seamen and the Queen's House*, London: Yale University Press, 2000, p. 58.

15 S. Muthesius, *The English Terraced House*, New Haven and London: Yale University Press, 1982, p. 149.

16 M. Stratton, 'Shining through the Fog: Terracotta and Faience', in H. Hobhouse and A. Saunders, *Good and Proper Materials: The Fabric of London Since the Great Fire*, London: Royal Commission on the Historical Monuments of England, 1989, p. 26.

17 Summerson, 1, p. 218.

18 J. Wilton-Ely, 'The Rise of the Professional Architect in England', in S. Kostof (ed.), *The Architect: Chapters in the History of the Profession*, New York: Oxford University Press, 1977, p. 183.

19 See R. Middleton, 'Chambers, W., *A Treatise on Civil Architecture*, London, 1759', in J. Harris and M. Snodin, *Sir William Chambers: Architect to George III*, London and New Haven: Yale University Press, 1996, pp. 68–76.

20 J. Musgrove (ed.), *Sir Banister Fletcher's A History of Architecture* (17th edn), London: Butterworths, 1987, p. 840.

21 J. M. Crook, 'The Pre-Victorian Architect: Professionalism and Patronage', *Architectural History*, XII, 1969, pp. 66–71.

22 R. Blomfield, *Richard Norman Shaw, R.A.*, London: Batsford, 1940, p. v.

23 Saint, *Shaw*, p. 4.

24 A. Service, *Edwardian Architecture and its Origins*, London: Architectural Press, 1975, p. 331.

25 L. Campbell, 'A Call to Order: The Rome Prize and Early Twentieth-century British Architecture', *Architectural History*, XXXII, 1989, pp. 131–51.

26 A. Sutcliffe, *Paris: An Architectural History*, New Haven and London: Yale University Press, 1993, pp. 171–2. The thirty distinguished architects selected by Miranda Newton in her *Architects' London Houses*, Oxford: Butterworth, 1992, all passed through a complete, formal training programme.

27 Crook, 'Pre-Victorian Architect', p. 66.

28 J. Summerson, *The London Building World of the Eighteen-Sixties*, London: Thames and Hudson, 1973, p. 21.

29 Crook, 'Pre-Victorian Architect', p. 66.

30 J. Harvey, *English Mediaeval Architects: A Biographical Dictionary down to 1550* (2nd edn), Gloucester: Alan Sutton, 1984, p. 206.

31 J. Harris and G. Higgott, *Inigo Jones: Complete Architectural Drawings*, New York: Drawing Center, 1989, p. 191; J.

Summerson, *Architecture in Britain, 1530 to 1830* (5th edn), Harmondsworth: Penguin, 1969, p. 77.

32 See R. Hewlings, 'James Leoni c. 1686–1746: An Anglicized Venetian', in R. Brown (ed.), *The Architectural Outsiders*, London: Waterstone, 1985, pp. 21–44.

33 *Ibid.*, pp. 22–3.

34 J. Fowler and J. Cornforth, *English Decoration in the* *Eighteenth Century*, London: Barrie and Jenkins, 1974, pp. 46–8.

35 Colvin, p. 48.

36 Sir Francis Dashwood quoted in D. Watkin, *Athenian Stuart: Pioneer of the Greek Revival*, London: Allen and Unwin, 1982, p. 45.

Selected Bibliography

PRIMARY SOURCES

J. Badeslade and J. Rocque, *Vitruvius Britannicus*, New York: Blom, II, 1967.

W. Besant, *East London*, London: Chatto and Windus, 1912.

C. Campbell, *Vitruvius Britannicus*, New York: Blom, I, 1967.

J. Harris and G. Higgott, *Inigo Jones: Complete Architectural Drawings*, New York: Drawing Center, 1989.

Inigo Jones on Palladio, Newcastle: Oriel Press, 1970.

London County Council, *Survey of London*, London County Council, xv, 1934.

The Modern Builder's Assistant, London: Robert Sayer *et al.*, 1742.

W. Pain, *The Builders' Companion*, London: Robert Sayer, 1762.

People and Cities, London: British Road Federation, n.d. [1964].

Reconstruction in the City of London, Corporation of London and Batsford, 1944.

Royal Commission on Historical Monuments (England), *An Inventory of the Historical Monuments in London*, II: *West London*, London: HMSO, 1925.

Royal Commission on the Historical Monuments of England, *Survey of London*, London: Athlone Press, XVII, 1991.

Sebastiano Serlio on Architecture, trans. V. Hart and P. Hicks, New Haven and London: Yale University Press, 2005.

G. Stamp (ed.), *Personal and Professional Recollections by the Late Sir George Gilbert Scott*, Stamford: Paul Watkins, 1995.

J. Stow, *Survey of London*, London: Dent, 1956.

Tutte l'opere d'architettura, et prospetiva, di Sebastiano Serlio Bolognese . . ., Venice: Giacomo de' Franceschi, 1619.

C. Wren, *Parentalia*, London: C. Wren, 1701.

SECONDARY SOURCES

P. Ackroyd, *London: The Biography*, London: Chatto and Windus, 2000.

C. Amery, *Wren's London*, Luton: Lennard Publishing, 1988.

— and D. Cruikshank, *The Rape of Britain*, London: Paul Elek, 1975.

D. Arnold (ed.), *The Georgian Villa*, Stroud: Alan Sutton, 1996.

D. Atwell, *Cathedrals of the Movies*, London: Architectural Press, 1980.

T. Baker, *London: Rebuilding the City after the Great Fire*, Chichester: Phillimore, 2000.

R. Banham, *The New Brutalism: Ethic or Aesthetic?*, London: Architectural Press, 1966.

F. Barker and P. Jackson, *London: 2000 Years of a City and its People*, London: Cassell, 1974.

T. Barnard and J. Clark (eds), *Lord Burlington: Architecture, Art and Life*, London: Hambledon Press, 1995.

X. Baron (ed.), *London 1066–1914: Literary Sources and Documents*, 3 vols, Robertsbridge: Helm Information, I, 1997.

C. Barron, *London in the Later Middle Ages: Government and People, 1200–1500*, Oxford University Press, 2004.

—, *The Medieval Guildhall of London*, Corporation of London, 1974.

P. Bayer, *Art Deco Architecture*, London: Thames and Hudson, 1992.

S. Bayley, *The Albert Memorial: The Monument in its Social and Architectural Context*, London: Scolar Press, 1981.

G. Beard, *The Work of Christopher Wren*, Edinburgh: John Bartholomew, 1982.

S. Beattie, *A Revolution in London Housing: LCC Housing Architects and their Work, 1893–1914*, Greater London Council and Architectural Press, 1980.

P. Beaver, *The Crystal Palace, 1851–1936: A Portrait of Victorian Enterprise*, London: Hugh Evelyn, 1970.

R. Blomfield, *Richard Norman Shaw, R.A.*, London: Batsford, 1940.

J. Bold, *John Webb: Architectural Theory and Practice in the Seventeenth Century*, Oxford: Clarendon Press, 1989.

—, *Greenwich: An Architectural History of the Royal Hospital for Seamen and the Queen's House*, New Haven and London: Yale University Press, 2000.

— and E. Chaney (eds), *English Architecture, Public and Private*, London: Hambledon Press, 1993.

M. J. Bolsterli, *The Early Community at Bedford Park*, London: Routledge, 1977.

A. Bolton, *The Architecture of Robert and James Adam*, 2 vols, London: Country Life, I, 1922.

F. Bond, *Westminster Abbey*, London: Henry Frowde and Oxford University Press, 1909.

P. Booth, *Planning by Consent: The Origins and Nature of British Development Control*, London: Routledge, 2003.

F. Borsi, *The Monumental Era: European Architecture and Design, 1929–1939*, London: Lund Humphries, 1987.

J. Bowsher, *The Rose Theatre: An Archaeological Discovery*, Museum of London, 1998.

S. Bradley and N. Pevsner, *London 1: The City of London*, London: Penguin, 1999.

—, *London 6: Westminster*, London: Penguin, 2003.

R. Branner, 'Westminster Abbey and the French Court Style', *Journal of the Society of Architectural Historians*, XXIII (1), 1964, pp. 3–18.

G. Bremner, '"Some Imperial Institute": Architecture, Symbolism and the Ideal of Empire in Late Victorian Britain, 1887–93', *Journal of the Society of Architectural Historians*, XLII (1), 2003, pp. 50–74.

N. Brett-James, *The Growth of Stuart London*, London: Allen and Unwin, 1935.

P. Brimblecombe, *The Big Smoke: A History of Air Pollution in London since Medieval Times*, London: Routledge, 1987.

British Architecture, London: Academy Editions, 1982.

F. Brown, 'Continuity and Change in the Urban House: Developments in Domestic Space Organisation in Seventeenth-century London', *Comparative Studies in Society and History*, XXVIII, 1986, pp. 558–90.

R. Brown (ed.), *The Architectural Outsiders*, London: Waterstone, 1985.

S. Brownill, *Developing London's Docklands: Another Great Planning Disaster?*, London: Paul Chapman, 1990.

T. Bruning, *Historic Pubs of London*, London: Prion Books, 1998, 2000.

N. Bullock, *Building the Post-War World: Modern Architecture and Reconstruction in Britain*, London: Routledge, 2002.

R. Burdett (ed.), *City Changes: Architecture in the City of London, 1985–1995*, London: Architecture Foundation, 1994.

J. Campbell, *Brick: A World History*, London: Thames & Hudson, 2003.

L. Campbell, 'A Call to Order: The Rome Prize and Early Twentieth-century British Architecture', *Architectural History*, XXXII, 1989, pp. 131–51.

R. Carter, 'The Drury Lane Theatres of Henry Holland and Benjamin Dean Wyatt', *Journal of the Society of Architectural Historians*, XXVI (3), 1967, pp. 200–16.

Centre for Urban Studies (ed.), *London: Aspects of Change*, London: MacGibbon and Kee, 1964.

G. Chadwick, *The Works of Sir Joseph Paxton*, London: Architectural Press, 1961.

Prince Charles, *A Vision of Britain*, London: Doubleday, 1989.

B. Cherry and N. Pevsner, *London, 2: South*, Harmondsworth: Penguin, 1983.

—, *London 3: North-West*, London: Penguin, 1991.

—, *London 4: North*, London: Penguin, 1998.

B. Cherry, C. O'Brien and N. Pevsner, *London 5: East*, New Haven and London: Yale University Press, 2005.

G. Cherry and L. Penny, *Holford: A Study in Architecture, Planning and Civic Design*, London: Mansell, 1986.

J. Cherry and N. Stratford, *Westminster Kings and the Medieval Palace of Westminster*, London: British Museum Press, 1995.

P. Clark (ed.), *The Cambridge Urban History of Britain, II: 1540–1840*, Cambridge University Press, 2000.

— and R. Gillespie (eds), *Two Capitals: London and Dublin, 1500–1840*, Oxford University Press, 2001.

B. Clarke, *Parish Churches of London*, London: Batsford, 1966.

A. Clifton-Taylor and A. Ireson, *English Stone Building*, London: Victor Gollancz, 1983.

H. Clunn, *The Face of London* (6th edn), London: Simpkin Marshall, 1935.

G. Cobb, *The Old Churches of London*, London: Batsford, 1942.

D. Cole, *The Work of Sir Gilbert Scott*, London: Architectural Press, 1980.

H. Colvin, *A Biographical Dictionary of British Architects, 1660–1840* (2nd edn), London: John Murray, 1978; (3rd edn), New Haven and London: Yale University Press, 1995.

—, *Royal Buildings*, London: RIBA, 1968.

— (ed.), *The History of the King's Works*, 7 vols, London: HMSO, 1963–82.

Contemporary British Architects, Munich: Prestel, 1994.

D. Cottam, *Sir Owen Williams, 1890–1969*, London: Architectural Association, 1986.

A. Crawford, *C. R. Ashbee*, New Haven and London: Yale University Press, 1985.

J. M. Crook, *The British Museum*, London: Allen Lane, Penguin, 1972.

—, *William Burges and the High Victorian Dream*, London: John Murray, 1981.

—, *The Dilemma of Style: Architectural Ideas from the Picturesque to the Post-Modern*, London: John Murray, 1987.

—, *The Greek Revival: Neo-Classical Attitudes in British Architecture, 1760–1870*, London: John Murray, 1972.

—, 'The Pre-Victorian Architect: Professionalism and Patronage', *Architectural History*, XII, 1969, pp. 62–78.

—, *The Rise of the Nouveaux Riches: Style and Status in Victorian Architecture*, London: John Murray, 1999.

D. Cruickshank and P. Wyld, *London: The Art of Georgian Building*, London: Architectural Press, 1975.

J. Curl, *Victorian Architecture: Its Practical Aspects*, Newton Abbot: David and Charles, 1973.

W. Curtis, *Denys Lasdun: Architecture, City, Landscape*, London: Phaidon, 1994.

A. Dale, *James Wyatt*, Oxford: Basil Blackwell, 1956.

T. Davis, *The Architecture of John Nash*, London: Studio, 1960.

Designing the Future of the South Bank, London: Academy Editions, 1994.

R. Dixon and S. Muthesius, *Victorian Architecture* (2nd edn), London: Thames and Hudson, 1985.

K. Downes, *English Baroque Architecture*, London: Zwemmer, 1966.

—, *Hawksmoor*, London: Thames and Hudson, 1970.

—, *Christopher Wren*, London: Allen Lane, Penguin, 1971.

S. Durant, *The Decorative Designs of C. F. A. Voysey*, Cambridge: Lutterworth Press, 1990.

H. Dyos, *Victorian Suburb: A Study of the Growth of Camberwell*, Leicester University Press, 1961.

T. Eaton, *Plundering the Past: Roman Stonework in Medieval Britain*, Stroud: Tempus, 2000.

N. Ellin, *Postmodern Urbanism*, Oxford: Blackwell, 1996.

English Heritage, *London Suburbs*, London: Merrell Holberton, 1999.

A. Eyles and K. Skone, *London's West End Suburbs*, Sutton: Keytone Publications, 1991.

A. Forsyth, *Buildings for the Age: New Building Types, 1900–1939*, London: HMSO, 1982.

J. Fowler and J. Cornforth, *English Decoration in the Eighteenth Century*, London: Barrie and Jenkins, 1974.

J. Friedman, *Inside London: Discovering London's Period Interiors*, New York: Prentice Hall, 1988.

L. Frost and E. Jones, 'The Fire Gap and the Greater Durability of Nineteenth-century Cities', *Planning Perspectives*, IV (3), 1989, pp. 333–47.

E. Gee, *A Glossary of Building Terms used in England from the Conquest to c. 1550*, Frome Historical Research Group, 1984.

D. Gentleman, *London*, London: Weidenfeld and Nicolson, 1985.

M. Girouard, *Sweetness and Light: The 'Queen Anne' Movement 1860–1900*, Oxford: Clarendon Press, 1977.

— (ed.), 'The Smythson Collection of the Royal Institute of British Architects', *Architectural History*, V, 1962, pp. 21–184.

P. Glanville, *London in Maps*, London: Connoisseur, 1972.

V. Glasstone, *Victorian and Edwardian Theatres*, London: Thames and Hudson, 1975.

J. Gloag, *The English Tradition in Architecture*, London: A. and C. Black, 1963, 1975.

W. Godfrey, *A History of Architecture in London*, London: Batsford, n.d. [1912].

J. Gold, ' "Commoditie, firmenes and delight": Modernism, the MARS Group's "New Architecture" Exhibition (1938) and Imagery of the Urban Future', *Planning Perspectives*, VIII (4), 1993, pp. 357–76.

R. Gradidge, *Edwin Lutyens: Architect Laureate*, London: Allen and Unwin, 1981.

L. Grant (ed.), *Medieval Art, Architecture and Archaeology in London*, London: British Archaeological Association, 1990.

W. Grimes, *The Excavation of Roman and Medieval London*, London: Routledge, 1968.

P. Guillery, *The Small House in Eighteenth-century London*, New Haven and London: Yale University Press, 2004.

R. Gunther, *The Architecture of Sir Roger Pratt*, Oxford University Press, 1928.

P. Hall, *London 2001*, London: Unwin Hyman, 1989.

P. Hammond, *The Tower of London*, London: Department of the Environment, 1987.

J. Harris, *Sir William Chambers: Knight of the Polar Star*, London: Zwemmer, 1970.

—, 'Sir William Chambers and his Parisian Album', *Architectural History*, VI, 1963, pp. 54–90.

—, *The Palladian Revival: Lord Burlington, his Villa and Garden at Chiswick*, New Haven and London: Yale University Press and Royal Academy of Arts, 1994.

—, *William Talman: Maverick Architect*, London: Allen and Unwin, 1982.

— and M. Snodin (eds), *Sir William Chambers, Architect to George III*, New Haven and London: Yale University Press, 1996.

R. Harris, *Discovering Timber-Framed Buildings* (3rd edn), Princes Risborough: Shire Publications, 1993.

V. Hart, *Nicholas Hawksmoor*, New Haven and London: Yale University Press, 2002.

—, *St. Paul's Cathedral*, London: Phaidon, 1995.

J. Harvey, *Conservation of Buildings*, London: John Baker, 1972.

—, *English Mediaeval Architects: A Biographical Dictionary down to 1550* (2nd edn), Gloucester: Alan Sutton, 1984.

—, *Henry Yevele, c. 1320 to 1400*, London: Batsford, 1944.

M. Hebbert, *London: More by Fortune than Design*, Chichester: John Wiley, 1998.

C. Hines, *Art Deco London*, Twickenham: Park House Press, 2003.

P. Hinton (ed.), *Excavations in Southwark 1973–76: Lambeth 1973–79*, Museum of London, 1988.

Historic Buildings of London, London: Academy Editions, 1975.

H.-R. Hitchcock, *Early Victorian Architecture in Britain*, London: Architectural Press, II, 1954.

H. Hobhouse, *Thomas Cubitt, Master Builder*, London: Macmillan, 1971.

—, *A History of Regent Street*, London: Macdonald and Jane's, 1975.

—, *Lost London*, London: Macmillan, 1971.

— and A. Saunders, *Good and Proper Materials: The Fabric of London since the Great Fire*, London: Royal Commission on the Historical Monuments of England, 1989.

C. Holden and W. Holford, *The City of London: A Record of Destruction and Survival*, London: Architectural Press, 1951.

E. Hollamby, *Red House*, London: Architecture Design and Technology Press, 1991.

E. Howe, *Roman Defences and Medieval Industry: Excavations at Baltic House, City of London*, Museum of London Archaeology Series, 2002.

C. Hussey, *The Life of Sir Edwin Lutyens*, London: Country Life, 1953.

M. Ignatieff, *A Just Measure of Pain: The Penitentiary in the Industrial Prison, 1750–1850*, Harmondsworth: Penguin, 1978.

L. Ison, *English Architecture through the Ages*, London: Arthur Barker, 1966.

A. A. Jackson, *Semi-Detached London*, London: Allen and Unwin, 1973.

C. Jencks, *The Language of Post-Modern Architecture* (6th edn), London: Academy Editions, 1991.

—, *Modern Movements in Architecture* (2nd edn), London: Penguin, 1985.

—, *Post-Modern Triumphs in London*, London: Academy Editions, 1991.

—, *The Prince, the Architects and New Wave Monarchy*, London: Academy Editions, 1988.

R. John and D. Watkin, *John Simpson: The Queen's Gallery, Buckingham Palace, and Other Works*, London: Andreas Papadakis, 2002.

E. Jones, S. Porter and M. Turner, *A Gazetteer of English Urban Fire Disasters, 1500–1900*, Norwich: Geo Books, 1984.

— and C. Woodward, *A Guide to the Architecture of London* (3rd edn), London: Seven Dials, 2000.

M. Jourdain, *The Work of William Kent*, London: Country Life, 1948.

H. Kalman, 'Newgate Prison', *Architectural History*, XII, 1969, pp. 50–61.

A. Kelly, 'Coade Stone in Georgian Architecture', *Architectural History*, XXVIII, 1985, pp. 71–95.

A. Kelsall, 'The London House Plan in the Later 17th Century', *Post-Medieval Archaeology*, VIII, 1974, pp. 80–91.

D. Kendall, *The City of London Churches: A Pictorial Rediscovery*, London: Collins and Brown, 1998.

D. King, *The Complete Works of Robert and James Adam*, Oxford: Architectural Press, 1991.

B. Klatt (ed.), *GLC/ILEA Architecture, 1976–1986*, London: Architectural Press, 1986.

C. Knowles and P. Pitt, *The History of Building Regulation and London 1189–1972*, London: Architectural Press, 1972.

S. Kostof (ed.), *The Architect: Chapters in the History of the Profession*, New York: Oxford University Press, 1977.

W. Kuyper, *Dutch Classicist Architecture*, Delft University Press, 1980.

O. Lancaster, *A Cartoon History of Architecture* (2nd edn), London: John Murray, 1985.

J. Lang, *Rebuilding St. Paul's after the Great Fire of London*, London: Oxford University Press, 1956.

R. Leacroft, *The Development of the English Playhouse*, London: Methuen, 1988.

B. Little, *Catholic Churches since 1623*, London: Robert Hale, 1966.

N. Lloyd, *A History of English Brickwork* (repr.), New York: Blom, 1972.

—, *A History of the English House*, London: Architectural Press, 1975.

H. Louw, 'The Origin of the Sash Window', *Architectural History*, XXVI, 1983, pp. 49–72.

— and R. Crayford, 'A Constructional History of the Sash-window, c. 1670–c. 1725', Part 1, *Architectural History*, XLI, 1988, pp. 82–130; Part 2, XLII, 1989, pp. 172–239.

J. Lubbock, *The Tyranny of Taste: The Politics of Architecture and Design in Britain, 1550–1960*, New Haven and London: Yale University Press, 1995.

J. McKean, *The Royal Festival Hall*, London: Phaidon, 1992.

E. McKellar, *The Birth of Modern London: The Development and Design of the City, 1660–1720*, Manchester University Press, 1999.

J. Mackie, *The Earlier Tudors, 1485–1558*, Oxford: Clarendon Press, 1952.

R. Macleod, *Style and Society: Architectural Ideology in Britain, 1835–1914*, London: RIBA Publications, 1971.

B. Malament (ed.), *After the Reformation: Essays in Honour of J. H. Hexter*, Manchester University Press, 1980.

M. Marmaras and A. Sutcliffe, 'Planning for Post-war London: The Three Independent Plans, 1942–3', *Planning Perspectives*, IX (4), 1994, pp. 431–53.

P. Marsden, *The Roman Forum Site in London: Discoveries before 1985*, London: HMSO, 1987.

R. Maxwell, *New British Architecture*, London: Thames and Hudson, 1972.

R. Merrifield, *The Roman City of London*, London: Ernest Benn, 1965.

E. Mills, *1946–1953: The New Architecture in Great Britain*, London: Standard Catalogue Company, 1953.

G. Milne, *The Great Fire of London*, New Barnet: Historical Publications, 1986.

—, *Roman London: Urban Archaeology in the Nation's Capital*, London: Batsford, 1995.

N. Moffett, *The Best of British Architecture, 1980–2000*, London: Spon, 1993.

E. Morris, *British Town Planning and Urban Design: Principles and Policies*, London: Longman, n.d.

J. Morris, *Londinium: London in the Roman Empire*, London: Weidenfeld and Nicolson, 1982.

T. Mowl and B. Earnshaw, *Architecture without Kings: The Rise of Puritan Classicism under Cromwell*, Manchester University Press, 1995.

P. Murray and M. Stevens (eds), *Living Bridges*, London: Royal Academy of Arts, 1996.

J. Musgrove (ed.), *Sir Banister Fletcher's A History of Architecture* (19th edn), London: Butterworths, 1987.

S. Muthesius, *The English Terraced House*, New Haven and London: Yale University Press, 1982.

—, *The High Victorian Movement in Architecture, 1850–1970*, London: Routledge and Kegan Paul, 1972.

I. Nairn, *Counter-Attack*, London: Architectural Press, n.d.

—, *Outrage*, London: Architectural Press, 1955.

D. Neumann (ed.), *Film Architecture: Set Designs from Metropolis to Blade Runner*, Munich: Prestel, 1999.

J. Newman, 'Nicholas Stone's Goldsmiths' Hall: Design and Practice', *Architectural History*, XIV, 1971, pp. 30–39.

M. Newton, *Architects' London Houses*, Oxford: Butterworth, 1992.

P. Oliver, I. Davis and I. Bentley, *Dunroamin: The Suburban Semi and its Enemies*, London: Pimlico, 1981.

D. Olsen, *Town Planning in London: The Eighteenth and Nineteenth Centuries*, New Haven and London: Yale University Press, 1982.

W. Page (ed.), *The Victoria History of London*, London: Constable, I, 1909.

D. Palliser (ed.), *The Cambridge Urban History of Britain*, I: *600–1540*, Cambridge University Press, 2000.

F. Parker and P. Jackson, *The History of London in Maps*, London: Barrie and Jenkins, 1990.

C. Percy and J. Ridley, *The Letters of Edwin Lutyens to his Wife Emily*, London: Collins, 1985.

N. Pevsner, *London I: The Cities of London and Westminster*, London: Penguin, 1957.

S. B. Platner, *A Topographical Dictionary of Ancient Rome*, Oxford University Press, 1926.

M. H. Port, 'The New Law Courts Competition, 1866–67', *Architectural History*, XI, 1968, pp. 75–93.

K. Powell, *New Architecture in Britain*, London: Merrell, 2003.

—, *New London Architecture*, London: Merrell, 2001.

—, *Richard Rogers, Complete Works*, 2 vols, London: Phaidon, 2001.

—, *World Cities: London*, London: Academy Editions, 1993.

C. and J. Riding (eds), *The Houses of Parliament: History, Art, Architecture*, London: Merrell, 2000.

J. Robinson, *Buckingham Palace: A Short History*, London: Michael Joseph, 1995.

—, *The Wyatts: An Architectural Dynasty*, Oxford University Press, 1979.

R. Rowsome, *Heart of the City: Roman, Medieval and Modern London revealed by Archaeology at 1 Poultry*, Museum of London, 2000.

J. Ruch, 'Regency Coade: A Study of the Coade Record Books, 1813–21', *Architectural History*, XI, 1968, pp. 34–56.

D. Ryan, *The Ideal Home through the Twentieth Century*, London: Hazar, 1997.

A. Saint, *The Image of the Architect*, New Haven and London: Yale University Press, 1983.

—, *Richard Norman Shaw*, New Haven and London: Yale University Press, 1976.

A. Saunders, *The Art and Architecture of London*, Oxford: Phaidon, 1984, 1988.

M. Saunders, 'Samuel Sanders Teulon, 1812–1873: A Pragmatic

Rogue', in R. Brown (ed.), *The Architectural Outsiders*, London: Waterstone, 1985.

S. Sawyer, 'Sir John Soane's Symbolic Westminster: The Apotheosis of George IV', *Architectural History*, XXXIX, 1996, pp. 54–76.

J. Schofield, *Medieval London Houses*, New Haven and London: Yale University Press, 1995, 2003.

D. Schubert and A. Sutcliffe, 'The "Haussmannization" of London?: The Planning and Construction of Kingsway-Aldwych, 1889–1935', *Planning Perspectives*, XI (2), 1996, pp. 115–44.

A. Service, *Architects of London and their Buildings from 1066 to the Present Day*, London: Architectural Press, 1979.

—, *Edwardian Architecture: A Handbook to Building Design in Britain, 1890–1914*, London: Thames and Hudson, 1977.

—, *Edwardian Architecture and its Origins*, London: Architectural Press, 1975.

P. Shand, *Modern Theatres and Cinemas*, London: Batsford, 1930.

J. Shepherd, *The Temple of Mithras, London*, London: English Heritage, 2002.

F. Sheppard, *London: A History*, London: Oxford University Press, 1998.

R. Simon (ed.), *Somerset House: The Building and the Collections*, London: British Art Journal, 2001.

R. Simpson, 'Classicism and Modernity: The University of London's Senate House', *Bulletin of the Institute of Classical Studies*, XLIII, 1999, pp. 41–96.

G. Spain and N. Dromgoole, 'Theatre Architects in the British Isles', *Architectural History*, XIII, 1970, pp. 79–90.

B. Spiller, *Victorian Public Houses*, Newton Abbot: David and Charles, 1972.

G. Stamp (ed.), *Personal and Professional Recollections by the Late Sir George Gilbert Scott*, Stamford: Paul Watkins, 1995.

— and A. Goulancourt, *The English House, 1860–1914: The Flowering of English Domestic Architecture*, London: Faber and Faber, 1986.

H. Steele and F. Yerbury, *The Old Bank of England, London*, London: Ernest Benn, 1930.

D. Stillman, *English Neo-Classical Architecture*, 2 vols, London: Zwemmer, 1988.

R. Stonehouse and G. Stromberg, *The Architecture of the British Library at St. Pancras*, London: Spon Press, 2004.

D. Stroud, *George Dance, Architect, 1741–1825*, London: Faber and Faber, 1971.

—, *Henry Holland: His Life and Architecture*, London: Country Life, 1966.

H. Stutchbury, *The Architecture of Colen Campbell*, Manchester University Press, 1967.

J. Summerson, *Architecture in Britain, 1530–1830* (5th edn), Harmondsworth: Penguin, 1969.

—, *Architecture in England since Wren* (rev. edn), London: British Council, 1948.

—, *Georgian London* (3rd edn), London: Barrie and Jenkins, 1978.

—, *Heavenly Mansions*, London: Cresset Press, 1949.

—, *The London Building World of the Eighteen-Sixties*, London: Thames and Hudson, 1973.

A. Sutcliffe, *Paris: An Architectural History*, New Haven and London: Yale University Press, 1993.

— (ed.), *Multi-Storey Living: The British Working-Class Experience*, London: Croom Helm, 1974.

J. Tarn, *Five Per Cent Philanthropy: An Account of Housing in Urban Areas between 1840 and 1914*, Cambridge University Press, 1973.

R. Tavernor, *Palladio and Palladianism*, London: Thames and Hudson, 1991.

W. Te Brake, 'Air Pollution and Fuel Crises in Pre-industrial London, 1250–1650', *Technology and Culture*, XVI (2), 1975, pp. 338–45.

P. Thorold, *The London Rich: The Creation of a Great City from 1666 to the Present*, London: Viking, 1999.

I. Toplis, *The Foreign Office: An Architectural History*, London: Mansell, 1987.

G. Tyack, '"A gallery worthy of the British people": James Pennethorne's Designs for the National Gallery, 1845–1867', *Architectural History*, XXXIII, 1990, pp. 120–34.

A. Vince, *Saxon London: An Archaeological Investigation*, London: Seaby, 1990.

N. Warburton, *Ernö Goldfinger: The Life of an Architect*, London: Routledge, 2004.

C. Warncke, *De Stijl, 1917–1931*, Cologne: Taschen, 1998.

M. Warner (ed.), *The Image of London: Views by Travellers and Emigrés, 1550–1920*, London: Trefoil Publications, 1987.

D. Watkin, *Athenian Stuart: Pioneer of the Greek Revival*, London: Allen and Unwin, 1982.

—, *A History of Western Architecture* (3rd edn), London: Laurence King, 2000.

—, *The Life and Work of C. R. Cockerell*, London: Zwemmer, 1974.

—, *The Rise of Architectural History*, London: Architectural Press, 1980.

B. Watson (ed.), *Roman London: Recent Archaeological Work*, Portsmouth, R.I: Journal of Roman Archaeology, 1998.

H. Webster (ed.), *Modernism without Rhetoric: Essays on the Work of Alison and Peter Smithson*, London: Academy Editions, 1997.

G. Worsley, *Classical Architecture in Britain: The Heroic Age*, New Haven and London: Yale University Press, 1995.

D. Yarwood, *The Architecture of England from Prehistoric Times to the Present Day*, London: Batsford, 1963.

FILM, CD, DVD AND VIDEOTAPE

Andrea Palladio: atlante delle architetture, DVD, Venice: Marsilio, 2002.

The Arsenal Stadium Mystery, 1939.

Betjeman's London, videotape, Green Umbrella, n.d.

London from the Air, DVD, Isle of Man: Duke, 2001.

The Lost Betjemans, videotape, HTV, 1994.

Richard III, 1995.

This Happy Breed, 1944.

Index

Illustration Credits

Contemporary photographs of sites in London are by and the copyright of the author. Other holders of photographic copyright are gratefully acknowledged in respect of the following illustrations:

Bank of England: 127

Colchester Museums: 8

English Heritage/National Monuments Record: 15, 141, 143, 337

Guildhall Library © Corporation of London: 9, 10, 11, 14, 20, 27, 28, 33, 41, 53, 54, 55, 60, 61, 62, 64, 65, 113, 120, 121, 122, 201, 208, 225

London Metropolitan Archives: 93

© The Museum of London: 3, 6, 7, 13, 34, 36, 45, 98, 114, 126, 161, 294

National Gallery, London: 4, 107

National Monuments Record: 5, 17, 26, 30, 31, 48, 49, 223

National Monuments Record © Crown copyright. NMR: 39

Simmons Aerofilms: 67, 136, 138, 145, 222, 253, 257, 259, 289, 296, 311

Toledo Museum of Art, Ohio: 328